Identity Politics on the Israeli Screen

Identity Politics
on the Israeli Screen

Yosefa Loshitzky

UNIVERSITY OF TEXAS PRESS, AUSTIN

First edition, 2001

Requests for permission to reproduce material from
this work should be sent to Permissions, University
of Texas Press, Box 7819, Austin, TX 78713-7819.

⊗ The paper used in this book meets the minimum
requirements of ANSI/NISO Z39.48-1992 (R1997)
(Permanence of Paper).

Library of Congress Cataloging-in-Publication Data

Loshitzky, Yosefa.
    Identity politics on the Israeli screen / Yosefa
    Loshitzky.—1st ed.
            p.   cm.
    Includes bibliographical references and index.
    ISBN 0-292-74723-3 (alk. paper)—
    ISBN 0-292-74724-1 (pbk. : alk. paper)
    1. Motion pictures—Israel—History.   2. Jews
    in motion pictures.   3. Holocaust, Jewish (1939–
    1945), in motion pictures.   4. Jewish-Arab relations
    in motion pictures.   5. Arabs in motion pictures.
    I. Title.

PN1993.5.I86 L37   2002
791.43'095694—dc21   2001017137

To the memory of the thirteen Palestinians, citizens of the State of Israel, who were killed by the Israeli police in October 2000

Contents

Acknowledgments

I wish to thank the following institutions for their financial support: the Authority for Research and Development at the Hebrew University of Jerusalem and especially Shula Woltz and Ofer Kela, who were very helpful in obtaining and securing this support; The Levi Eshkol Institute for Economic, Social and Political Research, Faculty of Social Sciences at the Hebrew University, and its director Yoram Bilu; and the Shaine Center for Research in Social Sciences, Faculty of Social Sciences at the Hebrew University, and its director Michael Shalev. I also thank the following institutions and persons for lending me stills: Israel Film Archive/Jerusalem Cinematheque, its director Lia Van Leer, and head of research and library services Costel Safirman and his deputy Nirit Avni; Tsipi Reibenbach; Havakuk Levison, Amos Gitai, and Ilan Moscovitch; Yehuda (Judd) Ne'eman; Dani Setton and Set Productions; Nissim Dayan; Shmuel Hasfari, Hanna Azulay Hasfari, and Yoram Kislev, H.L.S. Ltd.; Dan Wolman; Nicole de Castro; Daniel Wachsmann and Amnon Rubinstein.

I am also deeply grateful to Haim Bresheeth for his support; to Levana Nir for allowing me to use her interesting work; to Jessica Bonn for her intelligent comments; to Amy Kronish for her helpful tips; and to Marilyn Kulik, director of the Spielberg Archive, Hebrew University, and Hillel Tryster, her deputy, for their help and generosity. Special thanks goes to John Downing for his invaluable insight and perceptive reading and to Jim Burr, the Humanities Editor of the University of Texas Press, whose faith in my project and persistent support brought this book into being.

Some of the material used in this book has already appeared in print in somewhat different form and appears here courtesy of the following publishers. The analysis of *Don't Touch My Holocaust* appeared in *The Politics of War Memory and Commemoration: Contexts, Structures, and Dynamics,* edited by T. G. Ashplant, Graham Dawson, and Michael Roper (Routledge, 2000), and in *Visual Culture and the Holocaust,* edited by Barbie Zelizer (Rutgers University Press, 2001). A slightly different version of chapter 4 appeared under the title "Authenticity in Crisis: *Shur* and New Israeli Forms of Ethnicity," in *Media, Culture, and Society* 18, no. 1 (January 1996): 87–103 and is reprinted by permission of Sage Publications Ltd. The analysis of *My Michael* in chapter 5 appeared under the title "From Orientalist Discourse to Family Melodrama: Oz and Volman's *My Michael*," in *Edebiyat: A Journal of Middle Eastern Literatures* 5, no. 1 (1994): 99–123.

Introduction

Hybrid Victims

■ These I will remember.
Eileh ezkerah.

I asked to take leave of my father and he granted his
permission and left. An Arab sailor in Haifa lifted me
to the soil and it granted him leave.
    The Holocaust of the Jews of Europe and the
Holocaust of the Arabs of the Land of Israel are but
one Holocaust of the Jewish people. The two
Holocausts stare one another straight in the face.

Of these I will speak.
Eileh adaber.

Avot Yeshurun, *HaShever HaSuri Afrikani*
(The Syrian-African Rift: Poems)

A transition from a "politics of ideas" to a "politics of identity" is perhaps the major change that Israeli society has experienced in recent years.[1] Sociologists, historians, political scientists, cultural critics, journalists, political commentators, and public intellectuals all offer different interpretations of this shift including reasons for its periodization. When exactly did this change occur? Was it the result of a single dramatic event or an inevitable by-product of the long and painful process of building a new society? Or perhaps it is just a normal manifestation of an identity crisis that Israel is undergoing fifty years after its establishment. In an immigrant society aspiring to be a Jewish state rather than a state of its citizens, the issue of collective identity becomes all the more important for its members, and questions of identity related to the dialectics democratic versus theocratic, Western versus Oriental, collectivist versus liberal capitalist, or Jewish versus civil are constantly raised in an atmosphere of heated public debate verging—some would claim—on a culture war.

Although Edward Said claims that the issue of identity, and especially what he sees as the obsessive academic preoccupation with it, "is boring,"[2] one cannot ignore the feeling that this "obsession"—what Stuart Hall calls "a veritable discursive explosion in recent years around the concept of identity"[3]—becomes an issue when it is in crisis. It is also clear that despite Israel's tendency to see itself as unique, its contemporary crisis of identity is neither unique nor exclusive. The issue of identity, as Hall observes, has been *the* issue of the twentieth century. It defines contemporary politics and has become a site for contestation for many of this century's struggles. "We live in a world where *identity* matters," Paul Gilroy observes. The word identity itself, he elaborates, "has acquired a huge contemporary resonance, inside and outside the academic world. . . . Principally, identity provides a way of understanding the interplay between our subjective experience of the world and the cultural and historical settings in which that fragile subjectivity is formed."[4] This interplay explains the reason why some contemporary writers argue that the notion of identity should also be analyzed in the context of globalization. In a world where the boundary-setting capacities of the nation-state have been eroded, "the distinctions between inside and outside, citizen and alien, self and other"[5] are rendered problematic. The new kind of social space that has been created in our world—through the growth of crisscrossed economies and cultures—produces growing tension between local and global identities, and between heterogeneity and homogeneity.

This book is not a sociological work, nor does it pretend to provide an all-encompassing, comprehensive explanation for the social, political, and cultural processes that are currently making their mark on Israeli society. Rather, it deals with the reflection, projection, and construction of debates revolving around Israeli identity in one of the major forms of visual representation of Israeli society: cinema. In conceptualizing Israeli cinema as a representational form of identity construction I follow Hall's argument that we should think of identity "as a 'production' which is never complete, always in process, and always constituted within, not outside representation."[6] Sameness and difference, the main components of laying claim to identity, are marked symbolically through the representational system of cinema that both projects and reproduces the social, political, and cultural inclusion or exclusion of certain groups of people.

Ella Shohat's classic book, *Israeli Cinema: East / West and the Politics of Representation*,[7] was a breakthrough in its treatment of Israeli cinema as a representational system through which Israeli-Zionist ideology has been reproduced and perpetuated, particularly around the question of the Orient (as related both to the Palestinians and to Mizrahi Israelis). Since the publication of Shohat's pioneering work, Israel has undergone some dramatic changes, among them the Intifada (the Palestinian popular uprising), the beginning of the peace process, the Oslo Accords, the assassination of Prime Minister Yitzhak Rabin, the rise to power of Binyamin Netanyahu's Likud-dominated government, and the growing power of the religious and religious-ethnic parties. In addition, due to a lack of relevant films on the topic at the time of the book's writing, Shohat did not devote substantial space to the representation of the Holocaust, which I, like many other Israeli scholars, see as the main formative force in the shaping and construction of Israeli identity. The present book, obviously influenced by my own identity politics as a child of Holocaust survivors who lives in Israel, aspires to fill those gaps left by Shohat's otherwise very comprehensive book. Unlike Shohat's book, however, this book is not a historical and ideological in-depth study of the overall corpus of Israeli cinema from its inception. Rather, it is an attempt both to discuss the projection and negotiation of Israeli identity through an analysis of major Israeli films, particularly from the 1980s and 1990s, that constitute unique sites of struggle over identity formation and meaning and to open and broaden further the public space for debating this issue. The chapters in this book all deal, in different ways, with the question of identity, including notions of fluidity and contingency—that is, identity as formed in particular historical circumstances.

Identities in contemporary Israel, as in most of the contemporary world, derive from a multiplicity of sources—nationality, ethnicity, social class, gender, sexuality, and religion—that may conflict and thus lead to a society marked by fragmentation and polarization, which is the current state of affairs in Israel. This book focuses on three major foundational sites of the struggle over Israeli identity: the Holocaust, the question of the Orient, and (in an ironic historical twist of the "Jewish question") the so-called Palestinian question. The films discussed here raise fundamental questions about the identity of Jewish Holocaust survivors and their children—the "second-generation" Mizrahim (particularly the second generation of Mizrahi Israelis) and Palestinians. The book does not treat each identity group as a separate and coherent entity but rather attempts to see the conflation and interplay (and conflict) between them.

All the identities represented in the films that I discuss are marked by victimhood. And indeed, as in the multicultural wars dividing the contemporary ethnic landscape of American society, so in Israel discussion of racism is often displaced by competition over victimization. Contemporary Israeli identity politics is based on perceived and real victimhood that demands recognition and acknowledgment of victimization. The 1998 appeal for forgiveness by Ehud Barak from the Mizrahim for the way they were treated by the former Mapai (a predecessor of today's Labor Party) is a case in point.[8] What connects the Mizrahim with Holocaust survivors and Palestinians is a strong sense of being victimized by the Zionist state.[9] In recent years the hegemonic Israeli-Jewish narrative has been oscillating between the former myths of voluntary sacrifice and heroism on the one hand and the emerging appeals for recognition of involuntary past suffering on the other. To a large extent, Israeli society has become a society that thrives on victimhood and elevates it to the level of "civil religion." This was most evident in the recent Likud-dominated government, which viewed itself as a coalition of past victims or, in the language of contemporary Israeli journalistic rhetoric, a coalition of minorities composed of previously oppressed and stigmatized groups (ultra-Orthodox, Mizrahim, Russian immigrants, and the Israeli Right).[10] This coalition points to the centrality of victimology in contemporary Israeli identity politics, which, ironically, fails to acknowledge Israel's primary victims—the Palestinians. In fact, the basis of the identities of the Mizrahim and the Holocaust survivors resembles that of the Palestinians—the experience of spatial/geographic and cultural/spiritual displacement.

Identity, particularly in the case of extreme forms of national and/or ethnic conflict, is marked by inclusion and exclusion, "us" and "them." The three main identities discussed in this book are thus viewed as constantly playing off each other, as well as against an imaginary and imagined Israeli collective identity (Sabra, Ashkenazi, associated with Israeli leftist politics). Their struggle for hegemony, or at least recognition, is in most cases a struggle for the recognition of suffering and victimhood rather than voluntary heroic sacrifice.

Israel, as portrayed in this book, is the meeting point of conflicting and conflating identities. Hence Israel is represented not only as a site of contention and struggle but also as a site of meeting and negotiation, voluntary or not. Reality and necessity in history have turned Israel into a meeting point, or even melting pot, of conflating identities. Yet, these identities, according to Hall, pronounced in a different context "far from being eternally fixed in some essentialized past, . . . are subject to the continuous 'play' of history, culture and power."[11]

The historical encounter between the Israelis (the new Jews) and the Holocaust survivors who (voluntarily or not) immigrated to Palestine/Israel is one example of what Hall is referring to. Some of the films discussed in this book echo conflictual moments associated with this traumatic meeting, which has been insightfully described by Idith Zertal as "the return of the diaspora in its role as the unconscious of Zionism."[12] In Amos Oz and Dan Wolman's *My Michael* (see chap. 5) Hanna Gonen's insanity and abnormality is projected, screened, and reflected by the character of Duba Glick, the crazy Holocaust survivor and a character who populated the childhood space of the second generation. Dan Wolman's *Hide and Seek* (see chap. 6) similarly includes the story of the crazy, dirty, and stinking Holocaust survivor, Yankush, whose neighbors force him to take a shower despite his horror and shouts of "gas, gas." The violence practiced by the "vatikim" (oldcomers) and the Sabras against this particular Holocaust survivor is a prelude to the violence afflicted by members of the Haganah (the crème de la crème of the Zionist Yishuv) on the Jewish and Arab homosexuals in *Hide and Seek*. As my analysis shows, in Israeli cinema, violence as well as different practices of "purification" are constantly inflicted and forced on the "others" excluded from Israel's imagined collective identity.

In contemporary Israeli cinema, there is a growing openness to marginal and minority identity groups, and a transition to self-representation of these groups—as in the film *Shchur* (1994) and the second-generation Holocaust films (see chaps. 3 and 4)—is already taking place. This book, however, does not explore all the issues related to the representation of minority groups in Israeli cinema. It does not deal with the rise of religion as a major force in Israeli society, culture, and politics; the new wave of immigration from the former Soviet Union; the Ethiopian immigration; and foreign workers, which as yet are not salient topics in Israeli film. It also does not discuss contemporary tensions between global (mostly American) and local identities. The representation of women in Israeli cinema, as well as Israeli films made by women, are not discussed in this book as a special topic. However, a feminist critique is vigorously employed throughout the book and particularly in chapters 4–6.

As identity politics is intimately linked with the politics of representation, I chose to open this book with a Hollywood-produced film: *Exodus*. The construction of the new Jew by American popular imagination, as reflected in *Exodus*, influenced the construction of and focus on the Sabra by dominant Israeli cinema, particularly in what Shohat calls the "heroic-nationalist genre." In chapter 1 I outline the characteristics of the "new Jew" as established by Hollywood's cinematic epic *Exodus*, which has become an inspiring model text for this genre in Israeli cinema. The discussion approaches the film as an attempt to construct a Zionist myth, exploring the film's ideological tensions in its attempt to reenact the foundational Exodus narrative to support the Zionist project and to eliminate the "Palestinian question." I show how the film reinforces the universalist and liberationist reading of the Exodus myth while suppressing its reading as a paradigmatic narrative of colonization.

In chapter 2 I provide an overview of the space that the Holocaust occupies in Israeli collective memory and consciousness, as well as its place in the process of negotiating and constructing Israeli identity. I focus on the establishment of the second generation as an identity group and explore the philosophical, national, and ethnic roots of Israeli society's recognition and acceptance of these children of Holocaust survivors and Jewish refugees as a distinct generational entity. The discussion also explores the brief history of the representation of the Holocaust in Israeli cinema where, like in many other domains of Israeli culture, it has been silenced and repressed for many years. A significant change can be traced in the late 1980s only with the appearance of Orna Ben Dor's documentary *Because of That War* (1988), which deals with Israeli musicians Yehuda Poliker and Ya'akov Gilead, both children of Holocaust survivors. Poliker and Gilead's joint rock album, titled *Ashes and Dust*, introduced the Holocaust as a legitimate theme in Israeli popular culture, and together with Ben Dor's film it helped establish the second generation as an identity group.

In chapter 3 I analyze in depth the representation of the Holocaust in three major documentary films made by second-generation Israeli filmmakers: Orna Ben Dor's *Because of That War*, Asher Tlalim's *Don't Touch My Holocaust* (1994), and Tzipi Reibenbach's *Choice and Destiny* (1994). Using the notion of postmemory as elaborated by Marianne Hirsch, I discuss the films as constituting a social and cultural document on Israeli society by projecting the society's attitude toward the memory of the Holocaust and articulating the role that the Holocaust plays in shaping Israeli identity. I also suggest that what Hirsch calls the aesthetics of postmemory, a diasporic aesthetic of temporal and spatial exile that needs simultaneously to rebuild and to mourn, is at the center of these films.

Chapter 4 reverts to the second generation of Israeli Mizrahim, studying in depth the film *Shchur* (1994), written by Hanna Azulay Hasfari, a child of Moroccan immigrants to Israel, and directed by her Ashkenazi husband, Shmuel Hasfari. *Shchur,* told from the point of view of its woman protagonist Rachel, the youngest and only Sabra child of a family of Jewish immigrants from Morocco, is the first "art film" associated with Oriental ethnicity. The film is groundbreaking particularly because it is the first Jewish North African film made in Israel about what has come to be known in Israeli public discourse as "second Israel"—namely, culturally and economically poor Israel dominated by Mizrahi "mentality" and concentrated in remote development towns and in the slums of Israel's big cities.

In chapter 5 I explore yet another aspect of Orientalism in Israeli culture through the examination of the novel and film *My Michael*. Unlike more traditional analyses of the novel and the film, this chapter, written from a feminist perspective, locates the two texts within the context of colonial-Orientalist discourse. Through a comparison of feminist/colonialist discourses in *My Michael,* as well as its positioning in the context of other colonial texts (some of which have also been adapted into colonial and postcolonial films), I suggest a new reading of one of the canonical texts of both Israeli literature and Israeli cinema.

Chapters 6 and 7 comprise a discussion of the fears of "forbidden love" between Israeli Jews and Palestinians as they are expressed and transgressed in the relatively large group of films in Israeli cinema that deal with this theme. In these chapters I expose the sexual economy and ideology deeply embedded in these love stories and trace a line of progression from *My Michael* to the recent *Day after Day* (1998) by Amos Gitai—a clear transition from fantasy to materialization of fantasy. I argue that although *Hide and Seek,* with its open treatment of doubly forbidden love (homosexual and interracial), features perhaps the ultimate transgression in this genre, *Day after Day,* with its matter-of-fact treatment of its protagonist Mosh/Mussa, the Palestinian-Israeli hybrid (the son of a Jewish mother and Palestinian father), is the most transgressive film. *Day after Day* is the only optimistic film in the forbidden love genre because it implicitly suggests that the existence of the "hybrid fruit" promises that an Israeli multicultural and binational identity has the potential to become unforbidden. It is on this utopian note that the book ends.

Identity Politics on the Israeli Screen

CHAPTER ONE

Screening the Birth of a Nation

Exodus Revisited

■ Terror, violence, death: These are the midwives
of all new nations.

Akiva (the leader of the Irgun) to Ari Ben Canaan
in Otto Preminger's *Exodus*

■ After the Six-Day War there was a certain sense of
pride . . . like you didn't have to associate yourself
with Woody Allen; you could identify with Paul
Newman.

Lester Friedman

His masculine naked torso bathed in moonlight and gently wrapped in white
soft foam created by the light waves of the Mediterranean Sea, a necklace with
a big star of David adorning his neck—this is how Ari Ben Canaan (Paul
Newman), the protagonist of Otto Preminger's *Exodus* (1960), first "penetrates" the film spectator's space of desire. This sensual image of male beauty,
a doppelgänger to Sandro Botticelli's *Birth of Venus*, has engraved, for many
years to come, for world audiences at large and the American in particular,
the definite and ultimate image of the birth of the "new Jew." Like Elik—the
protagonist of Moshe Shamir's *Bemo Yadav* (*With His Own Hands*, 1954),
considered by critics and scholars to be the prototypical Sabra in the literature of the Palmach generation, a mythic Sabra, a Rousseau-like "noble savage" born from the sea—is Ari Ben Canaan: a powerful eroticized counter-
image to the diasporic Jew epitomized, perhaps, by the on- and offscreen
image of the neurotic, intellectual, urban "persona" of Woody Allen. If Elik
was a projection from the inside of a fantasized Sabra, an ideal ego constructed by nascent Israeli manhood, then Ari Ben Canaan is the ultimate external validation of this fantasy. Ari Ben Canaan, personified by the handsome Newman, demonstrated that the way the new Jew was represented to

himself was not far from how he was perceived by others. Self-representation and "objective" perception, self-projection and projection of the "other," narcissistic fantasies and fantasies of the "other" have thus become one in the long and traumatic historic affair between the Jew and the non-Jew. Hence it is for the birth of the mythic "new Jew" that the *Exodus* film stands. And it is in the filmic image of Newman, the actor who appeared to cinema audiences of the 1960s as a Greek god reborn as Hollywood star, that this mythic hero found such intensity of expression.[1]

Although *Exodus* is not an Israeli film, it has become an inspiring model text for the heroic-nationalist genre in Israeli cinema.[2] As Yael Munk observes, almost at the same time that *Exodus*, Hollywood's ultimate Zionist epic, used Paul Newman as the iconic Sabra, the film *They Were Ten* (1961) was released in Israel starring Oded Teomi in a no-less-heroic role, evidence of the compelling new Jewish image that Preminger's film created. A comparison between the two actors/characters reveals many similarities. Both are handsome European-looking men whose devotion to the Zionist project of establishing a Jewish state is total, and both are admired by women who despite their courage occupy a less central place in the narrative. Both films are loaded with symbolism of sacrifice and sanctification of death, and both came to be known as the ultimate shapers of the image of the new Israeli (identified with the Ashkenazi male.)[3] It is important, therefore, to note that Paul Newman (whose family name ironically fits into the film's ideological scheme) in the role of Ari Ben Canaan has become a model of pride for both Israeli and American Jews. Furthermore, the influence of *Exodus* has surpassed the sphere of images and idealized self-images and infiltrated into the territory of "high politics," reinforcing the view of America and Israel as mirror images of the promised land.[4]

My study of *Exodus* approaches the film as a conscious cinematic attempt to turn history into a contemporary Zionist myth in order to create a new national tradition of modern Israeli society. *Exodus*, I suggest, constitutes an interesting locus of ideological tensions and contradictions because it, like the biblical story, is a story of origin, or genesis. My reading of *Exodus* is centered around the question of how the film reenacts the foundational Exodus narrative to support the Zionist project of establishing Israel and to eliminate the "Palestinian question." A close reading of the film reveals new meanings and opens the way for fresh interpretations of the "mythical structure" of the Palestinian-Israeli conflict and its representation in Hollywood cinema and later in Israeli cinema. In particular, I attempt to show that the film reinforces the universalist and liberationist "classical reading" of the Exodus myth (thereby universalizing Zionism itself) while suppressing the potential threat of reading this mythical archetype as a paradigmatic narrative of conquest, colonization, and domination (the ethnic cleansing and oppression of the native Canaanites and, by implication, of the indigenous Palestinians).[5] This chapter aims to explore the ironies of this contradiction.

The Birth of a Nation: On Boats, Wombs, and Tombs

The story of the ship *Exodus,* which acts as the immediate historical reference in Preminger's film, is currently the subject of heated debate in contemporary Israeli historiography.[6] The story of the *Exodus* affair, and more accurately its interpretation, oscillates between competing historical narratives, and is a site of struggle in what has come to be known as the post-Zionist debate, a debate that has moved from the academic arena to the forefront of political controversies in Israel.[7] It is beyond the scope of this study to describe this debate; suffice it to say that it plays a role in contemporary critical discourse launched by Israeli historians, sociologists, and cultural critics on the dominant narratives of the Israeli nation that sustain the cohesion of its imagined community. The historical traumas of the past—the Holocaust, the 1948 war (known in Israel as the War of Independence), the Palestinian refugee problem, the massive immigration of Jewish survivors and refugees from Europe after World War II, as well as the mass immigration of Oriental Jews to Israel in the early fifties, and the different wars that Israel has endured since its establishment—have now emerged as important components in the contemporary Israeli culture war. How to narrate the nation has become a major theme in current Israeli political and public life, which shows a growing resistance to the former official memory. New forms of social memory are constantly constructed and deconstructed in an atmosphere that challenges traditional history and state-imposed myths. The *Exodus* affair occupies a major space in the contestation, raising fundamental issues of Israeli identity and the collective, cultural memories generated by the national past. Although the film *Exodus,* an example of what Alison Landsberg calls "prosthetic memory,"[8] is not an explicit part of this debate, it provides a fertile ground for reflection.

The ship *Exodus* was purchased in the United States by the Mossad (the organization in charge of illegal immigration of Holocaust survivors and refugees from Europe to Palestine).[9] From the very start the Exodus was incarnated as a symbol of the "haapla" (illegal immigration to the British mandate of Palestine) and a public relations tool for the Zionist movement. The ship set out from France with 4,500 Jews from displaced persons camps in Germany, among them pregnant women and hundreds of infants. Upon arriving in Haifa on July 18, 1947, while still outside Palestinian territorial waters, it was attacked with live ammunition by British soldiers. Three passengers were killed, including a small boy, and dozens were injured. The British unintentionally maximized the Zionist propaganda value of the *Exodus* by sending the passengers back to France instead of diverting them to the refugee camps in Cyprus. The French did not force the passengers to disembark against their will, and only a few left the ship. The drama lasted three weeks, drawing enormous media attention. Sympathy for the *Exodus* passengers reached its peak when the British government announced that the illegal travelers would be returned to Germany. In September 1947, two months after leaving the displaced persons camps situated across Europe, the passengers of the *Exodus* found themselves on the shores of Germany, in two fenced-in compounds not far from Lübeck. The journey of the *Exodus* with its heavy symbolism had served its purpose from a Zionist point of view: it had helped persuade the world that the Jewish people needed their own state.

The story of the ship *Exodus*, regardless of its interpretation by Zionist and/or post-Zionist historians (the latter accuse Ben-Gurion and the Zionist leadership of the Yishuv of manipulating and exploiting the suffering of Holocaust survivors in order to serve the political ends of the Zionist movement), demonstrates the power of revisiting and revitalizing national symbols and myths. Such myths, interestingly, can be reappropriated not only by the nation itself but also by the so-called enemy of the nation. And indeed the symbolism of national rebirth embedded in the historical tragedy of the *Exodus* did not escape the Palestinians. In 1987, a few months before the outbreak of the Intifada, the Palestine Liberation Organization planned to send a ship named *Safinat al-Awda* (Boat of Return) with Palestinian refugees and Israeli and European peace activists from Cyprus to Israel. On February 15, 1987, just days before embarkation, while the boat was still in Limassol, the Mossad blew it up. By appropriating Israel's own national symbols, the PLO was hoping to draw worldwide attention to the suffering of the Palestinian people and to Israel's denial of the right of return to their homeland, Palestine. This commuting of national symbols also emphasized the transformation of the Jews, the former victims, into oppressors.[10]

"To envision an abstract concept such as nation," Ilana Pardes, following Benedict Anderson, observes, "requires poetic power, a metaphoric leap that

Fig. 1 *A metaphor of national birth: The* Exodus *in Haifa (1947). Courtesy of Israeli Government Press Office Photography Department.*

would make the transition from one into a multitude more comprehensible."[11] Hollywood's *Exodus* provides this "metaphoric leap" by predominantly imagining the nascent modern Israeli nation as a person, or better still as a handsome American actor, Paul Newman, who plays the character of Ari Ben Canaan, the "new Jew." But the handsome Newman is not the only metaphor of the birth of the modern Israeli nation in *Exodus*. The ship *Exodus*, which in the Zionist narrative of the birth of the state of Israel plays such a crucial role, is also used as a metaphor of birth. The ship not only evokes Moses' cradle and the crossing of the water, which are part of the Exodus myth, but it follows an interesting and unexplored cinematic tradition of the "boat film" genre (a claustrophobic countergenre to the more personal and open space–oriented "road film") that mobilizes boats, ships, and submarines as metaphors of national birth and death in films such as *Potemkin* (1925), *Das Boot* (The Boat) (1984), *Titanic* (1997), and others.[12] As closed spaces, enclaves surrounded by water—the ultimate heterotopias, according to Michel Foucault[13]—ships, boats, and submarines are associated with a womb that can also become a tomb as the famous case of the *Titanic* shows.[14] In fact, the founding myth of America (a birth story that echoes the Exodus myth) is associated with two ships: Columbus's ship *Santa María,* which discovered the New World, and the *Mayflower,* which brought the first white settlers to New England. Hence *Exodus,* recalling these mythic ships (which themselves invoke the myth of ancient Israel) could only evoke sympathy in an American audience through the identification between America and Israel as the two promised lands.[15]

Redemptive Zionism

Three major "others" are appropriated in *Exodus* through a process of "redemptive Zionism": the "old Jew," who becomes a Zionist American "new Jew" (the American Sabra); the indigenous Arab, who becomes a Zionized Palestinian; and the Holocaust survivor, who becomes a Zionist martyr.

The Zionization of the American

The Zionization process of the American Jew and non-Jew alike in *Exodus* is embodied through three of the main characters in the film: Ari Ben Canaan, Kitty Fremont (Eva Marie Saint),[16] and Karen Hansen (Jill Haworth). The casting of Paul Newman as the ultimate "new Jew" plays on the tension between difference and sameness. Newman's "classic" looks, invoking the beauty of an ancient Greek sculpture, are a far cry from the stereotype of the old Jew. His salient Americanness redeems him for the American Jewish male from racial and ethnic difference, and makes him a source of narcissistic identification. To use Laura Mulvey's insightful phrase, the male spectator identifies more easily with "the production of ego ideals as expressed in particular in the star system, the stars entering both screen presence and screen story as they act out a complex process of likeness and difference (the glamorous impersonates the ordinary)."[17] This complex mechanism of spectatorial identification enables the American Jewish male to overcome the split in his identity caused by the perceived pressure of Zionism to identify with Israel even more than with his own country.[18] The Americanization of the new Jew and the cinematic construction of the Sabra as an American star embody, as Ella Shohat observes, "the virility of both the Sabra soldier and the American fighter, merging both into one myth, reinforced and paralleled by the close political and cultural Israeli-American links since the sixties. Israel, in conjunction with Hollywood, in other words, made possible the filmic transformation of the passive Diaspora victim into the heroic Jew."[19]

6

If the character of Ari Ben Canaan solves the problem of identification for the American Jew, then the other protagonist of the film, Kitty—the Waspish, soft anti-Semite—solves the problem for the American non-Jew. In the narrative and ideological economy of the film Kitty is used as a mediator between the non-Jewish American audience and the Jewish Zionist project. Kitty is from Indiana, a midwestern state, traditionally perceived as part of the heartland of America. She is blond and admits to "feeling strange among Jews." Yet, eventually she falls in love with Ari Ben Canaan, or the Hollywood version of the ultimate model Sabra. This celebration of what Shohat perceptively describes as "the cognitive transformation and the recruitment of the Wasp American woman"[20] to Zionism can also be read as an allegory of the growing involvement of the United States in the Middle East beginning in the 1960s, and of America's increasing support for Israel. Significantly Kitty is cast as a nurse. Her ideological function is indeed to nurture, as she heals the traumatized Holocaust survivors through her work in a camp in Cyprus, and saves the life of the Zionist hero Ari Ben Canaan. Her nurturing function fits the self-image of America as the omnipotent healer of weak nations. At the beginning of Kitty's initiation into "redemptive Zionism," when she is still infected by slight anti-Semitism, the only person with whom she admits not feeling strange is Karen, her younger blond double, a Holocaust survivor whose Aryan / Waspish look makes her a perfect candidate for American citizenship. Although potentially Karen possesses all the qualities that could have turned her into a model American citizen as Kitty's adopted daughter, she ultimately chooses Zionism over the American dream and sacrifices her young life for her new chosen homeland.

It is fitting that *Exodus*, as a parable of the "love story" between America and Israel, recruits Kitty, the all-American woman, to mediate between the American audience and the "alien" Jewish people as Ari Ben Canaan's lover. Symbolically the film, with its portrayal of both sympathetic and nonsympathetic British military personnel, also signals the new reality in the Middle East after the failure of the 1956 Suez operation. The disappearance of Britain as the former key imperialist power broker in the Middle East, followed by the emergence of America and the Soviet Union as the new superpowers in the region, is presented through the love story between Ari and Kitty. This love story is portrayed as an educational process whereby Kitty "learns to love the Jews" and respect them. Her initial "soft" anti-Semitism is gradually transformed into total love, admiration, and devotion.

Exodus is only one example of the cultural manifestations of the love story between America and Israel that became more pronounced in the 1960s. As

Rachel Weissboard observes,[21] a wave of novels and films such as *Ben-Hur* (1959) that dealt with Jewish liberation stories emerged at that time in the United States and enjoyed immense popularity with American audiences. On the Israeli front, the former Israeli literary canon of the time, inspired by Russian and Soviet literature, began to decline, and a new interest in America in general and American popular culture in particular began to develop. To a certain extent these changes in cultural taste also reflected political changes related to the role of Israel in the new Middle East of the Cold War, with the Soviet Union becoming an ally of the Arab countries and the United States an ally of Israel.

The Zionization of the Arab

Exodus transforms the Israeli-Palestinian conflict into a utopian reconciliation by following Hollywood's epic tradition of personalizing historical conflicts. The film portrays the conflict through the story of Taha (John Derek), the son of the Mukhtar of Abu Yesha, an Arab village neighboring the fictitious Kibbutz Gan Dafna. In a speech delivered by Barak Ben Canaan (Lee J. Cobb) to the group of children survivors who join Gan Dafna, he states that "we [Arabs and Jews] live as brothers." In this Zionist speech, Barak presents a picture of the Jewish settlement of Palestine even more radical than the official Zionist version. According to Barak's rendition, the Mukhtar voluntarily gave the land of his village to the Jews to build a village where Arab and Jewish youth could work and study together. The obvious message of Barak's speech is not that the Zionists took Arab lands but to the contrary: the Arabs (their brothers) gave them the land because they knew that the Jews would bring progress to the region. To further strengthen this version of enlightened colonialism, Ari and Taha are presented in the film as "brothers" who sanctify and validate their voluntary brotherhood through a ritual of blood mixing that imbues their bond with a "biological" and historical status.

The culmination of the "Zionizing" of Taha is seen in his sanctification as a Zionist martyr along with Karen, the young and pure Holocaust survivor. Their common sacrifice, symbolized by their shared funeral and grave (obviously fictional since according to Jewish law Jews cannot be buried with non-Jews), enables the old/young nation to be reborn. The act of martyrdom performed by the Palestinian Taha (he is ultimately murdered by Arabs for collaborating with the Jews) reconciles the iconography of the three great monotheistic religions. Although Taha is a Muslim, the scene where he is found dead is rich with Judeo-Christian symbols. A Star of David is tattooed in blood on his bare chest (echoing his blood oath to Ari) and his dead naked body is positioned in a crucifix-like way. Karen, the young, Aryan-looking Holocaust survivor, who is also killed by Arabs and who represents the "pure one" in the film's ideological economy, is like Taha a "sacrificial lamb" whose martyrdom redeems the nation. What is most curious about this scene is that it suggests that the hybridization of the Palestinian and the Holocaust survivor constitutes the moment of the birth of modern Israel. Paradoxically, and against the conscious Zionist intentions of the film, the one grave shared by Karen and Taha may lead the viewer to acknowledge the victimization of the Palestinian, as well as that of the Holocaust survivor. A corollary to this point could be that in the Palestinian collective consciousness the Holocaust occupies a significant role, since the memory of the Holocaust is "forced" upon them by the European "exodus." This scene might unwittingly imply that the Zionist state was literally built on the graves of the Palestinians and the Holocaust survivors, a suggestion that is not too far from current trends in post-Zionist critique. The inclusion of Taha, the "Zionist" Palestinian, in the birth of the modern Israeli nation thus affords a multiplicity of readings. The dominant reading suggests a legitimation of Zionism through the symbolic annihilation of Palestinian identity and selfhood, whereas a subversive, "against the grain" reading would suggest that the film acknowledges that the Zionist state was established on the graves of the Palestinians and the Holocaust survivors. The burial scene (mandatory for cinematic epics about national births—e.g., *Gandhi* [1982], *Malcolm X* [1992], and *Schindler's List* [1993], perhaps more than any other scene in the film, makes manifest the historical contradictions inherent in the Palestinian-Israeli conflict. A subversive reading of this scene would suggest that Taha and Karen are too pure to bear the tragic contradictions of history generated by the competing narratives of the Palestinians and the Israelis. According to the dominant reading, however, Taha and Karen must die because they "contaminate" the Zionist project of creating a "new Jew." As an Arab, Taha, even though he is a martyr for the Jewish cause, has no place in a community dominated by Zionist values. Karen too, despite her purity and sacrifice, came from "there"—from the land of the "old Jew," the Holocaust victim. The "new Jew," the American Sabra, *Exodus* suggests, can be reborn only on the grave of the impure ones: the Palestinian and the Holocaust survivor.

The Zionization of the Holocaust Survivor

Paradoxically, the moment of the birth of the modern Israeli nation according to *Exodus* is also a moment of death. And indeed, as Ilana Pardes suggests, "[n]ational birth, much like individual births . . . takes place on a delicate bor-

Fig. 2 *The Palestinian as a Zionist martyr: the executed Taha (John Derek) in a publicity still for Otto Preminger's epic version of Leon Uris's best-seller,* Exodus.

der between life and death."[22] The oscillation in the burial scene of Taha and Karen alternately as signifiers of life and death recapitulates the story of the birth of ancient Israel, a story of trauma and recovery. The story of the birth of modern Israel is also based on recovery from the trauma of the Holocaust, which constitutes the thematic and ideological core of the film *Exodus* as much as it constitutes the formative myth of modern Israeli identity. In the Zionist narrative the illegal immigration of European Jewish survivors and refugees to Palestine during the British mandate (the European "exodus") is described as if it were an inseparable part of the Holocaust.

Three Holocaust survivors in the film metaphorize this story of trauma and recovery: Dov Landau (Sal Mineo), whose fictional character is loosely based on the historical figure of Dov Gruner;[23] Karen, the Aryan-looking young survivor; and her mentally traumatized father. Only the two young survivors, Dov and Karen, are "purified" by "redemptive Zionism" from Jewish victimhood associated with the Holocaust. The ideological logic embedded in their "purification" from the humiliation of victimhood also necessitates their transformation into heroes and martyrs of Zionism. Karen's father, however, who represents in the ideological scheme of the film the "old Diaspora" Jew, and a "contaminated" Holocaust survivor, is beyond Zionist redemption. He is therefore doomed to remain in an insane asylum in a catatonic state. The scene of the meeting in the asylum between Karen and her silent, mute survivor father epitomizes the trauma of the Holocaust. Although physically alive, emotionally the father is dead. He is traumatized by the Holocaust to the extent that he is unable to communicate with his surroundings, even with his own daughter. The father's silent presence represents not only the trauma but also the symbolic threat that the survivors posed to the nascent Jewish state — the threat of "contamination," of "diasporic weakness," and of Jewish vulnerability. In a society where military heroism was the priority, there were conscious and unconscious fears that Holocaust survivors' stories could not be heard lest they turn the whole country into one "big insane asylum." [24] The father's silence thus represents the trauma, as well as the self-suppression and alienation experienced by the survivors in both pre- and poststate Israel. Only the young survivors can partially escape the "impurity" associated with the Holocaust. Dov is purified in the ceremony through which he joins the Irgun (the Etzel underground) and thus symbolically regains his Jewish phallus. Karen, who joins the kibbutz, and voluntarily relinquishes her dream to build a new and comfortable life in America, is killed by an "Arab gang" while defending her new homeland. Implicitly, the film suggests that the new homeland cannot accept the survivors as victims and therefore their only redemption lies in heroism and martyrdom.

In keeping with the ideological and cognitive scheme of the film, which constructs historical compromises between political rivals (Palestinians and Israelis, Israelis and Diaspora Jews), the two young Holocaust survivors, Dov and Karen, represent (through their friendship and love) the film's reconciliation between the Jewish Zionist Right and Left. The film tends to blur the internal conflicts between the Right and the Left (the Irgun and the Haganah, respectively) and to show them as marginal. The leaders of the two military undergrounds, Akiva (David Opatoshu) and Barak Ben Canaan, are biological brothers, as if the film wanted to say "it is all in the family." In his meeting with Ari Ben Canaan Akiva tells him: "In your optimism you are Haganah, in your methodology you are Irgun, but in your heart you are Israel." The representation of the conflict as familial fits Hollywood's tradition of personalizing history and reducing politics to family romance. Contemporary, highly divided Israeli society continues this trend by calling for reunification under the banner of "Ahdut Israel" (the unity of Israel) and "Am Israel" (the people of Israel).

Despite their initial resistance to Zionism, both Karen, who dreams about America, and Dov, who rejects his Jewish compatriots, eventually join the two major Zionist political entities. Karen joins the kibbutz associated with the Zionist Left, and Dov joins the Irgun, associated with the Zionist Right. Their choosing of sides also represents the traditional schism between the Israeli Left and Right with regard to the interpretation of the Holocaust. The Left's attempt to use the Holocaust to construct a moral paradigm that celebrates humanism and racial tolerance is represented by Karen, the blond "child of light" who was saved by the Danes and therefore, unlike Dov, trusts the non-Jewish world despite the Holocaust. Dov Landau, on the other hand, the young, dark and slightly misanthropic survivor, represents the "lessons" that the Right derived from the Holocaust: isolationism, mistrust of the "goyish" world, fetishistic militarism, and ultranationalism.

Dov's initiation into the Jewish Right is portrayed in the film in a dramatic scene, verging at times on Holocaust pornography, at times on spectatorial voyeurism. In this scene, during the course of a brutal interrogation by Irgun members and their leader Akiva, Dov reveals his "dark secret": his subjection as a sexual slave by the Nazis in Auschwitz. Following his revelation, Akiva forgives Dov and he is redeemed by the Irgun from his humiliation as a Jew and a man through a special purification ceremony that doubles as his rite of initiation into Zionist nationalism. His shame-broken manhood, his phallic pride, and his "normal Jewish heterosexuality"[25] are regained in this ceremony in which he swears to sacrifice his life for the nation on a Bible, Menorah, and a rifle, three fetishes that, when combined, symbolize phallocentric, homophobic, nationalist, and militarist Judaism.[26] The ceremony conveys the message that only through armed struggle can lost Jewish pride be regained, and diasporic humiliation revenged. Dov's initiation into the redemptive national struggle, and his acceptance, despite his contamination, by the phallocentric Zionist collective, is portrayed in this scene as the only way to counter and overcome the shame of the Holocaust. It is not an accident, therefore, that in *Exodus* the Arabs replace the Nazis, and the delayed revenge for the humiliation inflicted by the Nazis is displaced into the struggle against the Arab (the local "goy"). The equation in the film between the Nazis and the Arabs (later developed in a number of Israeli films affiliated with the nationalist-heroic genre) occurs in the scene when a mysterious Mephistopheles-like elegant Nazi officer, wearing a white Panama hat and white gloves, and evoking the glamorized colonialist attire depicted in *Casablanca*, incites Taha to attack Kibbutz Gan Dafna, invoking the historic visit of the Jerusalem mufti Haj Amin Al-Husseini to Berlin where he reclaimed a promise of Nazi support.[27]

The Hollywoodization of Zionism

The discussion of the cinematic rhetoric used by the film to provide its preferred liberationist reading reveals a multiplicity of ideological ruptures between "history" and "legend." To use Yael Zerubavel's words regarding the construction of the Tel Hai myth, Preminger's *Exodus* shows that at times the historical and legendary aspects of the commemorative narrative can be seen as essentially complementary.[28] *Exodus* combines a psychohistorical approach (the view that personal history is no less important than public history) with the epic genre. As an epic film exploring both individual and national psychohistory, *Exodus* invokes the difficulties associated with the representation of national struggles in cinema.[29] As a psychohistorical film, *Exodus* renders the Israeli-Palestinian conflict through its characters' psychology, as well as through a dialectical process of political argumentation whereby each party to the conflict (personified by a psychologically motivated character) presents his or her version of the political and historical events. Part of the fascination of the film thus derives from its highly eclectic mélange of elements and influences borrowed from a variety of cinematic, literary, and theatrical traditions such as the thesis play, the psychohistorical epic, the melodrama (with a leaning toward the woman's melodrama),[30] the war film, and the action film. The "historical" approach used by *Exodus* brings to mind Hayden White's view—partially indebted to Jacques Lacan—of "narration and narrativity as the instruments by which the conflicting claims of the imaginary and the real are mediated, arbitrated, or resolved in a discourse." For White, who studies the relationship between narrative and history, "narrativity, certainly in factual storytelling . . . is intimately related to, if not a function of, the impulse to moralize reality." Hence, every story "is a kind of allegory" that "points to a moral, or endows events, whether real or imaginary, with a significance that they do not possess as a mere sequence."[31] In preferring the imaginary to the real, *Exodus* surpasses the boundaries of realism and "history" and becomes a moral drama on Zionism.

The promotion of Zionism as a liberation movement by *Exodus* was an imperative because in 1960 when the film was released the propagation of the myth of Palestine as "a land without the people"[32] prior to Zionist settlement was no longer tenable, creating a need to rewrite the history of the Palestinian-Israeli conflict for the international community and the American audience in particular. Following a long, colonialist tradition, the film presents Zionism as fulfilling a "civilizing mission" with regard to the indigenous Arab population (the "Canaanites" of the biblical narrative). To further strengthen this reading the film shows that the native Arabs actually welcomed the Jews and even gave them the land of Palestine voluntarily as an act of gratitude for the progress they brought to this undeveloped corner of the world. Furthermore, in line with another colonialist practice the film appropriates the natives by implying that the new Jews are in fact the real "Canaanites."[33] It is therefore not an accident that Newman's surname in the film is Ben Canaan, which literally means "child of Canaan," or "native of Canaan." Moreover, the "Canaanization" of the Jew is supplemented by the "Zionization" of the indigenous Arab Taha, whose enthusiasm for the Jewish settlement in Palestine elevates him to the level of a martyr for the Zionist movement. Finally, transforming the old European Jewish victim into a new heroic Jew, the film uses the "shadow of the Holocaust" to further justify Zionism. To strengthen the idealization of the Zionist project, *Exodus* naturalizes differences and tensions, in particular those between the Irgun and the Haganah, the vatikim (oldcomers) and the newcomers—the Holocaust survivors and refugees from Europe. These tensions existed within the Jewish community during the years that the film depicts, and still permeate the political life of contemporary Israel. Full of intentional historical mistakes and conscious mingling of fact and fiction, the film constructs an idealized cinematic representation of the foundation of the state of Israel, naturalizing differences and symbolically annihilating "others."

The kind of history refracted by imagination that *Exodus* so beautifully constructs paved the way for other Hollywood narratives that celebrate Zionism: such films as *Judith* (1965), *Cast a Giant Shadow* (1966), and Steven Spielberg's *Schindler's List* (1993), which is perhaps the "master" of Hollywood Zionized narratives. Both *Exodus* and *Schindler's List*, to use Saul Friedlander's words in a different context, "suggest a mythic link between the destruction of European Jewry and the birth of Israel—i.e. catastrophe and redemption . . ."[34] Both narratives submit the experience of the Holocaust to the Zionist perspective, which sees the creation of the State of Israel as a process of Jewish redemption culminating in the creation of a new Israeli identity free of the burden of the Jewish Diaspora.

CHAPTER TWO

Surviving the Survivors

The Second Generation

- Here stands the station Treblinka
  Where millions will not buy you a return ticket.

  From a song performed by Israeli pop artist
  Yehuda Poliker; adapted from a poem by
  Wladyslaw Szlengel, the bard of the Warsaw Ghetto.

- The Holocaust is no longer our family secret—
  no longer a taboo.

  Anne Karpf, author of *The War After: Living with the
  Holocaust*

This chapter is an elaboration of the political and cultural manifestations of the "mythic link" suggested between the Holocaust and the establishment of the State of Israel. The chapter examines the space that the Holocaust occupies in Israel's public life and historical consciousness. In particular it examines the sociocultural phenomenon of the second generation, thus providing a prelude to chapter 3, which closely analyzes three trauma-saturated documentaries made by second-generation filmmakers.

The memory of the Holocaust and its victims has always been a locus of controversy in the Israeli public sphere. As Israeli historian of the Holocaust Yechiam Weitz observes, it was "accompanied by unending political strife. These debates were always harsh, bitter, full of tension and emotional. Occasionally, they were violent and even deadly." [1] Another Israeli historian, Dina Porat, notes that sometimes it seems that the controversy over the Holocaust is over, but it is just a short break. A single letter to the editor, a short press article, a movie, or a television program is enough to either rekindle the discussion as national-moral soul-searching or refuel the historical debate between the Right and the Left. Undoubtedly, she admits, it is one of the most painful and complex issues on the Israeli public agenda, and it seems sometimes that everybody is participating in it: those who experienced it firsthand, those who lived in Palestine during the period, and those born in its wake.[2]

The Zionist view of the Holocaust is predicated on the perception of the State of Israel as the most suitable monument to the memory of European Jewry, the secular redemption.[3] Indeed, the decision of the United Nations in 1947 to divide Palestine into two states, one Arab and one Jewish, was directly connected to Western guilt regarding the extermination of Europe's Jewish population. It was also an attempt to solve the Jewish refugee problem. Ben-Gurion's statist ideology regarded the Holocaust as the logical culmination of Jewish life in exile. Consequently, during the 1950s the Holocaust occupied a marginal place in Israeli public discourse and survivors were subject to alienation, latent repression, and self-suppression.[4] Zahava Solomon claims that in a fragile Israel after the war when survival, economic growth, and military heroism were the priority and weakness was shunned, Holocaust survivors were not encouraged to recount their experiences, thereby turning them into "immigrants in their own land."[5] A turning point in Israel's attitude toward the Holocaust occurred as a result of Adolf Eichmann's trial in 1960. As Haim Gouri observes, "Holocaust survivors were finally given the chance to speak" and overnight "they became the focus of national attention." The Eichmann trial, says Gouri, "'historic' in the fullest sense of the term, compelled an entire nation to undergo a process of self-reckoning and overwhelmed it with a painful search for its identity."[6]

The June 1967 war opened a new phase in the perception of the Shoah, followed by an ideological polarization that reached its peak with the rise to power of the right-wing Likud Party in 1977. Since the early 1980s the memory of the Shoah has been institutionalized and ritualized in Israeli official discourse on the Holocaust, with a growing awareness of what came to be known as the "second generation." Organized visits of Israeli and Diaspora Jewish youth (known as the March of the Living) to the sites of the former death camps in Poland, and the appropriation of the symbols of the Holocaust (such as the yellow Star of David) by racist ultra-right-wing movements (*Kach* and *Kahana Hai*) have become a part of Israeli civil religion.[7]

Recently, Israeli public discourse on the Holocaust has shown greater openness toward the more contradictory and disturbing aspects of the Holocaust. The emergence of the Israeli "new historians"[8] and their revisionist reading of the history of the Israeli-Palestinian conflict, the corrosive effect of the Intifada on the Israeli public, and the start of the peace process with the Palestinians and Israel's Arab neighbors have synthesized the concerns of Israel's artistic, intellectual, and academic communities, encouraging the Israeli public at large to reexamine the space occupied by the Shoah in the grand narrative of Zionism. In an age that has been called "post-Zionist" by some Israeli scholars and intellectuals,[9] it is only natural that the contradictory "lessons" of the Shoah (if one can talk at all about the "lessons" of this catastrophe), such as Israeli attitudes toward the Palestinian "other," the disturbing charges of collaboration between Zionism and Nazism,[10] as well as the traditionally arrogant and patronizing attitude of Israelis toward the Jewish Diaspora have had to be publicly discussed and debated.

In Israel as in Germany—where most of the discussions on Nazi crimes against the Jews took place in the cultural and aesthetic spheres—art preceded purely political debate. Films such as Orna Ben Dor's *Because of That War* (1988), as well as the music of Yehuda Poliker, have opened a new space in Israeli public discourse to the formerly suppressed plight of the Diaspora survivors and to the effect of their lived experience on their sons and daughters, the "second generation." In a play such as *Arbeit Macht Frei vom Toitland Europa* (*Work Frees from the Death Land of Europe*) the Israeli's and the survivor's selves are disturbingly mirrored in their Palestinian other. Moti Lerner's controversial play *Kasztner* was recently adapted into a television drama, *The Kasztner Trial* (1995), by the filmmaker Uri Barabash—the director of *Beyond the Walls* (1984)—and scandalized the Israeli public even prior to its actual broadcasting due to its revisionist post-Zionist reading of the affair, and particularly its demythification of the heroic figure of the Hungarian/Palestinian parachutist Hannah Senesh.[11]

The challenge of demythification presented by cinema, theater, and television drama is not confined to the cultural realm. A transition from representation to "life" has already occurred: in 1994 Polish President Lech Wałesa invited Yasser Arafat (as a Nobel laureate) to attend the commemoration of the fiftieth anniversary of the liberation of Auschwitz. As expected, this invitation—which further strengthens the symbolic link between the Israeli self and its Palestinian mirror/other—elicited a great deal of controversy among Holocaust survivors, especially in Israel. Amid the roar of these vociferous objections, Boris Goldstein, the head of the committee organizing the commemoration, announced on November 17, 1994, that the invitation to Arafat had been withdrawn.

An even more dramatic affair arose around Arafat's planned visit to the United States Holocaust Memorial Museum in Washington, D.C. The idea to invite Arafat to visit the museum was initiated in January 1998 by Aharon

Miller, Dennis Ross's deputy to the U.S. peace delegation. Ross and Miller, who are members of the museum's board of directors, convinced Arafat that the visit would assist the peace process with Binyamin Netanyahu's government. But activists in the Jewish community put pressure on the museum's directors warning the board not to invite "Hitler's double." It would be shameful, they claimed, for a museum that commemorates the memory of Hitler's victims to host Arafat in a manner reserved for world leaders and heads of state. As a result of this pressure Walter Reich, the director of the museum, and Miles Lerman, the head of the board of directors, told Arafat that he could visit the museum, but only as a regular visitor. The museum's decision sparked a heated controversy, and consequently the directors of the museum reconsidered the cancellation and reinvited Arafat as an official visitor. Arafat refused to accept the renewed invitation and did not visit the museum. He promised, however, that he would visit the museum on another occasion. On March 31, 1998, Arafat made a private visit to the museum of "Anne Frank's House" in Amsterdam. He said that he wanted to learn firsthand about the suffering of Anne Frank and her family during the Holocaust.[12]

The debates involving the Holocaust became more pronounced as the fiftieth anniversary of the end of World War II approached. Among the more salient Holocaust controversies of 1995 were an auction by a Tel Aviv store called "Zodiac Stamps," which presented a catalog in which Holocaust exhibits such as soap allegedly made of human fat, and "authentic" yellow stars were on sale;[13] the visit to Israel of the archbishop of Paris, Monsignor Lustiger, a Jew who was converted to Catholicism as a child in hiding during the Holocaust; the visit of the Israeli soccer team to Auschwitz; and the debate between Irit Linor (a popular writer, journalist, and filmmaker), Moshe Zimmerman (professor of German history at the Hebrew University), and Moshe Zukerman (history lecturer at Tel Aviv University) regarding the "right to hate Germans" provoked by the reactions in Israel to the defeat of the German soccer team in the Mondiale.[14] Another controversy in which Moshe Zimmerman, enfant terrible of Israeli academe, was involved was triggered by a comment he made in an academic conference that the children of the settlers reminded him of the Hitler Youth. Sixty-six right-wing faculty members of the Hebrew University published a petition in *Ha'aretz,* the daily broadsheet newspaper favored by Israel's liberal Left, in which they demanded that the university fire Zimmerman.[15] In response, left-wing faculty mobilized support for Zimmerman through the Internet and published petitions in the daily newspapers in defense of Zimmerman and academic freedom. Zimmerman, threatened by right-wing supporters, was assigned bodyguards by the police.

More recent controversies surrounded seven officers from the Israeli Defense Force (IDF) military academy who, while on an official visit to the extermination sites in Poland, spent seven nights in casinos in Kraków and Warsaw.[16] Debates about the uniqueness of the Jewish Holocaust continue to this day in Israel even as the *Historikerstreit* ("historians' debate") fades in the international arena.[17] Recently, the debate has focused in particular on the Armenian Genocide and the plight of the Roma people during the Holocaust.[18] The recent scandals surrounding the collaboration between the Swiss banks and the Nazis also had echoes in Israel. Yossi Katz, a historian from Bar Ilan University, revealed that Israel holds bank accounts of Holocaust survivors. In February 1997, in the midst of the Swiss banks affair, the Israeli government decided to stop its financial support to the "Amcha" organization (which supports survivors and their families). The decision to stop the aid to aging and sick survivors at a time when they needed it most was reached while the Israeli government was campaigning against the Swiss banks on the grounds that it is the legitimate representative of the survivors. Some survivors requested that they be individually compensated. It was, perhaps, the first time that survivors said that they did not want the Israeli government to represent them.[19]

In a provocative article published in *Ha'aretz* the day before the opening of an international conference on Holocaust Education at Yad Vashem,[20] Moli Brug, a sociologist from the Hebrew University, criticized Israelis for accepting the state's dominant ideological interpretation of the Holocaust.[21] This interpretation, according to Brug, is best exemplified by the expressions "MeShoah LeTkuma" (from Shoah to independence) and "Shoah VeGvura" (Shoah and heroism), which have come to signify the meaning of the memory of the Holocaust in Israel. When those expressions were coined, Brug claimed, they undoubtedly expressed an authentic collective feeling. For the survivors, the juxtaposition of the Shoah with Tkuma (independence) was an expression of their personal victory over the Nazi extermination machine; for the political leadership it was a proof of the victory of Zionism.

Speeches delivered by politicians during the 1996 state Holocaust Remembrance Day ceremony regarding the relationship between the establishment of Israel and the Holocaust, Brug claimed, bear testimony to the success of the state in nationalizing and monopolizing the memory of the Holocaust and constructing it as part of the Zionist redemption. The establishment of the State of Israel was, according to President Ezer Weitzman, "the will of the victims fully materialized," and according to Shimon Peres it was "the ultimate response of the Jewish people to the Nazi scheme." Yosef (Tomi) Lapid, a popular and populist right-wing journalist and politician who is himself a Holocaust survivor, wrote in the daily right-leaning *Ma'ariv* newspaper that "the Holocaust is the cosmic explosion from which the state of Israel was created." [22] In a sarcastic response to these statements Brug comments: "It is difficult to understand why the president and the former Prime Minister assumed that millions of non-Zionist or even anti-Zionist Jews wished to give us the state through their deaths." The linkage made between the Holocaust and the establishment of the State of Israel has, Brug claims, a mythic function. It reconstructs the Jewish code of existence and enables the integration of the ethos of "Yisrael HaMehudeshet" (the new Israel), as defined by Ben-Gurion in the Zionist national narrative, into the Zionist discourse, thus privileging Zionist pioneering over life in the Diaspora.

In his concluding remarks Brug appealed to the educational leadership in Israel to open new avenues for commemorating the Holocaust. Yad Vashem, he pleaded, should move its major Holocaust Remembrance Day ceremony from the Warsaw Ghetto memorial, the symbol of Holocaust military-style heroism, to the "Bikat HaKehilot" (valley of the communities), a witness to 1,000 years of Jewish culture destroyed by the Nazis. Yad Vashem should also, he passionately advocated, prevent the participation of soldiers in uniform in the commemoration ceremonies, and the personal, intimate dimension of Holocaust memory should be strengthened in order to emphasize the continuity of Jewish generations from the Holocaust to the present.[23] If those changes do not take place, he observed, there is a danger that the logic of "MeShoah LeTkuma" will continue to dictate a distorted reality in which the "Beirut bunker" (where Yasser Arafat was hiding during the 1982 Israeli invasion of Lebanon) becomes the "Berlin bunker" and Arafat and the PLO are "Hitler VeKalgasav" (Hitler and his brutal murderous soldiers). Brug asserted that the shaping of the memory of the Holocaust through association with the national war for liberation will ensure the perpetuation of the cult of the Holocaust and martyrdom and the cheapening of the term "Shoah." It will also threaten the uniqueness of the Holocaust as a historical event that bears universal lessons.

Brug's passionate appeal to "privatize" the Holocaust by breaking the state's monolithic practices of commemoration, as well as his plea to "demilitarize" it, not only reflects recent ideological and political changes in Israeli society but also echoes similar concerns raised by other Israeli scholars. Thus, for example, Weitz observes that in the first years of Israeli statehood the dominant tendency was to unify, standardize, and nationalize (if not politicize) the memory of the Holocaust.[24] The dominant position, best expressed by Ben-Zion Dinur, the minister of education and culture during the Second Knesset (1951–55), "gave preference to national and united Holocaust commemoration over and above the particularistic commemoration of individual movements."[25] Currently, he adds, with the growing fragmentation of Israeli society the tendency is to "privatize," "ethnicize," and/or "religionize" the memory of the Holocaust. Another Israeli historian, Gulie Ne'eman Arad, argues that the centrality of the Holocaust as a collective trauma in the rhythm of ritual and public life in Israel is being strongly contested as a result of a memory crisis that Israeli society has been undergoing for the past decade or more. There is, according to Ne'eman Arad, a conspicuous desire to privatize memory—to mourn private loss, rather than glorify collective gains. The invented ceremony of reading the names of relatives who perished in the Holocaust as part of Holocaust Remembrance Day ceremony is a noticeable example, she observes.[26]

Calls for alternative Holocaust narratives have also emerged in ultra-Orthodox circles, paralleling the rise of this group to a share of power in the 1994 elections. These calls for revised narratives have occasionally been met by rather hostile reactions from the secular Left. To give one example, Yigal Tumarkin, a left-wing artist, said: "Seeing them [the ultra-Orthodox], one can understand why the Holocaust happened." On September 12, 1994, Ariel Tzvi Rosenfeld, a law professor at Tel Aviv University, sued Tumarkin for his remarks. Ironically, Tumarkin designed the Holocaust monument in Kikar Malchei Yisrael.[27] Four years later, Tumarkin's comment was used as a basis for another, this time even greater, controversy. In January 1998 the board of directors of Yad Vashem decided to present Tumarkin with the Zusman Award, a special recognition given each year to an Israeli artist who expresses in her or his work the horrors of the Holocaust. The controversy broke out as a result of an article in the ultra-Orthodox newspaper *Yated Ne'eman*, which quoted the above comment made by Tumarkin in 1994, and called the decision to award him the prize a scandal. As a result of this "scandal," Yad Vashem backed down and reworked its decision. However, the award was ultimately given to Tumarkin by the Zusman Foundation, which criticized Yad Vashem for its withdrawal, asked it to return the money, and decided to award future prizes without the mediation of Yad Vashem. The Foundation spokesperson criticized Yad Vashem, saying that "we judge artists on the basis of their beliefs only, and not on the basis of their statements, which in Tumarkin's case have not even been confirmed."[28]

The religious struggle over the interpretation of the Holocaust was further intensified in 1997, playing a significant role in the political competition between rival religious factions, in particular between the Orthodox and the Reform. Yisrael Eichler, the editor of the Belz Hasidim's newspaper *HaMahane HaHaredi* (*The Haredi Camp*) accused Reform Jews of betraying and abusing the victims of the Holocaust.[29] This followed another accusation, voiced in 1996, that "[t]he Reform are to blame for the Holocaust."[30] One of the more extreme abuses of the Holocaust in the ultra-Orthodox attack on the non-Orthodox was an item in Agudat Yisrael's publication *Ha'Modia*, which compared screening movies in airplanes to the gas chambers because both cause "spiritual mass extermination."[31]

The blossoming of Holocaust memoirs in Israel in the past ten to fifteen years is further evidence of the country's changing culture of memorialization. Dina Porat delineates three stages in the evolution of this culture.[32] In the early years of the state Israeli society perceived the victims as an amorphous mass composed of an incomprehensible number of "six million" who were commemorated by state ceremonies. Later, she points out, those "six million" were conceived in terms of communities, which are more defined publics. They were memorialized by schools and by the "Yizkor" (commemoration) books of the destroyed communities. In contrast, the current, third stage of memorialization, similar to that proposed by Brug, is characterized by a personal attitude, and joined by the understanding that "each person has a name" and that each of the six million has his or her own story. The emerging memoir culture of the survivors is part of the process that places the individual and her or his story at the center. Porat's observation of the personalization of Holocaust Remembrance Day is one example. The gradual change in the attitude of Israeli society toward the Shoah and the survivors, as Porat and others have observed, includes also a more complex view of the notions of heroism, survival, and resistance. This view is more receptive to the survivors' voices and the complexities and multiplicities of their experiences. The survivors' voices found their most sensitive response among what came to be known as "the second generation."

What Is the Second Generation?

In 1942 on Yom Kippur my mother's family was taken to Treblinka, where her father and siblings met their horrible death. My mother, Doba, who escaped to the Soviet Union at the beginning of World War II, was the only survivor of her family. My name, Yosefa, is after my mother's father Yosef, who was murdered in Treblinka. My most powerful childhood memories are related to "Treblinka." Whenever my mother was upset with me, she would turn off the lights in our tiny Tel Aviv apartment, sit in the armchair in my parents' bedroom, and start crying and complaining in a monotonous, almost ritualized manner: "Why didn't they [the Nazis] take me to Treblinka? Why didn't I die in Treblinka?" Mesmerized and terrified by my mother's strange and incomprehensible behavior, I shrank in the corner of the room and silently prayed that she would turn the lights on and become "normal" again. Her feelings of guilt for being the only survivor of her family infiltrated my young Sabra consciousness and were grafted onto my own feelings of guilt for being a "bad girl" who upset her mother. For many years, like many other people of my generation, I resented anything that had to do with the Holocaust. I refused to listen to my parents' stories about their past, reproached them for speaking Yiddish (the language that epitomized the despised Eastern European Jewish Diaspora), and complained about not having the good fortune of being born to "normal" Sabra parents.

The turning point in my attitude toward the Holocaust was related to my own experience of the Diaspora, as a graduate student in the United States. Toward the end of my doctoral studies I began to be obsessed with my parents' past life in Poland and tried to fill the void in my family history. After finishing my studies and upon returning to Israel in September 1987, I heard on the radio a rock song titled "The Last Stop Is Treblinka." I was shocked. A rock song about Treblinka? This was too much for my newly acquired Holocaust sensibility. I regarded this song as blasphemy. It took me a while to recuperate from my reverse culture shock in an Israel that was so different from the country I had left in 1980. My recovery included familiarizing myself with the new second-generation Holocaust culture that had emerged in Israel during the mid- to late 1980s and of which Yehuda Poliker's song was a part if not a trigger. I also found out that my discovery of the Holocaust was neither unique nor strictly personal. Rather it was part of a sociocultural process in which many people of my generation were taking part. This generation came to be known as the second generation and was to have a profound impact on the portrayal of the Holocaust in Israeli cinema during the eighties and nineties, both shaping and reflecting the identity of this cohort group.

In his book *The Imaginary Jew*, the Jewish French philosopher Alain Finkielkraut wrote: "[T]he Judaism I had received was the most beautiful present a post-genocidal child could imagine. I inherited a suffering to which I had not been subjected, for without having to endure oppression, the identity of the victims was mine."[33] This sense of victimization gave him, Finkielkraut claims, a considerable advantage over the other children of his generation: the power to dramatize his biography. Except for his parents and two or three uncles and aunts, Finkielkraut has no family. And it was by miracle alone, he writes, that these few close relatives survived the general massacre of Polish Jewry. "I lived (and still live) surrounded by the vanished, whose disappearance increased my worth without managing to make me suffer."[34] Others, he bitterly writes, "had suffered and I, because I was their descendant, harvested all the moral advantage. . . . Since the actors had been annihilated, it was left to their narrator, their heir, their offspring to appropriate the reaction of their audience. . . . Lineage made me genocide's huckster, its witness and practically its victim."[35] And he continues: "I forged a tragic spectacle from the tragedy of my people, and I was its hero . . . but why accuse myself? My date of birth alone explains this propensity to bombast. . . . [T]he war's proximity at once magnified and preserved me; it invited me to identify with the victims while giving me the all but certain assurance that I would never be one. I had all the profit but none of the risk."[36] Although Finkielkraut never uses the term "second generation," he clearly refers to this group, which he ironically calls the "members of the brotherhood of Portnoys." For Finkielkraut, these "arm-chair Jews" who deny the contradiction between their sheltered, comfortable lives and their identification with their parents' suffering are "imaginary Jews."[37]

In a moving article, Marianne Hirsch, professor of French and comparative literature at Dartmouth College and a child of Holocaust survivors from Romania who immigrated after the war first to Vienna and then to the United States, says that along with many European Jews of her generation, she shares a sense of exile from a world they have "never seen and never will see, because it was irreparably changed or destroyed by the sudden violence of the Holocaust." Yet, she adds, this world—those countries from which their parents were exiled—will always be for the second generation "the place of identity, however ambivalent." As none of us (the second generation) knows the world of our parents, Hirsch observes, "[w]e can say that the motor of the fictional imagination is fuelled in great part by the desire to know the world as it looked and felt before our birth. How much more ambivalent is this curiosity for children of Holocaust survivors, exiled from a world that has ceased to exist, that has been violently erased. Theirs is a different desire, at once more powerful and more conflicted: the need not just to feel and to know, but also to re-member, to re-build, to re-incarnate, to replace and to repair."[38]

Compared to their parents, children of survivors, according to Hirsch, live at a greater temporal and spatial remove from that decimated world. "The distance separating them from the locus of origin is the radical break of unknowable and incomprehensible persecution; for those born after, it is a break impossible to bridge. Still, the power of mourning and memory, and the depth of the rift dividing their parents' lives, impart to them something that is akin to memory." Searching for a term that would convey its temporal and qualitative difference from survivor memory, Hirsch has chosen to call this secondary, or second-generation, memory "postmemory." The deep sense of displacement suffered by the children of exile, "the elegiac aura of the memory of a place to which one cannot return," creates, Hirsch observes, "a strange sense of plenitude, rather than a feeling of absence. . . . The fullness of postmemory is no easier a form of connection than the absence it also generates. Full or empty, postmemory seeks connection. It creates where it cannot be repaired. And, because even the act of mourning is secondary, the lost object can never be incorporated and mourning can never be overcome. . . . In perpetual exile, this/my generation's practice of mourning is as determinative as it is interminable and ultimately impossible."[39]

A similar sentiment is echoed by Israeli writer Eleonora Lev. In her first semiautobiographical novel, *First Morning in Paradise*, she writes: "In their unresolvable and incomprehensible orphanhood my parents told me nothing about the burning of the landscapes of their Europe, and although I obediently put up with my lack of knowledge, I could not get rid of my feelings of bitterness about everything that they prevented me from knowing. Like a demanding and deprived child I sensed that even the knowledge of these landscapes was cruelly taken away from me. But as you can see even this attempt to deprive me of this knowledge did not help and when darkness comes, stubborn longings for lost landscapes overcome me."[40]

In a spirit that recalled Hirsch's words, Yitzhak Laor, an Israeli writer and left-wing anti-Zionist activist, confessed: "I am suspicious about my ability to talk about the Holocaust as a part of me, as well as something which is not a part of me. I do not know, and will never know, where the border between the Holocaust that is 'part of me' and the Holocaust that is 'not part of me' lies. This border does not exist, although there is certainly something that is part of me and something that is not part of me."[41]

Finkielkraut, Hirsch, Laor, and Lev, like Henri Raczymow (*Contes d'exil et d'oublie*) and David Grossman (*See under Love*), are writers born after the Holocaust for whom this catastrophe is, as Geoffrey Hartman observes, "an absent memory." They, to cite the imploded language Hartman employs in a different context, "reconstitute the past from stories rather than direct knowledge." The eyewitness generation, as Hartman writes, "expressed a return of memory despite trauma; this 'second' generation expresses the trauma of memory turning in the void, and is all the more sensitive, therefore, to whatever tries to fill the gap." [42]

Second-generation "issues" have been detailed in psychological studies, principally in the United States and Israel.[43] According to Israeli psychotherapist Dina Wardi, the children born immediately after the Holocaust were not perceived by their survivor parents as separate individuals but "as symbols of everything the parents had lost in the course of their lives." [44] The survivor parent tries to reconstruct feelings of identity through her or his children. "By relating to the children as a kind of offshoot of themselves, the parents satisfy their inner need for identity and identification, but this prevents the children from being able to individuate themselves and to create a unique identity." [45] These children, "the memorial candles" of the Holocaust as Wardi calls them, "have been given the lifework of establishing intergenerational continuity." As the successors of the survivors, behind whom there are "ruin and death and infinite emotional emptiness," it is the obligation and privilege of the second generation "to maintain the nation, to re-establish the vanished family and to fill the enormous physical and emotional void left by the Holocaust" in their survivor parents' "surroundings and hearts." [46]

Indeed, one of the more interesting aspects of the second-generation phenomenon is related to the complex ways in which the memory of the Holocaust is transmitted through generational dynamics. The fact that some of the survivors are still alive provides us with a rare opportunity to observe the operation of memory in flux, its transmission from one generation to the next: from the survivors, to the second and third generations, with each generation creating and shaping a different kind of memory, as well as institutionalized forms of memorialization and commemoration. The generational aspect of the memory of the Holocaust becomes even more significant given the abnormality of the family structure in survivor families. As most survivors lost their parents in the Holocaust, their children, the second generation, do not have grandparents. In fact, only the third generation, the children of the second generation, enjoy full multigenerational continuity. They are, so to speak, the first "normal" post-Holocaust generation.

If we expand the narrow, psychological definition of who is entitled to inclusion within the category of the second generation, then we may as well talk about a second-generation "sensibility" that transcends the empirical status of the "real" children of Holocaust survivors and refugees. Thus, Steven Spielberg can be understood as a second-generation filmmaker, since *Schindler's List*, an anxiety-induced film motivated by fears of disappearance and consequent oblivion and denial, marks a shift in generational sensibilities toward the Holocaust. *Schindler's List* symbolically passes the torch from one generation to the next, reaffirming the role of generational identity in the symbolic memory culture of the Holocaust.[47] A very similar generational sensibility can also be detected in Finkielkraut's own confession that he began to reject his status as an "imaginary" Jew; that is, one who avoids "a negation that was difficult to face: the eradication of Diaspora Jewishness as an integral Jewish culture."[48] For Finkielkraut this rejection was not as a result of political change or the disappointment of Marxism, but came when he realized that his Holocaust survivor parents would one day die, and "with them, the knowledge of pre-war Jewish civilization he would never be able to possess."[49] Behind what Finkielkraut regards as the imaginary condition of post–World War II Jewish identity is the Holocaust—"the event that, despite its determining status, 'has no heirs.' An absence that haunts the rhetoric of postwar Jewish identity."[50] And indeed, the second generation, which, through intergenerational transmission, has inherited the role of guilty survivor, is now beginning to make its voice heard in an attempt to explore if not fill this haunting absence.[51]

Israeli Cinema and the Holocaust

When Finkielkraut discusses "second generation imaginary Jews," he does not neglect to remind his readers that his generation is also the generation of May 1968, the first to come of age in the age of television. "We grew up with the media age," he stresses, "from tender youth, the world as audiovisual spectacle has been our daily fare. Our coming of age was doubly transfixed, both by the century's grand struggles and by the incessant broadcast of images across the small screen."[52] The centrality of images in second-generation consciousness explains why film has become for many second-generation Israelis the main vehicle through which they articulate their Holocaust postmemory. Postmemory films work against the attempt to standardize and routinize an official monolithic memory of the Holocaust. They privatize memory rather than nationalize it, reflecting the current schism of Israeli society and its conflicts of identities. Israeli postmemory films, thus, constitute an identity-formation mechanism.

As both a mirror and complicit participant in the construction and perpetuation of dominant Israeli ideology, Israeli cinema, for many years, ignored the topic of the Holocaust. Although, as Roni Perchak observes,[53] many Israeli filmmakers come from survivors' families, the Holocaust occupied a marginal space in Israeli cinema. Most documentaries on the Holocaust that were produced for Israeli television were "educational" and designed for use as illustrative material in schools. Except for indirect allusions to Jewish refugees, and two feature films that directly deal with the Holocaust—*HaMartef* (The Cellar, 1963) by Nathan Gros and *Tel Aviv–Berlin* (1986) by Tsipi Trope—Israeli cinema has ignored this traumatic event in Jewish history. As Judd Ne'eman points out,[54] Holocaust representations in Israeli cinema appear in two historically separate stages, an early post–World War II stage and a late-1980s stage preceded by the production of Ilan Moshenzon's *Wooden Gun* in 1978. What Ne'eman calls "new wave" Holocaust cinema consists of a small number of films, such as *Tel Aviv–Berlin*, *Because of That War* (Orna Ben Dor, 1988), *The Summer of Aviya* (Eli Cohen, 1988), and *New Land* (Orna Ben Dor, 1994). The silence of Israeli cinema with regard to the Holocaust can be explained by the association of the Holocaust with diasporic consciousness and the "negation of exile"[55] practiced by Israeli Zionist ideology. An additional explanation might be that because cinema has traditionally been categorized as entertainment, it was not regarded by some as a suitable medium to deal with this topic.

The attitudes of Israeli filmmakers toward the Holocaust began to change in the late 1980s. The documentaries *Hugo* (1989) by Yair Lev and *Because of That War* by Orna Ben Dor and the feature fiction film *The Summer of Aviya* by Eli Cohen began to deal with the trauma of the survivors and their children. This tendency has intensified in recent years with four new documentaries. In three of them—*Choice and Destiny* (1993) by Tzipi Reibenbach, *Will My Mother Go Back to Berlin?* (1993) by Micha Peled, and *Daddy Come to the Amusement Park* (1994) by Nitza Gonen—the second generation explore and investigate their parents and the memory of the Holocaust through the movie camera. In the fourth documentary, *Don't Touch My Holocaust* (1994), director Asher Tlalim explores both the production and the performance of *Arbeit Macht Frei*, directed by Dudi Maayan and staged by the Acre Theater Group, and the roots and origins of the creators of this performance, as well as his own and Maayan's Moroccan roots.

In Israeli second-generation films the filmmakers focus both the camera and their own gaze toward their survivor parents.[56] Although these second-generation filmmakers have in common, as Yael Feldman observes, "a rejection of the collective model of representation that they inherited from their parents and cultural mentors," they seek "a close subjective encounter with the experiences that the ideology of that model of necessity suppressed."[57] Author David Grossman, for example, attempts "to release the Shoah from the shackles of the collective and reclaim it as a subjective experience" by "emplotting this long journey into the heart of the death camps as an intensely personal odyssey, triggered by a writer's block and traced to the particular pathology of (single) children of survivors." In a similar (post-Zionist?) spirit, second-generation documentary films express rebellion against Israel's nationalization of the Holocaust and its appropriation as collective property. These films attempt to denationalize the Holocaust by retrieving the private and expressing it as unique and personal. Eventually, however, their attempt to "privatize" memory results in a reconciliatory compromise between the private and the historical, the intimate and the collective. In a style reminiscent of the cinema verité tradition, the movie camera is used in these films as a valuable catalytic agent, a revealer of inner truth, which begins with the return to the private only to discover that the intimate is ultimately the collective. The camera in these films, as Perchak perceptively observes, is the instrument that shapes the family, the speech, the intergenerational encounter, and that finally expands the definition of the second generation by including the spectators as participants in this shared destiny, as well as in their role as witnesses.[58]

Hugo, made in 1989 as a graduation film in the Department of Film and Television at Tel Aviv University, transcended the status of student film and became the first documentary in the new genre of second-generation films to explore survivor parents. Hugo, the name of Lev's father in the film, deals with the problematic relationship between father and son—the protagonists of the film. This film made manifest a tendency that was to become typical of the second-generation films that followed it: the creation of a linkage between a crisis in the child-parent relationship and the parents' silence, which is rooted in the horror of the Holocaust. This silence is shattered through the power and mediation of the movie camera. The linkage is most evident in the scene where the camera focuses at length on the empty chair in which the mother sits while the father is telling his story and which she leaves from time to time. This empty chair, like the empty chair left by Jan Karski in Claude Lanzmann's *Shoah* (1985), becomes a metaphor of silence, a visual articulation of the impossibility of verbal articulation. The camera ultimately breaks the mother's silence toward the end of the film.

The presence of the camera in these films thus becomes an active presence that shapes the events and the protagonists' behavior. This has been most powerfully expressed in Gonen's *Daddy Come to the Amusement Park*, which documents a trip by the actor Shmuel Vilojni with his sister and father to his father's birthplace in Poland and to the extermination camp where his grandfather (whose name the actor Vilojni, known as "the memorial candle," bears) was murdered. The documentation of the visit is juxtaposed with clips of Vilojni performing stand-up comedy before a Tel Aviv audience, in which he satirizes his trip to Poland and his Jewish/Polish background. The fact that Vilojni is an actor was fully exploited in the film in a self-reflexive fashion. The camera continuously activated the actor, and encouraged him to externalize his moods, from his silliest moments, such as when he makes fun of a Polish soldier by marching along with him in a grotesque manner, to the more dramatic scenes, such as his emotional outbreak in Auschwitz, which was joined by his admission that he does not know who is indeed crying—he himself, or the actor within him. Vilojni's trip to Poland is consciously presented in this film as a roots journey, aimed not only at exploring the origins of his Jewish Polish family and its journey to death but also at getting to know his father and himself better. At the end of the journey the father confesses to his children that he has discovered that he has "two wonderful children," and the son confesses to finding a new father and a new "self." Old family tensions, in particular between the son and the father, end in a family reconciliation. The journey to Poland, the land of the murdered Jews, thus becomes, in Gonen's/Vilojni's film, an Oedipal journey that assumes healing therapeutic qualities. Gonen's, Reibenbach's, Lev's, and Peled's films express, as Perchack observes, an attempt to escape from the superficial effect of collective memory, and return to the realm of private, personal experience, through the witnessing of its singular and unique existence.[59] Yet, personal experience brings memory back into the all-engulfing bosom of the collective, leading toward a renewed recognition that what was experienced as private memory is ultimately shaped and mediated through film, which, along with architecture, is the most public art.

Don't Touch My Holocaust assigns another task to the medium of film. The film not only documents the performance of *Arbeit Macht Frei* and the trip of the actors' group to Germany; it also conducts another trip to Morocco, the birthplace of both Dudi Maayan, the playwright, and Asher Tlalim, the film's director. The act of making this film and the content of the theatrical performance itself link the discussion of the Holocaust to the Mizrahim and the Palestinians. Making Oriental Israelis and Palestinians part of the Holocaust "experience" challenges Zionist claims regarding the uniqueness of the Holocaust, and calls into question the implied Zionist dichotomizing mechanism that distinguishes between, on the one hand, those who directly, or indirectly through their families, experienced the horrors of the Holocaust and, on the other hand, those who remained outside it. The highly charged locus of the film is a cluster of seemingly unrelated and insignificant scenes, in which Tlalim's camera, while freely floating in the streets of Casablanca, lingers on a billboard of *Casablanca* the film, and later on a small movie theater in Tangier, where Tlalim was born. In this way Tlalim's camera testifies that cinema is not only the global producer of images, fantasy, and fiction but also the projection of conflictual identities that on the surface seem disparate and disconnected.[60]

CHAPTER THREE

Postmemory Cinema

Second-Generation Israelis Screen the Holocaust

■ I neither emigrated nor was deported. The world
   that was destroyed was not mine. I never knew it.
   But I am, so many of us are, the orphans of that
   world.

   Henri Raczymow

■ After the Catastrophe, Judaism cannot offer them
   any content but suffering, and they themselves do
   not suffer.

   Alain Finkielkraut

The recent tendency in Israel to privatize and ethnicize the memory of the
Holocaust is most evident in the wave of documentaries on the Holocaust
made by Israeli second-generation filmmakers in the late 1980s and early
1990s. The films presented in this chapter—Orna Ben Dor's *Because of That
War* (1988), Asher Tlalim's *Don't Touch My Holocaust* (1994), and Tzipi Reibenbach's *Choice and Destiny* (1993)—were selected because they represent
this tendency as well as the changing attitudes in Israeli society toward the
Holocaust and the survivors.

   Ben Dor and Reibenbach are both daughters of survivors, while Tlalim is
an Oriental Israeli. Despite differences in background and country of origin
(Ben Dor was born in Israel, Reibenbach in Poland, and Tlalim in Morocco),
the three directors belong to the same age group and have lived most of their
lives in Israel. Hence their films, despite being firmly rooted in their particular familial and ethnic milieus, transcend those differences and together constitute a form of social and cultural document on Israeli society with its multiplicity of views on the Holocaust. Among other themes, the films project
and screen Israeli society's struggle with Holocaust memory and, in turn, survivors' and their children's struggle with Israeli society. These films, therefore,

both construct and reflect the sociocultural phenomenon of participating in the process of negotiating and contesting Israeli identity.

What Hirsch calls the aesthetics of postmemory, a diasporic aesthetics of temporal and spatial exile that needs simultaneously to rebuild and to mourn, is at the center of these films. The films are constructed by an imagined collectivity of ghosts and shadows, and express loss and ambivalence toward their creators' "home" (both their real Israeli home and their imagined loved/hated diasporic home). In my analysis I explore what strategies these films devise to shape Holocaust postmemory and to reconstruct the lost world of their parents. My discussion is also concerned with the problem of how the films represent the second generation—to itself and to the dominant culture both in Israel and abroad. I attempt to examine a certain anxiety haunting Israeli second-generation films that insist not only on the significance of recovering memory but also on the acknowledgment that the very act of memory pays tribute to the culture of their parents that was destroyed by the Nazis, and further rejected and repressed by Israel's statist and antidiasporic ideology.

Because of That War (1988), Orna Ben Dor

The film *Because of That War* is based on a series of interviews and observations conducted with two Israeli second-generation musicians who work together, as well as with their Holocaust survivor parents. Yehuda Poliker is a popular Israeli rock singer whose Greek-born parents are Auschwitz survivors. Ya'akov Gilead, a composer, is the son of Polish Jews who also survived Auschwitz. In 1988 the two released an album titled *Afar ve Avak* (*Dust and Ashes*) whose topic is the Holocaust. It was the first album to use the Holocaust as a theme in Israeli popular music (in this case a mixture of traditional Greek music, pop, and rock), and was received enthusiastically by critics and young audiences alike. Orna Ben Dor's film, made during the same year, records testimonies of both artists, who describe their relationships with their survivor parents, and their parents, who reveal their Holocaust memories. In addition, the film documents live performances by Poliker, as well as moving meetings between the two survivor families.

Two motives were behind Ben Dor's making of her film. The main one was "to take the Holocaust out of the museum"[1] and make it more accessible to young Israelis. The second was to expropriate the Holocaust from the Israeli Right. This act of expropriation was made during the Intifada, which for many left-wing filmmakers, including Ben Dor, symbolized the inevitable result of the atrocities committed by Israel and supported by the Israeli Right (and Left in many cases) in the occupied territories.

The film also mirrors the conflation of the Holocaust and Ashkenazi-Sephardi dynamics in shaping identity and in the way it highlights the socioeconomic differences in the Gilead and Poliker families. Ya'akov Gilead's mother, Hellina Birenbaum, appears in the film as a highly skilled public performer. The camera follows her as she speaks to high school students of her Holocaust memories, documenting her "manipulation" of the students' emotional reactions to the reenactment of her experiences of the Holocaust. Despite restricting herself to the realm of her personal memory of the Holocaust, Hellina's act of memorialization in front of an audience attains the level of "performance." To put it crudely, Hellina "performs" like a "professional survivor." She perceives her public talks, delivered eloquently in a polished and highly articulate Hebrew, as an educational, pedagogical mission, a transmission of memory from one generation to another. Hellina, who is a writer and translator, is also filmed and interviewed in her spacious, well-equipped study sitting in front of her computer, evidence of her education and economic status, as well as of her transformation of her Holocaust experience into a lifelong vocation.

Unlike Hellina, Jacko Poliker, Yehuda Poliker's father, is filmed in the kitchen of his typically small and modest Israeli apartment. He stutters, his speech is dominated by silent pauses and hesitations, and his Hebrew is poor and broken. From time to time he stops to search for the right word. His manner of speaking suggests that he is completely oblivious to the camera and the implied film audience. He speaks only to Ben Dor, the interviewer, while visibly struggling to convey his painful memories. Jacko Poliker's testimony is a "pure" and "authentic" transmission of his personal Holocaust memories. It is quite clear that this is his first "public" recollection of his memories, and his difficulty is evident. Also, his lower-class background, his lack of formal education, as well as his poor mastery of Hebrew all convey pure subjectivity, "authenticity," pain, and the emotional void created by his Holocaust experience. It is quite obvious to the Israeli viewer that under normal circumstances Hellina and Jacko could not have met due to class, gender, and ethnic differences. Their meeting in the context of Israeli immigrant society could have happened only through marriage relationships between their respective families, or as Holocaust survivors—because on the ramp of Auschwitz all Jews were equal, and in the survivors' post-Auschwitz life only the shared memory of that place could bring them together. In the case of Poliker and Birenbaum the two factors brought them together: the relationship between their children and their shared memory of the Holocaust.

The comparison that the film implicitly suggests between the two survivors—the educated, articulate middle-class Hellina, and the uneducated, inarticulate, lower-class Jacko—becomes therefore a semianthropological document on the Israeli survivors' community. Furthermore, the comparison between the survivors, their children and the different ways they present their Holocaust stories provides an indirect, self-reflexive commentary on the politics of the representation of the Holocaust, both in "real" life (Hellina's talks to high school students, for example) and in the different modes of popular culture, such as music and film, that seem to be the second generation's choice. After all, Gilead and the younger Poliker selected music as their preferred means to communicate their and their parents' experiences of the Holocaust, and Orna Ben Dor, also the child of Holocaust survivors, chose cinema.

Moreover, the stories of both Poliker and Gilead about their relationships with their parents reinforce the psychological studies on children of Holocaust survivors. These stories convey to the Israeli public, perhaps for the first time, a full profile of children of survivors, thus establishing the notion of the second generation in Israeli public discourse. In fact, the documentary has generated a new genre of second-generation films, both professional as well as amateur "home Holocaust" films made by second-generation children who have interviewed and documented their survivor parents, particularly during joint "roots trips" to Poland. In this way the film has introduced the formerly psychological rubric of the second generation to the sociocultural sphere as well. The acknowledgment of the existence of the phenomenon of the second generation has thus moved away from the narrow circles of the psychotherapeutic community and survivor families to the Israeli public at large. Finally, the voice of the survivors was "given voice" by their children, whose prominence in Israel's cultural life ensured its infiltration into Israeli public consciousness.

The film's success both capitalized on and reproduced the success of Gilead and Poliker's album. At first songs from the album were broadcast only during Holocaust Remembrance Day or on special occasions,[2] but eventually as the songs acquired "hit" status they were broadcast more frequently, even on normal radio programs, thus accelerating the process of normalization and routinized assimilation of reflection on the Holocaust into the fabric of everyday Israeli life.[3] The assimilation of Poliker and Gilead's Holocaust "hits" into Israeli mainstream culture signified a change in the perception of the Holocaust by the Israeli public. The Holocaust was no longer perceived as "another planet" requiring a "new language," but rather a human event that could be represented through terms and concepts borrowed from everyday life. Similarly, it can also be argued that the Holocaust was certain to become "normalized" because it had been abused, cheapened, and instrumentalized in the Israeli public sphere, or because of the aging of the generation of the survivors and the need to find new modes of representation by the second and, today, third generation. This need is further strengthened by global post-modern tendencies to assimilate the Holocaust into popular culture, of which Steven Spielberg's *Schindler's List* is a prime example.[4]

Don't Touch My Holocaust (1994), Asher Tlalim

Asher Tlalim's documentary *Don't Touch My Holocaust* is about the play *Arbeit Macht Frei vom Toitland Europa* (*Work Frees from the Death Land of Europe*), which was performed by the Acre Theatre in Acre, Israel, for three years (1993–96) and traveled in Germany.[5] The film is a mélange of direct presentation of some scenes from the theatrical performance, interviews conducted with the actors, a reenactment of the actors' encounters with people from their past, and a documentation of the group's visit to Germany. The theatrical performance itself was a participatory journey through seven installations and tableaux. Part museum tour, part coach trip, part school play, part confession, part concert recital, part reconstructed ghetto, and part testimonial, it led its audience through an overwhelming five-hour experience of total theater, using an intimacy conceivable only in live performance.

The performance exploited all the senses and made its audience involuntarily complicit in the disturbing theatrical experience by making it an uncomfortable participant observer. The actors who made this performance are "total" people who mingle life with art, pushing both to the extremes. Their encounters with the audience affected the performance and were assimilated into each individual show. Current political events were continuously integrated into the play as well, thus making it more relevant and responsive to Israel's stormy public life. For example, in one of the scenes, an Independence Day dinner, the actor Muni Yosef, who only a few minutes before had been a crazy beggar, plays a typically supermacho Israeli male who boasts about screwing women and hunting "Arabushim" (a derogatory name for Arabs) while silencing his submissive wife. A day after the peace treaty with Jordan was signed, Yosef updated his performance, describing how he had just returned from the ceremony after screwing Queen Nur and harassing Bill's (President Clinton's) security guards.

The personal journey of Smadar (Madi) Yalon-Maayan (the principal actress and then-wife of playwright Dudi Maayan) into her past as part of the work on the play epitomizes the totality of the performance and its blurring of the boundaries between life and art, reality and performance. Her self-training for this role involved working through her private mourning for her father, a Holocaust survivor who after his liberation from the camps immigrated to Israel (where, according to Madi, "he wasted his life"). In Tlalim's film, Madi speaks about her experiments with self-starvation as a preparation for her role in the play as a *Musslman,*[6] during which she lost so much weight that she had to be hospitalized. She also tattooed a number on her arm, a significant number that indicated the date of her father's death. In the first scene in the theater space she touches this tattoo, either caressing it or trying to erase it.

The group members worked on the performance for six years. They collected materials for three years and performed the play for another three. *Arbeit Macht Frei* ran for three consecutive years, twice a week in the theater in Acre. Only thirty people were admitted to each performance, and tickets had to be reserved a year in advance. At three o'clock in the afternoon the thirty lucky spectators were driven in a luxury bus to the Holocaust museum of Kibbutz Lohamei HaGetaot (literally, "The Ghetto Fighters' Kibbutz"). Dudi Maayan, the head of the Acre group, said that it was essential for the audience to visit the museum first because the museum functioned as a transitory, preparatory stop before their imminent entrance into the unknown labyrinthine space of the theater, which recalled the sewage system of the Warsaw ghetto.[7]

Madi Yalon-Maayan, in the role of Zelma, a Holocaust survivor, guides the spectators among the "works" (*avodot*), the word she uses to refer to the museum's exhibits. In a fake and wearily didactic tone, and in a mixed language composed of broken Hebrew, German, Yiddish, and English, she discusses the exhibits and makes comments about the process of extermination, the destruction of trust between people, and the rise of fascism. "It is not a new invention," she says, "we too know a chosen people, Yes? Who can give me a contemporary example of a ghetto?" she asks the audience. "There is no need to be shy, nobody can see us here," she adds. "Soweto," somebody says. "Gaza,"[8] says another. "Very interesting," Zelma says, and comments, "Once in one of the groups I had a child, who said that here, in my heart, I have a ghetto."

Later Zelma takes the spectators to another hall where they can see wood sculptures of *Musslmen*. "This Musslmanchik," she says (in funny broken Hebrew), "whose stomach is glued to his back, I would have given a fortune to know where he hides a piece of bread. I'll give millions to know where his scream comes from." Hours later, toward the end of a typically Israeli dinner shared by the actors and the audience as part of the performance, the audience sees the actress Madi Maayan (Zelma in the museum) lying naked in a *Musslman*-like position on the dinner table and pulling a piece of bread out of her vagina. Then Khaled (the Israeli Palestinian actor Khaled Abu-Ali) takes over the role of the tour guide from Zelma and explains what happened in Treblinka using a wooden model of the camp. "I did not know about the Holocaust until four years ago," he says. "Only after visiting Yad Vashem did I begin to believe that it really happened. That people can indeed kill like that. I wish you could see me once guiding [Arab] youth from the surrounding villages, who are not familiar with the Shoah." The text that Khaled is performing is in fact not a fictional one. Khaled indeed became aware of the Holocaust only a few years before joining the cast, when he began leading groups of young people from Arab villages in Galilee around the museum. One of his guided tours is documented in Tlalim's film. The Arab youth in the tour say to the camera that the Jews suffered less than the Palestinians, that they at least were exterminated immediately, while the Palestinians are being slowly tortured.

The film *Don't Touch My Holocaust* begins with twenty minutes in which Tlalim tries to explore the meaning of the memory of the Holocaust for Israelis. He creates in this introduction what he calls "an inventory of the memory of the Holocaust." It is a sort of a retrospective tour de force of the lexicon of the Holocaust as it has been shaped by Israeli collective memory and is composed of the exploration of some key words, such as "Arbeit Macht Frei," that have come to symbolize the Holocaust.[9] Yet, as Tlalim insists, this inventory of institutionalized memory is represented "with love, from within," not in order to criticize and satirize Israeli society but in order to place it before a critical mirror. The film, as Tlalim explains, is structured like a psychoanalytic journey. "It is a journey deep into the soul."[10]

The significance of Tlalim's documentary is that it is not a simple documentation of the theater performance, but a film on memory and identity. As the director himself acknowledges: "All the films that I make are about memory." Tlalim perceives *Don't Touch My Holocaust* as a continuation of his series of six films on the 1973 war. In these films, as he has said, he tried to examine the trauma of war. In *Don't Touch My Holocaust* he confronts the question of how Israelis deal with memory: how they remember and how they forget. These questions, Tlalim explains, were triggered by a personal trauma that he went through during the 1973 war, in part related to the loss of his brother in the war. His film *Missing Picture* (1989) explores the notion of war trauma and its influence on its victims' daily lives. After Tlalim confronted the 1973 war trauma, he felt that the time was ripe for him to touch "the ultimate trauma which overshadows all the static memories of our daily life: the Holocaust."

Tlalim himself has no direct relationship with the Holocaust. He was born in Tangier and raised in Spain. Yet, he always felt that the division between the children of survivors and those of nonsurvivors, as well as between Ashkenazim and Mizrahim, is unjustified and in relation to the third generation is no longer important. Significantly, the shared diasporic roots of Casablanca-born Dudi Maayan, the playwright, and Tlalim, turned them immediately into close friends.[11] In the film *Don't Touch My Holocaust* the seeming paradox of Maayan and Tlalim, two Oriental Jews, commemorating the extermination of Ashkenazi Jews, is formulated as the question "What does a Moroccan have to do with the Holocaust?" which introduces Tlalim's documentation of his visit to his hometown, Tangier. The whole attempt "to penetrate deeper and deeper into memory in order to extract the beginning of it all" led, as Tlalim explains, "in unexpected directions." Tlalim traveled to Morocco to visit and shoot his and Maayan's childhood homes for the film.[12] Additionally, in the section that opens the film, he introduces the story of Muni Yosef, one of the actors, who was born in Iraq and was not familiar at the beginning of the production with the phrase "Arbeit Macht Frei." Yet, during the research period some of Yosef's repressions disappeared and he recalled that his childhood on Moshav Mazor was spent among survivors who founded the Moshav (a semicollective agricultural settlement). Tlalim's film documents his visit to Mazor and his meeting with one of the neighbors who tells him that she can still see Mengele performing a selection.[13]

The whole film *Don't Touch My Holocaust*, according to Tlalim,

is about looking at ourselves in the mirror. We look in the mirror and see ourselves as we are without putting the blame on the Germans and without adopting a victim's perspective. It is a film without Germans. We look at ourselves and try to see what we really look like. What is behind this film and all the other films that I have made is the belief that we are all ill, we all suffer from dark dreams. We all suffer from some childhood trauma and the only way to face it is to examine it. To look at ourselves and to make fun of ourselves. This is the way in which Madi who plays a survivor is looking at us, cruelly and yet lovingly. This is the way we look at our perversions and disturbances, painfully yet laughingly. I tried in this film to observe Israeli society mercilessly yet affectionately in an effort to understand what we are made of.

The dilemma behind the film, Tlalim said, is how to remember, both personally and collectively. Perhaps, he asserted, it would be better to live in amnesia. But this is impossible because the past always creeps into our life. "I have a problem with institutionalized ways of memorialization but the question is: what is the alternative? I see my children, the third generation, and the ways they are touched by the Holocaust. We need to relate to memory here and now, see ourselves as we live it now and not as it really happened. The film is structured like an internal journey and each spectator is invited to look at his own life. I call it 'The Mirror Way.'"

During *Arbeit Macht Frei*'s trip to Germany, Tlalim himself became an actor in the performance. *Arbeit Macht Frei* was a theater of process: once "I became an actor myself another dimension was added to this complex process. People wanted to see both the theatrical performance and the film, and a kind of dialogue was created between the two." In Germany the group used the Wannsee Villa, the place where the decision to implement the Final Solution was made, as a substitute for the guided tour in the Lohamei HaGetaot Holocaust Museum in Israel. The group was surprised by the salient absence of exhibits in the Wannsee museum that represented the actual catastrophe. They also discovered that the German "second generation" also wants to talk about the Holocaust, more than the Israeli group was willing to listen. One member of the audience told them his secret anxiety: to find a picture of his father in Nazi uniform in one of the museums. In one of the more cathartic journeys of the theater process, the actors are seen urinating on the site of Hitler's bunker and singing patriotic Israeli songs. While the Israeli Jews succeeded in exorcising some of their anxieties, Khaled, the Palestinian Israeli, felt constantly persecuted. According to Tlalim, the reactions to the performance in Germany were mixed. The Jewish audience was upset because the Germans as perpetrators were absent. The young non-Jewish Germans, on the other hand, were enthusiastic, and very interesting relationships developed between some of them and the actors.

One of the problems of Israeli society, according to Tlalim, is that it deals with the Holocaust only on the ceremonial level. This has brought about the trivialization and banalization of the memory of the Holocaust. In addition, assimilation of the Holocaust into modern Israeli society fails to assign a role to Jewish-Palestinian relations. Palestinian citizens of Israel have been excluded from the memory of the Holocaust.[14] This attempt at division is also related to the division between Ashkenazim and Mizrahim and, according to Tlalim, has resulted in a monopolization of the memory of the Holocaust by the children of survivors. This exclusionist attitude damaged the Arabs in particular. The message of Tlalim's film is that "the memory of the Holocaust belongs to us all." It was therefore very important for Tlalim to document through his film a guided tour in Arabic in the Lohamei HaGetaot museum conducted especially for Arab youth from the surrounding area. "I was shocked," Tlalim said, "by their reactions. Yet it is not them I blame, but the educational system that does not understand that every Israeli citizen has to confront this issue. Only when the system changes will people not make these silly comparisons between Israeli and Nazi soldiers and the Intifada and the Holocaust."[15]

According to historian Amnon Raz-Krakotzkin, the uniqueness of the performance of *Arbeit Macht Frei*, which was "one of the most overwhelming experiences provided by Israeli culture in recent years,"[16] is that it subverts and challenges the established memory of the Holocaust, while acknowledging that the Holocaust is the primary formative factor in the shaping of Jewish-Zionist consciousness. Furthermore, its point of departure is the creation of a sense of responsibility toward this memory. *Arbeit Macht Frei* enables its Israeli spectators to have a different kind of memory, one that is critically shaped against the existing one, and yet grows out of it. The unique use of the theatrical medium enables the creation of a dialogic relationship between the repressing present and the repressed past, turning the memory of the Holocaust into a basis for a completely different ethics.

Memory in *Arbeit Macht Frei* is "performed" by the characters of Zelma and Khaled who lead the narrative, while constantly changing and transforming in the course of the performance. Zelma, with a middle European accent and "broken" language, represents the victim, the one who came from "there" and whose memory has been absent from the traditional Israeli ideological framework that refers to the murder but not to the victims. Her "broken" language signifies a cultural positioning and not just the linguistic fact that her Hebrew speech is neither standard nor correct. Her cultural positioning as "marginal" is linked to the way in which her interpretation of the different exhibits in the museum leads to new and provoking insights regarding the Israeli-Palestinian conflict.

Zelma is later replaced by Khaled, who guides the spectators through a model of the Treblinka extermination camp. The identification of the Palestinian actor with the suffering of the Jews challenges the monopoly claimed by Zionism on the memory of the Holocaust and on the particularist Jewish lessons that it draws from it. The inclusion of Khaled in the ritual of remembrance assigns to the ritual a broad meaning, and gives the spectator a new and fresh perspective with which to understand some of the ideological assumptions of Israeli society.

The scene develops out of a torture scene in which Khaled is dancing completely naked on the wooden table based on the Treblinka model, thus uniting Khaled and Zelma into one image of memory. It is described by Israeli journalist Tzvi Gilat as "the closest thing to a nightmare which I have ever experienced in relation to any work of art."[17] The final scene of the play, located also at the end of Tlalim's film, serves as the ultimate expression of Maayan's and Tlalim's primal protest against exclusionist Holocaust memory.

The scene begins after the audience, along with the actors, have finished a very rich dinner and enjoyed wine and baklava (a sweet Middle Eastern pastry) as refreshments. They have descended one by one through a very narrow door that has been opened in the ceiling of the room where most of the performance takes place, to another space. It is a hybrid space evoking associations of both discotheque and gas chamber. An "Israeli folk dance festival" is projected on huge video screens, featuring Israeli singer Shoshana Damari, who in Israeli public consciousness is known as "the singer of the wars." Surrounding the video screens are various photographs and exhibits related to the Holocaust. At the corner of this space, one of the actresses, completely naked, is obsessively eating the remains of the dinner to the point of vomiting. Madi Maayan, completely naked, is crouching in another corner in a *Musslman* posture and Khaled, also naked, is dancing on a wooden table in another corner of the hall. It was only a few hours before on a similar table in the Lohamei HaGetaot Museum that Khaled explained to the audience that Jews were beaten to death every day in Treblinka. Now Khaled is beating himself with a club similar to the one that was used by the Ukrainians to beat the Jews in Treblinka, and invites members of the audience to come to the table and join the beating. Horrifying as it is, there are people (both in Israel and in Germany) who accept his "invitation" and beat him. Others use the bottle opener hanging from Khaled's neck in order to open bottles of beer.

The horrific party culminates with a slowly rising high-pitched sound emanating from the loudspeakers and changing respectively from wild drum beats to Israeli popular songs of the 1950s that celebrate the Zionist project of settling the land—all this while the eyes of Holocaust victims and of Herzl, the founder of Zionism, stare at the audience from images hanging on the walls. A tough attendant leads the audience to the exit (or entrance?) gate bearing the words "Arbeit Macht Frei," the famous slogan that welcomed the victims to Auschwitz. Khaled is still frantically dancing and beating himself, his naked body flooded with strong beams of blinding light thrown by powerful projectors. On the way to the exit the members of the audience see Khaled, exhausted from the physical and mental effort, collapse and cry cathartically,[18] while Madi Maayan, still naked, hugs and calms him down in a Pietà-like posture.

The Pietà image leads the spectators to acknowledge the victimhood and self-flagellation of Khaled, the Palestinian, as well as that of Zelma, the survivor whose repression in Israeli culture derives from his or her epitomizing the ultimate icon of the diasporic Jew, a mythic figure rejected by the ideology of the "negation of exile," which is at the core of Zionism. Thus, the memory of the victim, as Raz-Krakotzkin observes, becomes a focus for Jewish identity, which paradoxically enables the opening up of the memory of the Palestinian past. Yet, no memory, neither Jewish nor Palestinian, can retrieve the past. The common memory of victimhood, which this last scene so powerfully establishes, creates the conditions for a change of consciousness regarding the boundaries of discourse on and of memory.

The last scene of *Arbeit Macht Frei* also reestablishes a mirror effect, echoed by Tlalim's "mirror way" in *Don't Touch My Holocaust*. To look at one's self in the mirror is also to look at the other. And this act of looking is precisely the junction where the survivor and the Palestinian merge into what I call a "hybrid survivor." However, it is important to remember, as Raz-Krakotzkin reminds us, that the Palestinian actor does not represent an indigenous "Palestinian consciousness" but constitutes part of a play that was written by Jews and deals with Jewish consciousness (despite the dialogism and openness toward the "other" that characterizes this work of theater). Although the actor presents his point of view, its importance is that it shows the consciousness of the Jew from the point of view of the other. The distinction here is not between a "particularistic" versus "universal" memory, but between two patterns of memory that the language of Israeli culture creates. The Palestinian actor points out an essential observation: It is the fate of the Palestinians—more than other nations, excluding the Jews and the Germans, and in a different way, the Poles—that the Holocaust occupies such a significant role in their collective consciousness. And that is so because the memory of the Holocaust is "forced" upon them not only to justify Jewish settlement in Palestine, but to explain expulsion of the Palestinians and the negation of their right to freedom and self-determination. This dialectic process, based

Fig. 3 *An image of a Pietà: Khaled (Khaled Abu Ali) and Holocaust survivor Zelma (Madi Maayan) in Asher Tlalim de Bentolila's* Don't Touch My Holocaust, *based on the Acre Theatre's* Arbeit Macht Frei vom Toitland Europa. *Courtesy of Dan Setton Set Productions.*

upon a diasporic consciousness, opens up the possibility of seeing the extermination of the Jews as the point of departure in forging a new attitude toward the continuous oppression of the Palestinians, without reverting to the simplistic and senseless comparison made by the Arab youth in Tlalim's film between two kinds of national catastrophes ("holocausts"). The rupture in the existing Jewish consciousness, as Raz-Krakotzkin observes, makes room for a new definition of Jewish existence in Israel/Palestine. It is a definition that not only acknowledges the Arab existence but assigns to it a "surplus value." It is a definition that assumes full responsibility by acknowledging the wrongs done to the other and identifying with the repressed.[19]

As the Israeli critic Michael Handelzaltz claims, the final scene of the play, in which the naked Khaled is beaten by "volunteers" from the audience (Tlalim's film shows the beating in Germany) creates a reality of humiliation. The spectator who does not interfere to stop the suffering is as indifferent as the bystanders in the Holocaust. But had the spectator interfered he or she would have collaborated in the activity of the theater. The spectator, thus, is both an innocent and complicit observer. You (the spectator), Handelzaltz concludes his review, "are both observer and collaborator, there is no way out." [20]

The Acre Theatre Group left Tel Aviv, the cultural center of Israel, for Acre, an originally Arab town that today has become an Arab ghetto. Khaled claims that the theater experience helps him in his personal choice: beyond being an Arab, an Israeli, and a Palestinian, he has decided to be a human being. And over and over again he realizes what this means. From time to time people who beat him on the wooden table call him and ask for forgiveness. Only now, they explain, have they realized what they have done. "What kind of forgiveness are you asking for?" Khaled asks them. "You have become Nazis yourselves." "But you gave us a club and asked to be beaten," they respond. "And if I had given you a knife?" he replies.[21]

The actor Muni Yosef explained that the show gave him relief from his trauma. The performers collected materials for the show during the Gulf War. He and Madi experienced severe anxiety and were afraid that it could be the end of Israel.[22] Dudi Maayan said that he would like the Holocaust to be perceived as "the other planet," to use Ychiel Dinur (Ka-Tzetnik)'s phrase. Yet, according to Maayan, this planet should be viewed slightly differently from Ka-Tzetnik's. It is one among many planets. This planet, Maayan says, is here, it was a part of our lives and yet life goes on. Even the prime minister,[23] Maayan emphasizes, says that we are no longer a lonely people (*am levadad yishkon*). In Maayan's view, this is a revolution in the way Israel perceives itself, and we are seeing only the beginning of that revolution.

One of the scenes of the play is a satire on the institutionalized ceremonies conducted in Israeli schools to commemorate Holocaust Remembrance Day. While the actors perform a parody in the form of a mock ceremony, the background walls of the performance space are filled by video projections. One of them shows selection, another Israeli folk dances, and on the other two we see kibbutz children respond to a question about what they know of the Holocaust, while famous Israeli television broadcasters report the daily news. "Replace your television with a mirror" suggests Dudi Maayan in a flier distributed to the audience when they leave the theater. But as Gilat perceptively observes, "all those televisions are mirrors on which we are screened, and everything is difficult to watch: funny, saddening, comforting and disturbing at the same time." [24]

Viewing both *Arbeit Macht Frei* and *Don't Touch My Holocaust* is an unsettling, disturbing experience, especially for an Israeli audience.[25] Both these works create a moral dilemma for the ideal imaginary (and imagined) Israeli identity by using pornography, invoking Palestinian victimhood and Israeli racism in conjunction with the Holocaust, and making the audience complicit in the theatrical performance. In this way both the play and the film capture one of the confusing contradictions embedded in Israel's struggle with the memory of the Holocaust. The viewing experience may be too offensive for survivors. Although Tlalim has claimed that survivors were grateful to him for making this film,[26] my own (though limited) experience of survivors' reactions is different. At the Twelfth World Congress of Jewish Studies, where I presented a short version of this study, I illustrated my paper with an excerpt from the ending of the film that documents a performance of the Pietà scene in Germany. As the audience in my session was composed of survivors and academics (a very common mixture in Holocaust-related conferences held in Israel), I warned everybody, and in particular the survivors, that they might find the material offensive and therefore they should feel free to leave. Despite my warning, and despite the fact that I never suggested any comparison between the oppression of the Palestinians and the Holocaust, I was still bitterly attacked by one survivor for the sheer fact that I brought together the Holocaust and the Palestinian issue. The film was also attacked by the survivors in my audience for being pornographic, sensationalist, and scandalous.[27] Although I do not accept the survivors' judgment, I can fully understand their point of view. Indeed, after experiencing *Arbeit Macht Frei*, I told everybody how overwhelming this performance was and how important for understanding Israeli identity. Yet, I have always maintained that this performance was suitable for the second generation only. It should be emphasized time and again that both *Arbeit Macht Frei* and *Don't Touch My Holocaust* reflect a second-generation sensibility and are primarily aimed at a second-generation audience. The second-generation sensibility, after all, is based on the desire to fill a void, to imagine what David Grossman in *See under Love* calls "Eretz Sham" (the country over there), or to repeat Ka-Tzetnik's phrase "the other planet." Spatially and temporally distant from the historical Holocaust, the second generation has its own Holocaust that, not unlike "Grossman's Holocaust" and consciously so, exists in the realm of the imaginary, which does not strive to explore what really happened there, but how what happened "there" affects us here and now—how our imagined and fantasized Holocaust has been assimilated into our consciousness.

Choice and Destiny (1994), Tzipi Reibenbach

Choice and Destiny was directed and produced by Tzipi Reibenbach between 1988 and 1993.[28] It is 118 minutes long and in Yiddish. It was edited by Ziva Postac, the editor of Lanzmann's *Shoah*, and shot by David Gurfinkel and Avi Koren. The production took five years because there was neither private nor public support for it. As the director reveals, she was repeatedly asked, "A film in Yiddish? About your parents?" The first version lasted four hours, with the visit to Europe constituting its core. However, this version did not satisfy Reibenbach, so she reedited it. The focus of the revised version was a closely observed account of her parents' daily routine, combined with her father's recollection of his Holocaust memories. The film was thus shortened, and according to Reibenbach, "it is a film about a memory that is not willing to be forgotten, although 50 years have passed."[29]

The film documents the story of Reibenbach's parents, Itshak and Fruma Grinberg, during the Holocaust, and their life as a retired elderly couple in Israel today. The camera follows their daily routine from the moment they wake up until they go to bed, ready or not for a night's sleep that either comes or fails to come. The camera introduces the spectator into the couple's sphere of intimacy and is used as a catalyst to make them talk. We move along with it from one room to another in the survivors' modestly furnished, Israeli low-income "shikun" apartment and follow their daily activities. The father is a big man who was in his early eighties when the filming began. His movements and gestures are carefully measured, almost ritualized, and project strength and tranquillity. By contrast the mother, who is small and hyperactive, projects nervousness and restlessness. She is constantly on the move: preparing food, dusting furniture, watering plants, and arranging clothes in the closet. The spectator gradually recognizes the pattern of the couple's daily routine while observing them both individually and together. The impression that the couple conveys is that of a highly trained "team" that despite behavioral differences projects a harmony not disturbed even by the presence and proximity of the camera. Slowly the spectator learns to know the protagonists through observing their mundane existence.

Yet, the core of the film is not a voyeuristic penetration into the protagonists' life. The spectator quickly finds himself/herself fascinated by the father's story and transported to the time of the Holocaust, to the father's territories of personal memory introduced in his *mamalushen* (mother tongue), Yiddish. Through the father's memory, which has not faded with the passage of

Fig. 4 *Spheres of intimacy: Holocaust survivors Fruma and Itshak Grinberg in Tsipi Reiben-bach's* Choice and Destiny. *Photo by Havakuk Levison. Courtesy of Tsipi Reibenbach.*

time, the viewer arrives in the past and proceeds with the storyteller from one domain of memory to another—from one concentration camp to the next. The father's life narrative is gradually revealed to the spectator, and is followed by the movements of the silent mother, whose body cries out through her nervous activity.

Choice and Destiny was described by director Reibenbach as a "memory film. A film that speaks about the daily life of Holocaust survivors. . . . I visited Poland, Czechoslovakia, and Austria," Reibenbach said, "in order to better understand my parents' past, but I understood that I will find nothing there. If it is possible to understand or feel anything at all, you have got to look for it among the people still living among us."[30] Reibenbach herself was born in Poland, shortly after the war. When she was three years old her parents decided to immigrate to Israel, and they settled in Lod (originally an Arab town). Reibenbach decided to document their daily life in a realistic fashion.

> I returned to their flat in Lod, to the kitchen, the living room, the dining room, the bedroom and the bathroom. I documented all the minute details, the face-shaving and washing, and in particular the process of preparing the food, the

main activity at home and in the film. My father, who finally after 50 years found a sympathetic ear, collaborated willingly. There is no heroism or sentimentality in his manner of speech. He relates even the most horrific stories in a matter-of-fact tone. In his opinion, the daily routine of the Holocaust, even during the worst periods, was not sensational. Eventually it was a story of small accounts and weekly budgets. Toward the end of the film, when it seems that everything has happened, a miracle occurs: all of a sudden, without any warning, my mother begins to talk, and it happens with an overwhelming outburst of emotion, anger, and lamentation over her beloved murdered family.[31]

In a special issue of the *Ha'aretz* Friday supplement "Ashkenazi Anxiety," which discussed ethnic tensions between Mizrahim and Ashkenazim, Reibenbach, in an opinion piece titled "My Parents," wrote:

My parents arrived in Israel in 1950. They are Holocaust survivors from Poland. The Israeli establishment then was controlled by Ashkenazim. But not Ashkenazim like my parents. The descendants of the Biluyim and the pioneers, Holocaust survivors who immigrated to Palestine between 1945 and 1948 and were deported to Cyprus, the people of the Palmach generation—those were the real heroes of Israel. My parents were taken to transit camps (Ma'abarot)[32] and nobody wanted to talk to them in the languages they knew, Yiddish or Polish. The clerks asked them "why did you come?" An attitude of superiority, contempt, indifference and a lack of understanding—this was the treatment they received after they came from there. "You went like lambs to the slaughter, you did not fight or resist" was the dominant attitude toward the Holocaust survivors until the early 80s. My parents symbolized the Diaspora, they were despised. They did not have work, and whoever did not have the red book ('hapinkas haadom') or 'protektzia'[33] did not have a chance of supporting his family. How can you think about culture under such circumstances? My parents arrived in the Levant and their Europeaness stood out. The Sabra culture was the dominant one then, and it was not a spiritual culture. It was a very physical one.[34]

The film opens with Reibenbach's parents sitting in their small living room and listening to the Yiddish news program on the radio. Lech Wałesa, the Polish president, is heard requesting forgiveness from the Jewish people in his speech to the Knesset. In the scene that immediately follows, the parents are seen shopping in the open market of Lod. A muezzin is heard calling the believers to prayer, and a mosque is seen in the background. The editing that juxtaposes these two scenes gives visual and ideological expression to the parents' alienation from the Levant as previously discussed by their daughter. The parallel editing creates a striking visual meeting point between two cultures—that of the Eastern European Jewish survivors and that of the "local Easterners," the few Palestinians who remained in Lod after the mass expulsion from the town in 1948. Although the editing suggests incongruity and cultural and political tension, it also implies a sense of involuntary shared tragedy, the tragedy of the displaced and alienated. Both the survivors and the Palestinians are perceived as an "other" minority, whose tragic and repressed memories threaten the perceived "wholeness" of the Zionist state. Hence the opening scene establishes the survivors, for the spectator, as outsiders to the society that surrounds them. A sense of exile, both external and internal, permeates this scene, which becomes a visual metaphor of the physically and spiritually alienated existence of the survivors in Israel. It should also be mentioned at this point that many Holocaust survivors were, as a matter of government policy, settled in evacuated Palestinian homes in Arab towns like Jaffa, Haifa, Lod, and Ramla, thus forcefully grafting the memory of the Holocaust onto Palestinian national memory, and symbolically linking the Holocaust of the Jewish people (mostly Polish Jews) to the Palestinian *Nakba* ("catastrophe," as the 1948 war has been dubbed by the Arabs).[35]

In another scene the parents are seen watching the television news about the opening of the fifty-year commemoration of the end of World War II in Warsaw. This news item is followed by another about the murder of an Israeli lawyer in Gaza, thus reminding the spectator once again of the constant presence of the Israeli-Palestinian conflict shifting back and forth from the background to the foreground. In yet another scene the parents watch the evening news again. This time it is about the murder of Chris Hani, the leader of the Communist Party in South Africa. All these seemingly non-diegetic allusions can be read as an implied attempt to expand the boundaries of the discourse on the Jewish Holocaust and, if not to compare it to other acts of genocide or racism, then at least to make us (Israelis) aware of their existence.

Time in the Film and the Film in Time

Time is a significant component of *Choice and Destiny*. The sound of the clock plays a major role in the soundtrack. The tick of the clock opens and closes the film. The daily routine of the survivor couple is also based around the clock. Their day begins with the sound of the clock and ends with the winding of the clock before they go to sleep. Furthermore, the clock itself is used in the film as a repetitive visual motif. The clock is not only part of the decor, but becomes a major "actor" in the film. It divides the day into activity blocks that structure the family ritual, as well as the daily routine of the protagonists. The clock also creates a pause in the father's story and acts as a transitional device from the "past" to the "present" and vice versa. It is thereby utilized to bring the "outside" into the interior of the home. The clock creates continuity between the everyday routine and the lack of routine during the Holocaust period. As the director explains: "I did not use flashbacks, on the contrary, I brought the past into the present. Therefore it is a film about the present."[36] Indeed, the many transitions to the past that occur in the film are hardly noticeable, camouflaged as echoes in the survivors' lives where the past joins the present. The clock is also used as a decorative visual prop, a type of icon toward which the gaze (that of both the protagonists and the spectators) is very often directed. Beneath the clock the mother sits and listens intently to the father's stories. A line of continuity is thus created between the clock, the picture of the children that hangs beneath it, and the chair that the mother puts exactly underneath the clock and on which she, a silent and intent observer/spectator, sits and listens. This physical line establishes the temporal and spatial flow of family continuity and identity, creating temporality of the time "there" and the spatiality of the family "here."

In contrast to the present, which is usually "around the clock," time in the father's story has no meaning. The father tells his story without anchoring it in time. We do not know how old he was, how long he stayed in each camp, or when each of his stories took place. Time in his story is without boundaries; it floats and is unmarked. Only when the father is specifically asked about time does he relate to it: "Yes, we marched about for two weeks from Auschwitz to Prague," or "Yes, it was already towards the end of 1945."

Another relation to time arises from a question that Reibenbach asks her father—"why do you want to speak so fast?"—and from his answer—"because I will not live forever." Here we witness a recent phenomenon that characterizes Israeli (and also American and European) society: the attempt to document and record testimonies of Holocaust survivors before they disappear from the land of the living, as well as a willingness on the part of the survivors to tell their stories as a result of the change in attitude toward them and the Holocaust.

Language

The spoken language in *Choice and Destiny* between the father and the mother and between them and their daughter is a simple and basic Yiddish. This is despite the fact that the parents speak Hebrew, which becomes clear when they briefly converse with their grandchildren. Only the subtitles are in Hebrew. The choice of language is not accidental. First and foremost, this is the language spoken at home by the protagonists, as well as in the homes of many Holocaust survivors. Reibenbach's parents also know Polish, but her father, who, like so many other Polish Jews, hates Poles, refuses to speak it (although the mother has tried to speak Polish with her daughter). The parents listen to the radio news in Yiddish, read a Yiddish newspaper, and even attend Yiddish theater. Reibenbach says: "Hebrew was spoken outside, Yiddish is their language. This was my decision as a director. Yiddish is the language they feel at home with. They opened up more easily in Yiddish."[37]

In a conscious choice by the director, the use of the Yiddish language defines the cultural identity of the protagonists and provides a statement about their cultural and social belonging. The attitude expressed in the popular prestate slogan "Hebrew people, speak Hebrew!" attributed to language not only the functional role of communication, but also an ideological role marking and forming cultural and national collective identity. The Hebrew language is part of the identity of the Israeli who has severed his ties with the Diaspora and has created for himself a "proud identity," that of a productive new Jew. The choice of the parents to speak Yiddish informs the spectators about their background and indicates their particular identification (or lack of identification) with Israeli Zionist society. Their linguistic choice indicates that they did not immigrate to Israel out of Zionist or ideological motives. Reibenbach says that "[t]hey just wanted to rest. There, we were strangers. There were hopes about our Jewish homeland but the disappointments surpassed the expectations."[38] Reibenbach's testimony suggests that her parents were looking for empathy and sympathy but became disillusioned by Israeli reality. It is quite clear that the indifference (let alone the contempt) of Israeli society made it difficult for them to identify with the new country, its culture, language, and symbols.

The use of Yiddish in the film invokes other problems related to the identity of the second generation, whose members are torn between loyalty to their parents and identification with the Israeli society in which they were raised. "You understand what kind of problem I have always had with my parents. Yiddish is a language one is not supposed to speak. . . . I was ashamed of them, they are Diaspora Jews. I was always angry that I was not a Sabra," Reibenbach recalls.[39] Her decision to make a Yiddish-language film therefore carries a personal message of reconciliation with and acceptance of her parents. As is common with members of the second generation, she has gone through a therapeutic process: from feelings of shame to acceptance and pride. That the film, similar to *Because of That War*, was made out of love, compassion, and acceptance is very noticeable. Throughout the film the director introduces and initiates her parents into Israeli society and further reconciles with them. And so does the spectator. Hence the film parallels the change that the second generation has undergone as well as the change in the attitude of Israeli society toward the survivors. The very making of this film—the choice of protagonists, the selection of Yiddish, the depiction of the Holocaust survivor as a diasporic antihero figure whose physical existence is at the center of his life, and finally, the enthusiastic reception of the film—all are markers of this progression.

Body Language

The film makes use of the potential of film protagonists to "speak" through their bodies. The film medium, more than any other, seems suitable to this kind of "hero." Reibenbach's parents are simple, undistinguished Eastern European Jews, the common folk ("amcha") of Israeli society who have never been the protagonists of any cinematic representation of the Holocaust.[40] The father, who speaks laconically throughout the film in very factual and unemotional language, also expresses himself through his movements and gestures, which like his language are measured, controlled, and restrained.

The father describes the past horrors without providing any emotional or ideological interpretation. Although he uses the first-person narrative, he creates the impression that he is a sort of neutral observer who is not talking about himself. The most horrific events are recounted in a monotonous and emotionless voice. Sometimes the description is conveyed with a macabre sense of humor accompanied by a smile. For example, when he describes the daily ritual of counting the camp inmates, he says: "they counted us as if we were gold." Through his detached descriptions, which neither generalize nor provide any interpretative framework for the events described, he shields the spectator from the enormity of the horrors he experienced. For example, cannibalism, one of the phenomena experienced by the father in the camp, sounds like any other episode. With an expressionless face he speaks about bodies that arrived at the crematorium with parts of their buttocks missing because the Soviet inmates who transferred the corpses had cut them and sold the parts as horseflesh. His face is also expressionless when he describes the difficulty in removing the entangled bodies from the gas chambers.

When the father is asked by his daughter "What did you feel?" he answers: "I do not know what I felt . . . what we felt." Reibenbach reports that when she asked him how he managed to live with the daily burden of transferring so many bodies to the crematorium, he answered: "We were not human beings at that point, we were automatons. Our heads did not work at all; we worked mechanically, because otherwise it would have indeed been impossible to survive."[41] Victor Frankl, Holocaust survivor and existentialist psychologist, perceived apathy as a necessary defense mechanism against physical and emotional distress.[42] The father's detachment can be seen as a manifestation of the emotional repression of the past that made the recovery of the survivors possible. The fact that the father, at the age of eighty, tells his story for the first time is testimony to the lack of working through his trauma. His recollection of his past is perhaps only the beginning of the process of memorializing and mourning that is already too late.

The mother is silent throughout the film up until a dramatic outburst toward the end. Yet, even her silence speaks. Her lips are sealed, but her body tells her story. Her nervous movements express her feelings and reveal to the spectator the secrets of her mind and heart. "She listens to her husband, and at the same time, she feverishly cuts onions, furiously prepares gefilte fish, and obsessively dusts the shelves. She listens impatiently, as if saying to herself, "Why are you talking? Those who were not there will never understand."[43]

The mother's body language testifies to the existence of inner emotional turmoil, restlessness, inwardness that expresses silent protest, fear, and insecurity. She fortifies herself at home, and when the father goes out she obsessively locks the door with four locks, and even so still checks the door handle. This compulsive ritual is repeated in inverted form when the father returns. Yet, upon this return the ritual is less nervous than it was when he left the apartment because the mother smiles at him wholeheartedly (it is the first time in the film that we see her smile).

According to Reibenbach, the mother lives in constant fear. "She is afraid . . . today she is afraid even of peace." Fear and lack of basic trust in society, an isolationist attitude, and reliance on close family members only are the characteristics of Holocaust survivors. It is an internal defense mechanism adopted by many in order to overcome past memories. The mother clings to the house, she goes out only with her husband, and even then only to the market. She needs the sense of security that he gives her, as much as she needs to be surrounded by the objects of her kitchen, which provide her with a familiar and safe environment.

Given the mother's long silence, her outburst provides the emotional climax of the film. The outburst is followed by an emotional cry, manifested by her voice, facial expressions, and body movements. She erupts suddenly, like a volcano, and the words that emerge from her mouth are invested with pain, anger, and resentment. Despite her silence, her emotional involvement is greater than that of the father. She loses control, and her cry gives the film the emotional dimension that is lacking in the father's testimony.

The husband and wife seldom talk to each other; the few words they do exchange are related to everyday activities. Yet, this lack of verbal intercourse does not testify to a lack of communication or to an emotional distance. On the contrary, there is a closeness and harmony between them that does not require the mediation of words. The glances that they exchange while listening to the news about Lech Wałesa's appeal to the Jewish people for forgiveness are a case in point. Emotional closeness and affection are also expressed in the wife's maternal attitude toward her husband when he goes out. "Watch out! Be careful when you cross the street! Are you listening to me?" she says to him. Her welcoming smile to him upon his return is further evidence of their closeness.

The relationship between the couple is devoid of any evidence of physical affection. We never see them touch each other. The verbal and physical distance between them is also mentioned by their daughter: "My parents never touched each other or me." The audience during screenings in Europe also commented on this lack of physical touch in discussion with Reibenbach. According to the director, her parents' generation is not open about expressing emotions, which is evident in the group of Holocaust survivors who cared for their children's physical needs, such as food and clothing, but who were not very generous in giving them emotional warmth and providing physical contact. This is, according to Reibenbach, the origin of the sense of deprivation typical of the second generation.

Silence

The choice of silence as a pattern of behavior is typical of Holocaust survivors. Many reasons have been given for this "sonorous" silence. The standard explanation is that the survivors wanted to posit a demarcation line between the "there and then" and the "here and now." Separating themselves from the past enabled them to invest their energy in the tremendous effort required for establishing themselves in Israel both economically and socially. In addition to being immigrants, they were also survivors. They arrived in Israel during its early years, which were years of mass immigration and economic austerity. They wished to open a new chapter in their lives and to disconnect from the past. As the mother says in the film: "I have not told you anything. I did not want to talk at all. . . . I did not want to remember." But despite her silence she remembers and recalls, in particular during her long sleepless nights. The survivors knew that they would not be able to erase the past but hoped that through their silence they would spare their children and provide them with normal surroundings without burdening them with the past. Another explanation attributes the silence of the survivors to the negative, patronizing, and critical attitude of Israeli society toward them. It is hard to imagine the pain and insult experienced by the survivors on meeting the Israelis from whom they expected compassion and support.[44]

The father chose to break his silence and to tell the camera about his past. The mother, on the other hand, chose to continue her silence, but she could not maintain it. It seems that the father's story brought back feelings and emotions that were suppressed for years. When the mother has her emotional outburst, she, perhaps surprised by the power of her own anger, explains: "I have never talked. If I spill it all out now, maybe I'll feel better." And she adds, "Maybe I'll feel relief too; maybe I'll be able to fall asleep." In contrast to the father's seemingly rational and balanced decision to break the silence, the mother's outburst is uncontrolled. Both the choice of silence, as well as the choice to break the silence, derive from internal and external processes. The external reasons have to do with the change of attitude in Israeli society toward the Holocaust and the survivors.

Food

"'Yeder zach by unz Yidn drayt zich arum broyt un toyt.' 'Everything about us, Jews, circles around bread and death,' the popular Yiddish phrase runs, and this is what this film is all about," says the Israeli writer Aharon Meged.[45] The preoccupation with food, and the activities surrounding it, such as buying, cooking, and eating, as well as the descriptions of the father that always involve attempts to smuggle food into the camps—is the central focus of the film narrative, both in the past and in the present. It seems that the two parents are busy from the moment they wake up until they go to sleep with food and everything that it involves. The camera documents the different stages of food preparation and consumption: shopping in the market, cooking, and finally the moment of eating. In fact, a full fifty-five minutes of the film deal with the parents' preoccupation with food in the present, while fifteen minutes of the father's total story comprise anecdotes related to different ways in which he managed to acquire food in the camps. All together more than half of the film deals directly with food. "The whole story," Reibenbach said, "is about one more drop of soup or a bite of bread."

But the centrality of food is not expressed by film time alone. The camera concentrates on the couple's faces and hands while they prepare food, capturing the concentration and care invested in the process. The attention given

Fig. 5 *"Everything about us Jews circles around bread and death."* Holocaust survivors Itshak and Fruma Grinberg in Tsipi Reibenbach's Choice and Destiny *preparing a dish typical of traditional Eastern European Jewish cuisine. Photo by Havakuk Levison. Courtesy of Tsipi Reibenbach.*

to the food and the sensual indulgence in it are evident also in the parents' manner of eating. It makes the spectators themselves hungry, and indeed this was the director's intention.[46]

There is something repulsive and revolting about these endless rituals of eating. The spectator wonders: Why do they eat all the time? Why do they keep eating in silence? Is this the essence of their existence? The spectator's judgmental attitude is moderated by engagement with the father's stories, which put the parents' food obsession in perspective. Reibenbach notes that when the film was shown in Switzerland and France, some (Jewish) spectators left the screening in protest. One spectator in Paris said: "It is disgusting! They eat so much." In response the wife of a Parisian critic, who was in Birkenau when she was fifteen, yelled at her: "Bread is what matters! Look for the food!" One of the judges of the competition in France, a Russian Jew, asked Reibenbach angrily, "How dare you show him [the father] eating and talking about Birkenau?" Reibenbach's response is that whenever her father eats his associations go "there." The availability of food in the present reminds him always of the scarcity of food and the hunger of the past. The daily struggle of the father against hunger thus always appears in the background when food is shown in the present, but when he talks about death there is no food. The film editing thereby uses food and food associations to create transitions between the present and the past, here and there.

Food provides an answer to the constant hunger experienced in the camps. Hunger was the basic feeling. The mother, during her outburst, says, "We were hungry, it was an unimaginable hunger." The centrality of food in the parents' life transfers the high, spiritual, and abstract discourse on the Holocaust to the material level. The reverential rhetoric of the Holocaust, so typical of Israeli official discourse, is stripped down to its bare bones. The survivors' struggle comes down to basic bodily needs. Thus, the Holocaust is represented not as an abstract metaphysical struggle but as a very physical one. The film exposes the cruelty and brutality integral to the struggle for survival: cannibalism, drinking of urine, different methods of obtaining and concealing food, and total dedication to thinking about new "creative" ways to get food ("organiziren" as the father calls it).

The film thus implicitly raises uneasy questions regarding the issue of survival. Is the struggle for "one more drop of soup and one more bite of bread" the essence of the Holocaust for the survivors? The answer, of course, is complex. Many children of survivors have experienced their parents' attitude toward food in general, and bread in particular, as sacred. The prohibition against throwing away food, the compulsion "to finish everything that is on the plate," and the recycling of leftovers are basic life experiences of most survivor families and, to a certain extent, have spilled over into Israeli society at large. It is also possible that the consumerist, gourmet culture that has developed in Israel in recent years constitutes a generational reaction against the guilt-ridden food ideology practiced in survivor families. Food is used by the director and film editor as another device to sharpen the contrasts between the "then" and the "now," between the plenitude of the present and the shortage of the past, the routinization of the meals "here" and the risk, courage, and initiative involved in obtaining food "there."

Food and bread carry meaning that transcends physical existence. They represent the primary gratification of the human being, and hence the search for food carries with it an existential significance. Frankl, who experienced concentration camp life, writes that the desire for food was the major primitive drive, the axis around which all mental life in the camp revolved.[47] The centrality of food is also expressed through the story frame of the film, which opens and closes with the family's Sabbath meal. The food is an element that unites the family—the parents, the children, and the grandchildren. The documentation of the different stages of food preparation, possibly an anthropological attempt to record traditional ways of preparing dishes typical of Eastern European Jewish cuisine such as gefilte fish, chopped liver salad, kreplach, and challahs (the baking of which provides one of the narrative and emotional climaxes of the film) draws family members together as inheritors of a shared tradition.

More than anything, the family meal manifests the victory of the survivors. Not only have they survived, but they have also built their lives anew, establishing families and bearing children and grandchildren. In the light of these achievements their past struggle to survive even through the most horrific circumstances assumes meaning. Related to this meaning is the name of the film itself.

Choice or Destiny?

The life story of the father—one of the film's protagonists—oscillates between choice and destiny, between his personal choices and the fate imposed on him as a European Jew during the Holocaust. Fate is a recurrent motif in all of the father's stories, in which he implies, and sometimes explicitly claims, that he did not survive due to his courage and initiative, but due to destiny. It is not he who is presented as the main hero in his own stories but destiny itself. The father repeats this in many ways: "Every man has his own destiny," "I am alive due to destiny," "I got out of it, you understand? Destiny, that is, this is destiny!" He describes his arrival at Birkenau thus: "Sometimes they had water in the showers and sometimes gas. We had water." The meeting with Itche Eisenstein, who got the father out of the Roma camp in Auschwitz and thereby saved him from extermination, is also described as a stroke of luck, as is the typhus disease that saved him from extermination by the Sonder-kommando in the crematorium in Mauthausen.

Destiny is the explanation that the father gives to his daughter who presses him to provide an interpretation of the events. For himself the father accepts things the way they are without any need for further explanation. This accep-tance, this fatalism, also expresses his worldview and personality. Acceptance, the flip side of destiny, is a repetitive pattern in the father's story. "We knew that Auschwitz was the end." "We got used to it, there was nothing we could do, we waited to die." "We knew that we were going to die." This fatalism pre-vented him from escaping from Plasow and later from the death march, but it did not prevent him from continuing his daily struggle to get food.

The kind of fate that is invoked by the father is not identified with divine authority. He is not religious and does not mention God in his stories. There is something very "secular" in his type of destiny; indeed, Reibenbach con-firms that her father is a complete *epikors* (atheist). He does not ask questions or even suggest an implicitly philosophical framework that could assign meaning to the suffering and horrors that he endured and witnessed. This at-titude enables him to fall asleep at night and live in the present. In contrast, the mother does not accept her destiny. She asks questions, she cries "why?" and seems unable to find answers. She is left only with questions and is there-fore sleepless at night.

The other axis of the father's life is the limited choice he had. This is ex-pressed first and foremost in his will to live, in the preference of resistance, however meager, over surrender. His numerous stories about obtaining food testify to his determination to live. Even his choice not to escape from Plasow, or from the death march, derives from a rational calculation of what is the best way to stay alive. When his daughter insists and asks, "why didn't you es-cape? . . . [A]s a strong young man who didn't even look Jewish, why didn't you escape? You could have joined the partisans and fought: Why did you let them drag you from one camp to another?" He answers angrily, "You do not understand. There was no place to run away to. There was no village, no for-est; the Polish partisans killed Jews and there was no food." During the death march he had the opportunity to escape but he chose to continue: "We entertained the idea of escaping, but we had no food so we did not escape." These two choices, limited as they are, reflect the way of thinking and the behavior typical of many Jews during the Holocaust. Clinging to the familiar and the known, even if it happened to be one's tormentor, was a defense mechanism of the victim.

Choice and Destiny is different from all the other documentaries that have been made on the Holocaust. It is a Holocaust film that deals with life rather than death, and it happens in present-day Israel and not in the Europe of the past. It is a film that deals not with perpetrators and victims but with human beings. It is a Holocaust film that does not tell heroic stories, but narrates everyday routines. It does not mystify or sanctify the survivors but exposes the ugliness and brutality of the struggle for physical existence.

Through the gaze of the camera on the survivor couple, the Holocaust is seen differently and Israeli society is carefully examined. The narration of personal experiences, as well as the nonverbal elements of this narration, provides insights and understandings that cannot be obtained through other means, particularly scholarly studies. The "heroes" of the film represent many other survivors who seldom find their way into academic research or documentaries on the Holocaust, which tend to prefer either heroic figures (fighters, partisans, etc.) or accomplished individuals (artists, intellectuals, politicians and the like) over uneducated, ordinary survivors. The father and the mother are ordinary people, antiheroes. They did not escape, fight, or rebel during the Holocaust. The events described by them are neither monumental nor dramatic. They describe the everyday routine of life in the camps. And when they immigrated to Israel they continued to live as "undistinguished" people. Yet, they are representative of an integral constituency of Israeli society. What happened to the film's protagonists happened to many other survivors who live in Israel, and therefore the film transcends the particular and becomes a cultural document that explores the relationships between Israeli society, the Holocaust, and the survivors. Before the film premiere the director was concerned about reactions to the film, particularly how the representation of her parents would be perceived. After the screening she was kissed by survivors who told her that "this is the first time that a film has been made about *us*. It is not a film about your parents alone." [48]

The minimalism of *Choice and Destiny* reinforces its antiheroic stance. There is no story except for the one generated in the spectator's mind. The film does not use any recycled imagery from the collective iconography of the

Holocaust, but rather is rooted in contemporary Israeli reality and confined to a modest Israeli apartment. The film's intervention in the protagonists' life is minimal. The parents do not perform for the camera but continue their daily routine, the only significant exception being when Reibenbach dresses her father in old-fashioned European clothes and hat and makes him pose in front of the camera. This reenacting technique—reminiscent of that used by Lanzmann in *Shoah*[49]—contrasts the here and now (the underwear that the father—like many people of his generation who immigrated to Israel—wears in the tiny, hot apartment) with the there and then (Europe and its past elegance). The parents tell their story in their natural surroundings at home. The fact that their daughter, as director, constitutes their immediate audience creates a natural situation and unmediated contact between the interviewer and the interviewee, and consequently between the teller and the spectator. The camera never interferes, but always follows the protagonists closely and cautiously. The editing, however, is more interventionist than the cinematography. The cuts create transitions, parallels and contrasts, rhythms, tensions, and interest, hence helping to produce a multilayered sociocultural text.

The importance of the film lies elsewhere, in its being the expression of a maturing Israeli society that has become more receptive to the survivors and their plight. As a film made by the child of survivors, it reflects a change in the attitude of the second generation toward their parents, themselves, and the Holocaust. In addition to being a second-generation product, it is also the product of the generation of the survivors themselves, who after more than fifty years are willing to tell their story because today there are finally those who want to listen.[50]

Distance and Proximity

The films discussed here have contributed to the emergence not only of the survivors' voice but also of the second generation's voice as well as to acceptance by the second generation of themselves as secondary victims (both direct "victims" of their survivor parents and indirect victims of the Holocaust). This acceptance indicates changes in Israeli society, which has shifted from a society that prizes heroism to one that prizes victimhood. Paradoxically and tragically, however, the identification with the Jewish victim increases as the identification with the victims of Israel, the Palestinians, wanes. This contemporary Israeli dialectic of victimhood, perceptively captured by *Arbeit Macht Frei*, recalls the American elevation of the Holocaust into a master moral paradigm whereby an "easier" identification with the Jewish Holocaust is substituted for confrontation with America's own victims—Native Americans and African Americans.[51]

Second-generation Holocaust films counter the attempt to standardize and routinize an official monolithic memory of the Holocaust. They privatize memory rather than nationalize it. These processes are part of the current schism within Israeli society and its conflicts of identity, in which the Holocaust functions as an identity-formation mechanism. Yet, the collective spirit of the "Israeli tribe" is stronger than any attempt at individuation. To borrow the famous feminist slogan, in Israel the private is always public. Consequently, the phenomenon of second-generation Israelis going to Poland (in most cases with their survivor parents) to visit the former death camps in order to perform a "secular ritual" of pilgrimage, or "Holocaust tourism,"[52] has become part of Israeli civil religion. Similar journeys in search of lost diasporic identity are practiced by Moroccan second-generation youth who travel to Morocco to find their roots. The close relationships of the two trends is expressed in Tlalim's *Don't Touch My Holocaust,* which explores the complex issues of identity, memory, and ethnicity through the conjunction of the Holocaust with both Jewish and Arab "Orientals."

The films discussed here can also be seen as manifestations of a healing process, in particular with regard to the second generation, but also with regard to Israeli society as a whole. This is evident in *Because of That War,* and even more so in *Don't Touch My Holocaust,* which is dominated by the second-generation voice and completely ignores the survivors' voice. The survivors' voice in this film is transmitted through the sometimes perverse prism of their ventriloquist children whose "Holocaust" remains in the realm of morbid fantasy. In contrast, the realistic style adopted by Orna Ben Dor in *Because of That War* gives an equal voice to the survivors and their children. It respects the survivors' memories, but nevertheless shows compassion toward their children, who to a certain extent became their "victims." Indeed, *Because of That War* was the first Israeli documentary that used the children of survivors as protagonists in a Holocaust film and consequently helped establish the second generation as an identity group. Obviously, the status that Poliker and Gilead enjoy in Israeli youth culture aided identification with them as protagonists. Similarly, Vilojni's status as a popular actor and stand-up comedian helped his home movie–style roots journey to Poland to receive greater public exposure. *Choice and Destiny,* on the other hand, is mainly a film about the survivor parents. The survivors' child (director/interviewer Reibenbach) never says anything about herself. She is always in the background playing a very unintrusive role. Yet, despite its intimate, familial character, the film transcends the genre of a home movie and becomes a fascinating document about Israeli society and identity.

The play of distance and proximity in these films is also evident in their gender/parenting economy. It is fascinating to examine in these films who speaks and who keeps silent, who is absent and who is present, who is visible and who is invisible as an indication of how removed from or enmeshed in the Holocaust the film is. In *Because of That War* Gilead's father is absent. We see him briefly at a family dinner before the mother goes to Poland. We know only that he is also a Holocaust survivor. Poliker's mother, on the other hand, is always present in the frame, but she remains a silent presence. All we know about her is that she is also a survivor from Greece. In *Daddy Come to the Amusement Park* the mother is completely absent. We have no idea who she is and even if she is alive. The whole film concerns the Oedipal axis of father/son, and even the sister is used only to provide emotional support for her father and brother. *Choice and Destiny* is the most interesting film from the point of view of family dynamics. The silent mother erupts toward the end, creating a shift of narrative focus. Of all the films discussed here, *Don't Touch My Holocaust* is the most remote from the actual Holocaust. In this film Madi's father is the ghost behind it all. Both Tlalim and Maayan were initially attracted to the subject through their first wives, who happened to be daughters of survivors. Both used the Holocaust as a "tool" in their search for their own repressed Oriental identity, and both focused on a phantasmagoric Holocaust based on imagination rather than on testimonies or fact-oriented evidence. *Because of That War* is less remote due to its involvement with both the survivors and their children. Yet, the film focuses on the second generation whose identity is perceived as shaped by their relationships with their survivor parents. In terms of distance from the world of the Holocaust and the survivors, *Choice and Destiny* is the closest. The survivor parents are the unquestionable protagonists of the film, and the "curious" camera accords their faces, their silences, and their talk the respect and dignity that they deserve.

By ethnicizing and privatizing the Holocaust, the films discussed here, like other second-generation Holocaust documentaries made in Israel during the 1980s and 1990s, express the fragmentation of the Israeli Zionist narrative of the Holocaust into "small narratives" reflecting the struggle over hegemony in Israel's identity politics. Moreover, as most of these films express a leftist perspective, they manifest an attempt to expropriate the discourse on the Holocaust from the Israeli Right, which elevated it to the level of myth identified with right-wing ultranationalism. These processes of ethnicization, privatization, and expropriation signify that the memory of the Holocaust has become one of the most contested arenas of Israeli identity today.[53]

Memory of Generations, Generations of Memory: The Holocaust and Identity Formation

French philosopher and former *gauchiste* activist Alain Finkielkraut has managed, perhaps more than anyone, to capture the spirit of the second generation even though he never uses the term "second generation." In the great tradition of French confessional writing he analyzes, contemptuously, bitterly, even cruelly, and always candidly, the contradictions inherent in the collective psyche of what he calls the "imaginary Jew." This postwar generation, according to Finkielkraut, "shares a nostalgia for the dark intensity of events that preceded our births."[54]

In an article criticizing the notion of the second generation, the author Howard Cooper resists what he calls "the kind of generalizations one often finds in the more academic literature concerning the second generation." In the last twenty years in particular, he argues, "the 'second generation' has become for psychologists and psychotherapists a growth-industry."[55] Despite Cooper's claim that the "symptoms and conflicts of the second generation are neither unique nor exclusive to them,"[56] he still acknowledges the recognizability of the "toxic consequences"[57] for those born to survivor parents. "Sadly it may even prove to be true that—unless the work of detoxification is done—the inequity of that age is 'visited upon the children, and upon the children's children, even to the third and fourth generation' (Exodus 34:7)."[58] It should be pointed out that Cooper's critique of the notion of "the second-generation syndrome" is launched from a psychotherapist's perspective, although he views the psychotherapist's art, like that of the novelist, as a "fictive endeavor."[59]

Finkielkraut's bitter reproach against the duplicity and self-deception of the post-Holocaust generation is completely missing from Israeli literature and film. On the contrary, the view of the second generation as "memorial candles," "linking the parents back both to their pre-*Shoah* personal history as well as their collective settings,"[60] is perceived by the children as a "self-torturing price."[61] Momik, the hero of David Grossman's novel *See under Love* (1986), epitomizes what we might call the self-tortured second-generation child. In *See under Love* and Michal Govrin's novel *The Name* (1995), as Rachel Feldhay Brenner observes, the victim is transformed "into an integral component of

Israeli consciousness," and in both books the "issue is no longer the proper relationship of the Israeli with the victim of the Holocaust, but rather, facing and coming to terms with the consciousness of the Holocaust."[62]

Reflecting on the relationship between the Holocaust and Israeli identity, left-wing writer Yitzhak Laor has said:

> I know that the Holocaust defines me as an Israeli Jew. It also collides with the cruel oppression of the Palestinians, although the two phenomena, despite official Arab arguments, are not directly connected. I cannot connect these two things, but I confess that I cannot separate them either. I know that the Holocaust, or more accurately, Nazism, or even more accurately the humiliation endured by my father and transmitted to me by him as "an educational lesson," shaped my extreme moral attitude towards politics. I also know that the Holocaust defines me as an Ashkenazi, and consequently it redefines the Oriental Jew as less Israeli than me, because he "was not there." I know that the Holocaust defines me as the son of a German Jew, namely my economic status is better because, for example, money from German reparations helped my father to buy me an apartment. I know that the Holocaust defines me as a son of "Vatikim," those who left Europe before the foundation of the State. And this tension between oldcomers and newcomers was crucial in the establishment of cultural hegemony in Israel during its formative years.[63]

The relationship between the Holocaust and ethnic identity is particularly interesting. There is a sense that for many second-generation Israelis the Holocaust has become the locus of their Ashkenazi identity. In a letter to *Ha'aretz* in response to a special issue of its weekly magazine devoted to "HaHarada HaAshkenazit" (Ashkenazi Anxiety), Mira Hovav wrote:

> As a second-generation daughter of Holocaust survivors I would like to relate an anecdote which to me symbolizes the ethnic gap: My relatives, typical representatives of "melah ha'aretz" [the crème de la crème of Israeli society, literally "salt of the earth," descendants of pre-Holocaust immigrants]—came back from a vacation in Eastern Europe and were asked by a family member who was planning to go there to recommend places to visit. Among other things they described to her was a commemoration site for Jews who were murdered in the Shoah, and they went into laborious detail to describe its location and architecture which they found to be "very impressive." I thought to myself that if I ever saw this monument, I would try to find in it my grandfather, the lost youth of my mother, the pain that also exists inside me, rather than the name of the architect. It is my destiny that this monument be "mine"

in a way that it will never be that of "melah ha'aretz." The other half of the equation is that it is my destiny that this country [Israel] be mine in a way very different from theirs: they will always feel at home here, too much at home, nothing will challenge their feeling at home, whereas in me—although I am a Sabra—there will always be something of the diasporic anxiety. In contrast to what might be implied by what I say, I have no yearning to acquire this feeling at home which characterizes "melah ha'aretz." On the contrary, it is this diasporic Jewishness, which is like walking on a very thin rope, that I long for.[64]

Hovav's simple but powerful words beautifully capture Hirsch's notion of postmemory dominated by exilic consciousness and the longing for an irretrievable "home." Her feelings of displacement, internal exile, and homelessness, together with her nostalgic sentiment toward the Diaspora, echo Theodor Adorno's famous phrase "It is part of morality not to be at home in one's home."[65] Her exilic consciousness, therefore, places her in the Jew's "natural home," the spiritual Diaspora.

The interesting thing about this letter is that Hovav defines her identity not vis-à-vis an "alien" Oriental one but rather against an Ashkenazi one—that of the "oldcomers" ("vatikim"), the privileged, and the insensitive. A similar sensibility is expressed in Reibenbach's choice to use Yiddish, "the language spoken at home," as the language of *Choice and Destiny*. Reibenbach's parents chose to speak their mother tongue even in their new country, a country that put pressure on its newcomers to join the national Zionist melting pot and to adopt Hebrew as part of their new Israeli identity. The result of this pressure was that Yiddish became a despised, forbidden, and almost secret language spoken only inside the safe boundaries of the new "home" in the (old?) new homeland. Using Yiddish, Reibenbach not only reclaims her identity as the daughter of survivors and immigrants, but also publicly takes pride in her immigrant parents' forbidden language. For the second generation both Arabic and Yiddish were sources of humiliation and shame in their parents. But since the "return of the Jew" to the growing ethnicized landscape of Israeli society, these languages have become a source of renewed pride and have contributed to ethnic revival.

Further evidence of the functioning of the Holocaust as a factor in ethnic identity formation is the wave of reactions triggered by Ehud Barak's appeal for forgiveness from the Mizrahim for the way they were treated by the historical Mapai (now the Labor Party), of which Barak was recently the leader. Many of the negative reactions to his statement came from children of Holocaust survivors who claimed that their Ashkenazi parents were subject to a worse reception than that awaiting the Mizrahi immigrants. This reaction points to the centrality of victimology in contemporary Israeli identity politics where the former pride in making a sacrifice for the state has been replaced by charges of being victimized by the state.

While the insertion of the Holocaust into the current Israeli "victim contest" has also ethnicized it, the official trend reflects the state's resistance to "privatization" and "ethnicization" of the Holocaust. Organized tours to the former death camps, such as the so-called March of the Living, have become part of the curriculum of Israeli high schools, reflecting the attempt to limit its subversive or heterogeneous dimensions by suggesting a uniform and unifying memorial narrative.

The Third Generation

The noise in the Warsaw terminal was unbearable. "Those are the Israeli kids going back home," one of the women assistants in the duty-free shop told her colleague. . . . Students from the René Cassin high school in Jerusalem came back last week in high spirits from a journey to the death camps in Poland. On their T-shirts read the message: "René Cassin, Jerusalem—Trip to Poland." Another stage in identity-building has been successfully achieved. Children, like children—loaded with duty-free purchases, experiences, and souvenirs— exchanged loud impressions in the Warsaw terminal, which resembled a military absorption base more than a Polish airport. A huge Israeli flag was wrapped, like a scarf, around the neck of Yaki, a young Jerusalemite kid.[66]

This was the only picture that I had any enjoyment out of taking throughout the whole week I spent in Poland. It personally made me feel very proud to see two young Jews raise the Israeli flag at the end of the railway line in Birkenau. It felt like a real tribute to those who had died that Hitler had failed in his attempt at the final solution.[67]

The above quotations reflect perhaps the two polarized reactions to organized trips of third-generation Israelis to the former death camps. These dichotomized reactions also reflect the traditional schism between the Israeli Left and Right with regard to the interpretation of the so-called lessons of the Holocaust. The Left has attempted to use the Holocaust in constructing a moral paradigm that celebrates humanism, racial tolerance, and peaceful coexistence. Hence, Shulamit Aloni, the former Meretz minister of culture and education in the government of the late Yitzhak Rabin, echoed Yehuda Elkana's criticism of the organized tours that, she claimed, breed nationalistic, racist, and xenophobic feelings among Israeli youth.[68] The Right, on the other hand, has used the Holocaust in its justification and promotion of nationalistic pride, mistrust of the "Goyish world," fetishization of military force, and cultivation of the ideological trump cards of "the whole world is against us" and "what happened before can happen again." The lessons derived by the Right from the trauma of the Holocaust achieved tragic proportions with their campaign of hatred and incitement against Rabin's peace policy, which ended in his murder by a right-wing religious zealot.[69]

For the second generation, and especially for those who come from survivor families, the search for familial roots is an attempt to give meaning and create gestalt in the void left by the Holocaust. This search begins as a personal one and ends as a collective one. Yet, despite the spread of the phenomenon of second-generation Israelis searching for their roots, it has never been controlled or institutionalized by the state. In most cases the search has been confined to the boundaries of the nuclear family (rarely do the grandchildren participate) with the survivor parents acting as the "guides." This, of course, does not apply to the third generation and even to those whose grandparents are survivors. Most of them visit Eastern Europe, and Poland in particular, through organized high school trips that have already been institutionalized and integrated into the established curriculum. The second-generation trips thus manage to recapture and "reexperience" authentic personal memory far more successfully than those of the third generation. For the latter, the Holocaust is more a collective memory that weakens the link between public memory and personal experience.

In a satirical piece Doron Rosenblum, a columnist for *Ha'aretz* and a keen-eyed observer of Israeli society, discusses Israel's new culture of death and mourning, claiming that "the rituals of the sealed room during the Gulf War" and "the horror show of the distribution of gas masks" constitute a manipulation aimed at uniting "the collective Israeli psyche" through trauma.[70] Even Israel's wars and the army's confrontations, according to Rosenblum, have acquired a new meaning, embedded in a new and deep feeling of misery and victimization. The trigger for this change was perhaps, according to Rosenblum, introduced by Yossi Peled, former IDF commander of the northern region of Israel and a Holocaust survivor, who after a skirmish in the north gave the soldiers permission to cry over their fallen friends. Rosenblum claims that it was no accident that Peled emphasized his being a Holocaust survivor and that his "permission" was given at a time when the organized trips (the March of the Living) of Israeli youth to the former death camps were becoming so popular. Despite the vast differences between the experience of the persecuted Holocaust victim and that of the fighter for his own country, Rosenblum argues, the style of military commemoration is growing similar to the "crying rituals" initiated in visits to the former death camps. It should also be pointed out that the cumulative effect of the 1967 and 1973 wars, as well as that of the Gulf War, has been to "soften" Israeli attitudes toward the Holocaust. It is quite common among Israeli scholars to claim that what were perceived by the Israeli public as real threats to the existence of the state of Israel shed a new light on the victims of the Holocaust and created a growing sense of empathy and identification with them.

One of the more disturbing phenomena related to the Holocaust is its exploitability by the pornographic imagination. The combination of violence, death, and sexual perversity have become characteristic of exploitative Holocaust cinema and literature (seen in "high art," commercial popular culture, and explicit underground pornography). For second-generation Israelis, as Omer Bartov shows, the pornographic appeal of the Holocaust was "consumed" during their adolescent years in the early 1950s through the "illegitimate" literature of the Holocaust: "Stalag" pulp fiction and the writings of Yehiel Dinur (Ka-Tzetnik).[71] The third generation, however, has always been exposed to a highly charged, "extracurricular" (yet open and often "legitimate") pornographic discourse on the Holocaust that has also been part of the (non-Israeli) culture at large. Paradoxically, however, this generation (not unlike the second generation) is at the same time exposed to an elevating, if not reverential, educational approach toward the Holocaust that, as Ne'eman Arad observes, forces them "to live under the shadow of Auschwitz."[72] It is this strange combination, perhaps, that explains the seemingly irreconcilable manifestations of Holocaust culture recently observed among the third generation. On one hand there exists the official culture of visits to the former death camps with its latent "cult of the dead" undertone. On the other hand a "Holocaust counter-culture" has infiltrated different spaces of popular culture. A high school principal in Tel Aviv, for example, writes his own plays for Holocaust Remembrance Day using unsavory language and imagery. Seemingly crude, he claims that he is trying to counter the disrespectful behavior of his students when they are subjected to the falsified and cynical abuse of the Holocaust. This same principal had to move his "Yom Hashoah" remembrance ceremonies from his own high school to a movie theater in Tel Aviv because of the great demand for this particular ceremony.[73] In 1993 the very popular Tel Aviv weekend supplement *Ha'ir* dedicated an entire issue to what it called "Nitzulei Ha'shoah" (Exploitations of the Holocaust), implying, of course, that these have overshadowed the "Nitzolei Ha'shoah" (Holocaust survivors).[74]

As Ne'eman Arad observes, this trend is even present in state television broadcasts. The very popular satirical group HaHamishiya HaKamerit (the Chamber Quintet), for instance, mocked street-naming in memory of destroyed communities in exchange for sizable contributions to whatever municipality would name streets after them. It also ridiculed Israel's demands for privileges from President Clinton for the suffering of the Jews. It reserved even harsher criticism for Israel's begging for special consideration from Germans. This program, catering to what in Israel would be called the "Yuppie audience," also marketed the former death camps as preferable tourist sites to popular Turkey, since in the camps one can enjoy a shower every day.[75]

One of the most extreme and controversial manifestations of the third generation's revolt against the official memory of the Holocaust is related to the recent discovery that during Holocaust Remembrance Day in 1997 some jokes (about Auschwitz, the ghettos, tattooed numbers, etc.) were distributed over the Internet by Israeli youth. The controversy provoked by this discovery was demarcated along two axes: those who thought that this humor expressed a "healthy attitude" versus those who thought that the last great taboo had been broken.[76] It should be pointed out, however, that the introduction of "humor" (dark as it may be) into Holocaust youth culture is, perhaps, an intensification of already existing global and local tendencies to "popularize" the Holocaust. Popular culture has infiltrated even the most traditional fortresses of institutionalized memory, invading official custodians such as Yad Vashem, which, following the example of the Holocaust Museum in Washington, has since 1994 organized for the general public different (and "lighter") cultural activities during the holiday seasons such as "journeys to destroyed culture," book fairs, films, guided tours, Klezmer music, sound and light shows, exhibitions, special events, special activities for children, and so on. Encounters between Germans and Jews of the second and third generations have also contributed to the growing "normalization" of the Holocaust. As Hirsch perceptively puts it: "But as a third generation grows to maturity and postmemory becomes dissociated from memory, we are left to speculate how these images can communicate on their own."[77] As yet, film images of the Holocaust have not been produced by the Israeli third generation, which is still struggling to imprint its mark on the political and cultural spheres.

CHAPTER FOUR

Shchur

The Orient Within

- It is the story of all the Orientals. Everybody feels that *Shchur* is his story.

  Ronit Alkabatz—the actress who plays Penina, Rachel's sister in *Shchur*

- One could have treated the film with a certain level of tolerance, had it not stressed that it is the absolute fruit of the screenwriter's imagination; but her attempt to represent it as the reality of these people creates a feeling of rejection and repulsion.

  Orly Levi, Israeli model, daughter of David Levi—a Moroccan Jew and former minister of foreign affairs

Every once in a while, a film or literary work arrives on the cultural landscape and sparks debates on significant issues of history, representation, and national identity, the ramifications of which extend far beyond the boundaries of the individual work in question. Recent examples from the international scene include Salman Rushdie's *Satanic Verses* (1988) and Steven Spielberg's *Schindler's List* (1994). Within the Israeli national space, such polemics surrounded works like Amos Oz's *My Michael* (1967) and Sammy Michael's *Victoria* (1993). A more recent example is the experimental film *Shchur* (1994), written by Hanna Azulay Hasfari and directed by her husband Shmuel Hasfari.

Shchur's narrative is presented from the point of view of its woman protagonist Rachel, the youngest—and only Israeli-born (Sabra)—child of the Ben-Shushan family of Jewish immigrants from Morocco. The father is blind and the mother, who (with the eldest son Shlomo) manages the family affairs, practices *shchur*—the Moroccan Arabic term for sorcery or black magic—in order to solve the family's problems. Shlomo tries to help the family adapt to Israeli society by sending his younger siblings to different Ashkenazi boarding institutions. The eldest daughter is sent to an Orthodox yeshiva, the other son Avram is sent to a kibbutz, and the daughter Zohara is forced to marry her uncle Moshe, who is twenty years older than she. Shlomo also tries to convince his mother to hospitalize her retarded daughter, Penina, in a mental institution (which she finally does). Shlomo himself is preparing for the entry exams to the Sorbonne in Paris (a plan that finally fails). Rachel, the youngest daughter and the family's "promise" for a better life in the new country, manages to pass the entry exams to attend a leadership training program in Jerusalem for underprivileged Oriental Jews—an Ashkenazi establishment program held in the most prestigious boarding school in Israel. Rachel adopts the more Israeli-sounding—less Oriental and diasporic—nickname Cheli, and eventually becomes a successful television personality.

The film begins with a phone call Cheli receives from Shlomo while preparing for her television show. She is told that her father has just died and is asked to bring her sister Penina, whom she has not seen since she was admitted to a mental hospital twenty years earlier, to the funeral. Cheli takes her sister from the hospital and together with Cheli's own autistic daughter, Ruth, they set out for the father's funeral. In the claustrophobic space of the car, where an enforced intimacy with her retarded female relatives threatens to crush her fragile normal "Israeli identity," Cheli confronts her repressed childhood memories.[1] The film ends with an act of reconciliation between Cheli and Penina (whose name stands as a metonymy for traditional Jewish Moroccan culture) as well as between Cheli and her daughter (who symbolizes the ambiguity embedded in the future of the third generation of Moroccan-Jewish immigrants to Israel).

As the first experimental "art film" associated with Israeli Oriental ethnicity,[2] Shchur constitutes an ideological breakthrough in Israeli culture. Despite (or perhaps because of) the controversies it invoked, it has already been heralded as one of the most important Israeli films made in recent years. The fact that it won six prestigious awards from the Israeli Academy of Motion Pictures for its artistic merits and formal innovations only intensified the controversy centered around its social, cultural, and political messages.

Without being a documentary in the customary generic sense, Shchur constitutes a form of ethnic document through its unusual juxtaposition of fantastic realism with a simulacrum of anthropological-like observation of ethnic rituals and daily activities. The film's controversiality derives precisely from its "impossible" experimental combination of naturalism and fantasy, raw realism and highly aestheticized style that challenges and questions cultural no-

Fig. 6 *A metonymy for traditional Jewish Moroccan culture: Penina (Ronit Alkabatz) in Shmuel Hasfari and Hanna Azulay Hasfari's Shchur. Courtesy of Yoram Kislev, H.L.S. Ltd.*

tions associated with ethnicity in Israel. (For example, in Israeli cinema Moroccan identity has traditionally been associated with the "low" form of the *bourekas* films).[3]

The Israeli Reception of *Shchur*: Framing a Public Debate on Identity in Crisis

The representation of Oriental Jews in Israeli film and literature has always been problematic.[4] In many respects Israeli cinema is, as Israeli film critic Uri Kleine observes, an ongoing discussion on the question of Israeli identity. *Shchur* joins this discussion in a particularly complex and difficult way. Not only does it ask the question "Who is an Israeli?" but it locates it at the heart of a melodramatic human existence in which magic (*shchur*) is a source of broken, smothered, and split identity.[5] In previous Israeli ethnic films—no-

Fig. 7 *Penina (Ronit Alkabatz) is sexually harassed by a neighbor during the Shavout celebration in* Shchur. *Courtesy of Yoram Kislev, H.L.S. Ltd.*

Fig. 8. *An impotent patriarch: the blind father (Amos Lavi) in* Shchur. *Courtesy of Yoram Kislev, H.L.S. Ltd.*

table among them *Sallah Shabbati* (1964), *Casablan* (1973), *Salomonico* (1973), and the other *bourekas* films—it was much easier to decode the underlying ideology that motivated their creators. By contrast, *Shchur* positions the viewer at a complex and problematic vantage point. The spectator, offered different optional readings within the difficult and ambivalent ideological reality that the film depicts, is deprived of the outsider's privileged status. *Shchur* thus turns itself and the kind of spectatorship it generates into part of the problem of Israeli identity in crisis. The spectator, like the film's heroine, does not know whether to accept the reality described by the film or to reject it.

Azulay Hasfari portrays Rachel as someone who has become phony as a result of being severed from her past and family, and the Israeli identity with which she tries to mask herself is described as an invented construction. Unlike previous Israeli films that tried to confront the need to create an Israeli identity from within, *Shchur* represents the self-other relationship in Israeli society as a permanent distortion. The unresolved union between Israeliness and various ethnic traditions has created a distortion that passes from one generation to another. *Shchur* is the representation of this distortion. As a melodrama—the most suitable genre, according to Laura Mulvey, to be used "as a safety-valve for ideological contradictions"[6]—it acquires a wider aesthetic and political significance. A testimony to the film's importance in intellectual circles is the fact that Dov Alfon—who was born in Sus, Tunisia, and immigrated to Israel with his parents from France in 1972—invited eight young Israeli Orientals to see the film before its official release in 1995 and, as editor of the weekend supplement of *Ha'aretz* (a liberal Israeli daily newspaper favored by academics and known for its presumably high journalistic standards), published their reactions in the paper.[7] This symposium, in turn, triggered a public debate about the film and its relationship to national and ethnic identity. It should be noted, however, that the debate was almost exclusively confined to the public space of "professional" intellectuals and academics, both Oriental and Ashkenazi. The polarity of the debate was respectively represented by Dov Alfon and Sammy Smooha, an Israeli sociologist born in Baghdad who writes about ethnic conflicts and polarization in Israeli society. According to Alfon, "*Shchur*, one of the most important Israeli films ever made, destroys all the sacred values of the first generation of Orientals and invites the next generation to dance on their grave." The film, Alfon predicted, "will provoke debates because it has violated one of the sacred rules of Oriental art: always blame the Ashkenazim." Azulay Hasfari, according to Alfon, "unmasks the hypocrisy surrounding the self-image of North Africans and ridicules the prevalent stereotypes of the Moroccan family—their warmth and hospitality, sexual puritanism, religious tradition, and mutual support. Even the food is not very attractive." [8]

In her response to the debate in *Ha'aretz*, Azulay Hasfari (1995) said that her film aims neither to condemn nor to criticize Moroccan culture, the Ashkenazim, or the defeatist Oriental attitude that results from discrimination. *Shchur*, she said, seeks to describe a situation, to tell the story of a second generation, which in this specific case is a Moroccan second generation. In fact, she added, her initial intention was to tell about herself—about her own private pain—but it happened to touch the raw nerves of many people. In Azulay Hasfari's opinion, Cheli, the television star—a second-generation Israeli woman who was praised by some of the discussants in the *Ha'aretz* debate for her rebellion against her family—is, in fact, pathetic. She invokes more pity in her spiritual impoverishment than does her "primitive" family. Her spiritual legacy is epitomized by a cold external appearance, cold feelings, and emotional paralysis, to the extent that she cannot communicate with her own daughter, her future. "What confused me as a child," Azulay Hasfari commented, continues to confuse those (like Dov Alfon) who still "see in the Western polished figure of Cheli a model for success." [9] For Azulay Hasfari, the result of the unthinking cross-fertilization between East and West that occurred in Israel has produced a strange hybrid creature that, in order to survive in the new Israeli world, has to wear a mask that hides nothing, because there is nothing to hide. Unlike what many people think, says Azulay Hasfari:

> I don't define myself as Oriental. I wish I could. I am an Israeli. The new Israeli, who in most cases belongs to the second generation of immigrants from different countries, a product of a nascent culture, a rootless product. . . . The moment I decided that I would not judge my parents' culture, but rather try to understand what meaning it has for people who have lived it naturally, I understood that I was lost. I understood that what I was forced to do as a child was due to rules of the time which were repressive, and called on one to crush this culture. Because whether this culture is primitive or not, underdeveloped or not, it could still have been mine. [10]

As a second-generation Israeli writer epitomizing the difficulties experienced by immigrants in the transitional phase, Azulay Hasfari created a diasporic film that challenges the repression of ethnicity in official Israeli discourse. In Israel, as Walter Zenner observes, "the term *edah* (originally meaning congregation) which is roughly equivalent to 'ethnic group' implies a Middle

Eastern Jewish origin-group, one of *edot Hamizrah*. The euphemism for Arabs is *mi'utim* (minorities). In these cases, groups marked as 'ethnic' are seen as stigmatized, as somewhat foreign or inferior." [11] Originally, as Ammiel Alcalay suggests, "a component of the pejorative label used to institutionally categorize non-European Jews (*benei 'edot ha-mizrah*, 'the offspring of the Oriental ethnic communities'), the words *mizrah* ('East') and *mizrahi* ('Easterner') gradually took on qualities of pride and defiance as the *mizrahim* (plural: 'Easterners') came to describe themselves." [12] This newly restored pride in ethnicity is embedded in *Shchur*, as the first Jewish Moroccan film to be made in Israel. Yet, *Shchur*'s "ethnic pride" is based on a painful cinematic exploration of the roots of the history of rejection of ethnic identity by Moroccan Jews in Israel.

The rejection of ethnic identity, still common among second- and third-generation Oriental Jews, signifies, according to Yossi Yonah,[13] the ultimate victory of collective Israeli identity over different ethnic identities, primarily Ashkenazi and Oriental. According to Yonah, there is a latent association between the notion of Israeli identity and Ashkenazi origin. This association causes difficulties in the application of this identity to Orientals (and definitely to Arabs) as well as, to a certain extent, to women. In Israeli collective identity the Orientals are slotted as occupying a (constant) transitional phase from Oriental identity to an Israeli-Western one. The Orientals thus live in a paradoxical situation: their countries of origin constitute for the non-Orientals an obstacle in their attempt to acquire an Israeli identity. So, despite the fact that most of them try hard to achieve an Israeli identity and are officially identified as Israelis, they are not perceived as such either by the Ashkenazim or by the members of their own ethnic groups who internalized the Ashkenazi-dominated conception of Israeli identity.

Consciously or not, Rachel, *Shchur*'s heroine, understood that her ethnic background was a barrier to entering the "Israeli collective" and therefore she changed her ethnic genealogy and her name to Cheli so that she would be perceived as "pure" Israeli. The latent pressure to repress Oriental identity, Yonah argues, shows the manipulative/dialectical use made by Israel's dominant ideology of the notion of "Israeli collective identity." On one hand it is used as a way to deny the existence of economic, social, and ethnic differences ("We are all Israelis," "We are all Jews"). On the other hand, it is invoked to justify the very existence of these differences, by arguing that they derive from the fact that different sections of the population (a euphemism for ethnic communities like Oriental Jews, Arabs, and also Ethiopian Jews) have not yet fully acquired the Israeli identity with its affiliated value system and ethos, which are necessary components for social mobility. The manipulation of the notion of Israeli identity also explains why the debate over cultural pluralism in Israeli society still suffers from a lack of legitimacy (despite its increasing popularity in Israeli academic circles). The melting pot ethos remains dominant, blocking any development of politico-economic consciousness that may result in a claim for more equal representation of different ethnic groups in economical, political, academic, and cultural centers of Israeli society.

Shchur is part of this ongoing public discourse on the Israeli second generation's search for identity. This search is related to the repression of the Diaspora culture by Zionist consciousness, which is based on the "negation of exile."[14] Traditional Zionist contempt for Jewish diasporic culture played a decisive role in the definition of the status of Arab Jews and the shaping of the attitude toward the Arab culture they represented. The condition for joining the Israeli collective was the embracing of a cultural change and, consequently, the liquidating of ethnic collective memory and identity. As Azulay Hasfari commented: "I think that the film tells about the distress of the second generation of Oriental immigrants from a very personal point of view. I'm sure that many young people like myself feel this distress, this double identity, the big price they have paid in order to assimilate into Israeli society. I do not mean the Orientals only. We are all in the same boat. The Romanians, the Poles, the Iranians—we all want to be Western."[15]

On the part of Oriental Jews, and Moroccan Jews in particular, the Israeli search for identity has manifested itself in recent years through revival and remodification of Moroccan Jewish culture. These manifestations of ethnic renewal include cultural phenomena such as the revival of the cult of saints (*tzadikim*), including the establishment of new sacred sites of Jewish saints; the nationalization of Jewish Moroccan celebrations (*hilulot*) like the *Mimuna*; and the emergence of popular healers and practical Cabalists.[16] Most of these phenomena have taken place in development towns, "planted" communities founded during the 1950s and early 1960s on Israel's urban periphery and populated mostly by North African Jewish immigrants.[17] Today they house between one-fifth and one-sixth of the country's population. These "artificially-created locales"[18] are also the backdrop against which the drama of *Shchur* is enacted. The unidentified development town of *Shchur* is a synthetic composite of familiar landscapes associated with the iconography of the development town (dreariness, bare landscape, uniform and run-down housing projects).

In the domain of popular culture, the secular manifestations of the "return of the repressed" in the form of "ethnic renewal" have included the emergence of popular Oriental musicians known as "cassette singers," and the recent emergence of alternative, all-Oriental, low-budget cinema, also known as the "cassette films." Other manifestations of Moroccan ethnic renewal, especially in the realm of music, have adopted more elitist approaches that strive to expose the pure "authenticity" of Moroccan Jewish culture and to integrate it with other non-Western folk traditions (for example, the singer Shlomo Bar). These rites of ethnic revival reflect, according to Eyal Ben-Ari and Yoram Bilu, "the growing confidence of an emigré group in being part of the contemporary Israeli scene while, at the same time, indicating a strong sense of ethnic distinctiveness." [19] *Shchur*, with its challenging representation of Moroccan Jewish rites, can be seen as a symptom of this growing confidence.

Shchur signifies the emergence of a new genre in Israeli cinema: immigrants' stories. Despite the differences, as Amnon Lourd observes, it is hard to ignore *Shchur*'s relationship to the film *New Land* (*Eretz Hadasha*) (1994) by Orna Ben Dor, which deals with the hardships of immigration experienced by Eastern European Jewish children who survived the Holocaust and immigrated to Israel after World War II.[20] It is not altogether an accident that the protagonists of both films are children and that both were made by women of the second generation. The emergence of these immigrants' stories on the artistic front coincides with the emergence of a new post-Zionist discourse in Israeli academic circles. The rise of what has become known as "the new historians" and "the new sociologists" not only has revised some traditional Zionist narratives regarding the history of the relationship between Jews and Palestinians but also has transformed the dominant language used to describe the social and cultural fabric of Israeli society. Crucial to this transformation was the semantic shift in terminology used by these new revisionist schools, which no longer describe Israel as a state of *olim* but a state of *mehagrim* (immigrants). Whereas the use of the word *olim* expresses an underlying subscription to a melting pot, integrativist, and assimilationist ideology based on the Zionist-inspired assumption that *olim* have come to Israel voluntarily, driven by ideological (Zionist) motives, the use of the notion of "immigrants" implies an acknowledgment that the Jewish state of Israel is basically a multicultural society of immigrants dominated by ethnic diversity and social polarization.

Shchur is in fact the first Jewish North African film made in Israel by a mostly Jewish Moroccan crew. Nevertheless, as mentioned before, it was interpreted by some Oriental critics as self-degrading and exploitative. According to these critics, much like *Victoria* (the novel by Israeli Iraqi Jewish writer Sammy Michael that portrayed Jewish life in Baghdad), Azulay Hasfari's *Shchur* confirms the cultural underdevelopment of Oriental Jews. Without stretching the point too far, I would like to claim that the Israeli public debate surrounding *Shchur* (though confined mainly to intellectual circles) raises issues similar to those generated by the controversy surrounding the publication of Salman Rushdie's novel *The Satanic Verses*. The criticism leveled at Rushdie, it should be pointed out, went beyond the circles of Muslim fundamentalists. It was also shared by some secular intellectuals who define themselves as "cultural Muslims"[21] and who argue that Rushdie's novel offers the West more ammunition with which to attack Islam. That *The Satanic Verses* dealt with Islam in English, Edward Said suggests, "for what was believed to be a largely Western audience was its main offense."[22] On the other hand, the Muslim defenders of Rushdie claimed that Rushdie's fall into this Orientalizing misrepresentation of Islam is justified because "in making a 'bad old thing' the target of a post-modern cultural critical stance, *The Satanic Verses* repudiated the historicist restriction as *itself* another Orientalist withholding of the creative possibilities of Islam for its own self-understanding and self-criticism . . . the novel is of such obvious importance not only to Muslims' understanding of themselves but to how Muslims must expect and demand that others understand them."[23] A similar stance regarding the issue of self-representation was raised by Azulay Hasfari, who said in one of her interviews: "One needs courage in order to say 'We also have problems at home,' but without courage there is no real art. . . . The principle of drama is conflict. If we do not face ourselves and say, 'This is good, this is bad, this is what we are,' we'll never have real art. Indeed, there are many not so beautiful things in Moroccan culture. The film also represents painful things."[24]

The Anti-*Bourekas* and the "High Art" Paradox

The *bourekas* films, produced mostly by Ashkenazi filmmakers, formed a dominant genre within the Israeli film industry particularly between the years 1967 and 1977. Mainstream critics, as Shohat observes, "used the term 'bourekas' as a pejorative noun . . . condemning the films as 'commercial,' 'vulgar,' 'cheap,' 'dumb,' 'Eastern,' 'Levantine,' and even 'anti-cinema'."[25] Azulay Hasfari's film, however, despite dealing with what some regarded as "ethnic primitivism," escaped the fate of the *bourekas* films. To the contrary, the film enjoyed sweeping critical acclaim. Alfon argued: "*Shchur* could not have shaken so drastically our basic beliefs had it not been a truly quality film." [26]

Although *Shchur* borrows some topoi and visual icons from the tradition of the *bourekas* films, this tradition is revisited, to use Umberto Eco's phrase, "but with irony, not innocently," [27] recalling his definition of the postmodern "litterature citationelle." Hence, for example, the house of the "Ashkenazied" Cheli is an enormous space inhabited only by herself and her autistic daughter and is shot with blue colors suggesting an alienated, cold world, associated in the tradition of the *bourekas* films with Ashkenazi characters who are snobbish and hypocritical egoists. Another example is Azulay Hasfari's decision to give her heroine an autistic daughter, recalling the birth of a retarded child to the protagonist in Menahem Golan's *Queen of the Road* (1971), about a Moroccan prostitute in Tel Aviv (played by Gila Almagor, the Ashkenazi actress who plays the mother in *Shchur*). [28]

The shooting style of the outdoor scenes in *Shchur*, and particularly the sensual, almost pagan celebration of *Shavuot*, recalls Pier Paolo Pasolini's shooting style in some of the outdoor scenes in *Accattone* (1961), a film about the life and death of a thieving pimp living in Rome's poorest district, where the handheld camera renders a strong, realistic, and sensual portrayal of the life of the Roman subproletarian milieu. The pagan, folkish sensuality of the *Shavuot* celebration [29] stands in sharp contrast to the film's opening scene, which portrays an official, almost synthetic May First parade taking place on the main road of the dreary development town. This parade, complete with red flags and shot on a backdrop of graffiti of the Israeli "Black Panthers," [30] takes place in 1972 and its "aesthetic of imperfect cinema" evokes the "poverty" and "imperfection" of the Third World, [31] hence recalling the radical 1960s and 1970s modernist aesthetics typical of the highly politicized Jean-Luc Godard [32] and the radical Orientalism of Pasolini and Bernardo Bertolucci, the tourists of the exotic. [33]

To a certain extent, Shmuel Hasfari's borrowings from film culture associated mainly with a Southern European milieu turn *Shchur* into a "generic" film, a "southern" film that reveals affinities with films like Giuseppe Tornatore's *Stanno tutti bene* (*We Are All Just Fine,* 1990), a road film that portrays the journey of a father from the Italian *mezzogiorno* (the name for the country's undeveloped South) to his children in the highly developed and industrial North; and to Pasolini's and the Taviani Brothers' films occupied with the South. Indeed, the world of the development town, as represented in the film, seems closer to the Third World than to a modern Western society. Although Azulay Hasfari wanted to convey the aura of a green northern development town, different from the stereotypical image associated with the arid desert, the feeling is still that of a southern Israeli development town. The film's minimalist aesthetics (a fixed repertoire of colors divided by the blue/red-cold/hot scheme, economy of camera movements, ascetic mise-en-scène) thus reinforces the ideological dichotomy of poor South versus rich North that is a prevalent topos in current postcolonial discourse.

Yet, the quotational quality of *Shchur*, its affiliation with European art cinema and its a priori designation as a quality art film created a "broken dialogue" threatening its potential effectiveness as an educational tool and a truly popular vehicle for consciousness raising. The designated category of "art film" may have prematurely "castrated" the film's social and political meaning, as Esther Schely-Newman suggests.[34] It neutralized its potential subversion and popular appeal and triggered debates mainly in the highbrow spheres of Israeli public space (the debate in *Ha'aretz*, symposia at universities, feminist conventions, etc.). Unlike the highly popular *bourekas* films, *Shchur* failed to attract the masses or to create any grassroots manifestation of public protest or enthusiasm. As Israeli sociologist Sammy Smooha put it: "The making of *Victoria* into a bestseller and *Shchur* into the film of the year is an amazing phenomenon. Undoubtedly, due to their literary-cinematic quality, they were well-received by an audience with good taste."[35]

A Claim for Authenticity: Anthropology without Anthropologists and the Question of "Ethnographic Representation"

Without being a documentary in the traditional sense, *Shchur* constitutes a form of social document. It generated critical (but not so much popular) debate precisely because of what has been perceived in the Israeli public sphere as its claim for authenticity.[36] For a few years, Azulay Hasfari collected stories and narratives on black magic (*shchur*) rituals that have been practiced for centuries by Moroccan Jews. "Most of the stories in the film are real," Azulay Hasfari claims.[37] Yet, some scholarly authorities on Jewish Moroccan culture do not consider the film as an ethnographic document but rather as an interesting artistic form that takes a poetic license to use *shchur* as a generic term, lumping together magic, demons, and evil eyes, while disregarding the fact that *shchur* is only one category of affliction. The rites and practices in the film, according to Yoram Bilu, a psychological anthropologist, are a far cry from accurate representations of "*shchur*" practices as he encountered them in his fieldwork. They represent construction, based on memories and fantasies of a woman who even as a little girl looked at black magic traditions as esoteric and marginal. Add to this the liberty of a creative artist, Bilu argued, "and you get a very commendable movie but a very poor ethnography."[38]

The question regarding the ethnographic accuracy of the rituals and practices represented by the film is, definitely, beyond the scope of this chapter, let alone beyond the boundaries of my expertise. Whatever the film's ethnographic accuracy, pertinent to the matter at hand is the public perception and—in many significant cases as I shall later demonstrate—the Oriental intellectuals' perception of the film as a social document stating a claim for "the real." Much like *Sallah Shabbati*, a *bourekas* film that was a sweeping success among critics and audiences alike,[39] *Shchur* was received by critics (including Oriental intellectuals and academics) as if it were authentic anthropological testimony concerning Moroccan Jews. Part of what was perceived as the film's claim for authenticity was based on the fact that Azulay Hasfari used autobiographical elements in her film. Yet, this very claim for authenticity based on the author's personal memories and ethnic identity was also the catalyst for some of the harsher attacks by some Oriental intellectuals who claimed that Azulay Hasfari's portrayal of her own ethnic community reinforced racial prejudices and stereotypes. Notable among them was Smooha, who compared *Shchur* to Michael's *Victoria*. Michael claimed that his book integrated autobiographical details into its narrative fabric. Smooha's objection to *Victoria* was aimed precisely at this claim, which Michael used in order to verify the authenticity of his description in the face of the criticism leveled at him by Israeli Iraqi Jews for what they perceived as a distortion and misrepresentation of their community. Michael claimed that the Iraqi community in Israel has reached a stage of maturity and therefore can afford to absorb self-criticism. According to Smooha, both *Shchur* and *Victoria* provide "proof" of the cultural underdevelopment of Oriental Jews manufactured by the Oriental Jewish elite itself. It is no longer a testimony given by outside writers who deliver superficial impressions about Oriental Jews, or by researchers who report selectively; rather, it is a work based on personal confessions. The message of a film like *Shchur* is, according to Smooha, that cultural underdevelopment is a burden that Oriental Jews carry with them from their countries of origin, and which they can discharge only in modern Israel. It is a message that suggests that emancipation and progress are enjoyed solely by the second generation, which has grown up in Israel and passed through the Israeli school system and the army (IDF). In the final analysis, the discourse produced by this film, Smooha claims, suggests that there is no one to be blamed, there is no discrimination, there is no place for protest, there are no struggles over resources and power among ethnic groups, and the Ashkenazim are not a real party to this story.[40]

The questions surrounding the authenticity of the film and its appeal to the real (despite its fantastic/magic realist style) were at the heart of the critical and public debate generated by the film, and played a significant role in its reception by the third generation of North African Jewish immigrants. For this generation, the acceptance or rejection of the film's claim for authenticity and for truly representing Moroccan culture was crucial to understanding their national and ethnic identity. In a discussion of students of Kidma, a progressive all-Oriental school established in 1995 in the Hatikva community in Tel Aviv (a mostly poor Oriental neighborhood in South Tel Aviv) that integrates Oriental culture into its curriculum, the main question that bothered the (seventh grade) students was whether the world represented in *Shchur* is imaginary or real. Journalist Dalia Karpel, describing this discussion, wrote that "the young students sounded like anthropologists observing people from a different society."[41]

The Feminist Diasporic/Exilic Transnational Film

Although *Shchur* is an ethnic film recounting the story of the second generation of Moroccan Jews in the ethnically distinctive "polities" of the Israeli development towns, it transcends its local specificity and becomes part of the new emerging genre of diasporic/exilic transnational film.[42] Diasporan films, as Laura Marks observes, talk about the physical effects of exile, immigration, and displacement. Independent, hybrid, transnational cinema, with which *Shchur* is affiliated, is "a genre that cuts across previously defined geographic, national, cultural, cinematic, and meta-cinematic boundaries."[43] By linking genre, authorship, and transnational positioning, "the independent transnational genre allows films to be read and reread not only as individual texts produced by authorial vision and generic conventions but also as sites for intertextual, cross-cultural, and transnational struggles over meanings and identities."[44]

Shchur recalls recent examples of transnational feminist cinema, particularly Mufida Talal's *Les Silences du Palais* (Tunisia, 1994), but also (though to a lesser extent) Gurinder Chadha's *Bhaji on the Beach* (U.K., 1994). In both films, as in *Shchur*, the experience of exile is both physical and spiritual/mental. The women protagonists (as well as the actual authors) are displaced persons in terms of ethnic and class identity. All three films make use of the road film genre to make a feminist statement. In *Shchur* and *Les Silences* the trip to the father's funeral is a trip into the past and into the patriarchal culture from which both heroines have attempted to escape. The journey ultimately liberates both women from the past. In *Shchur* Cheli learns to accept her culture of origin and consequently manages to communicate with her autistic daughter. As a representative of the transitionary generation, she thus secures the vital ties between the past and the future through reconciliation with her Jewish Moroccan culture (epitomized by her sister Penina) and her future (represented by her autistic daughter). The heroine of *Les Silences*, on the other hand, commits an act of rebellion/emancipation after visiting her father's funeral. She decides not to have an abortion despite her lover's and society's pressures. In *Bhaji*, the one-day bus trip that three generations of lower-middle- and middle-class Asian women (in England defined as women from India, Pakistan, and Bangladesh) take from Birmingham to the working-class, seaside resort of Blackpool becomes an allegory of diasporic/exilic women's experience. The collective road trip is thus rendered a filmic social critique by an Asian woman director who is deeply linked to her community while being critical of many of its values, particularly its authoritarian approach to marriage and its intolerance of blacks.

In all three films motherhood is invested with pain and becomes a dialectical symbol of oppression and liberation alike. In *Les Silences* the female protagonist reaches a mature decision to have her baby, and in *Bhaji* the Asian medical student Hashida, who is the promise of her local ethnic Asian community (not unlike Rachel in *Shchur*) and who is made pregnant by her West Indian boyfriend, is finally reconciled with him. In all three films the women rebel against cultures in which the main criterion for the success of women is in the domestic familial domain. Another aspect common to all three films (and to the hybrid transnational film in general) is a fluid exchange of languages. In *Shchur* there are language shifts between Hebrew, Arabic, and French. In *Les Silences* the transitions are from Arabic (the native language) to French (the language of the colonizers), and in *Bhaji* the transitions are from English to different Asian languages.

The liberation of Rachel (in Western terms) as an Oriental woman, namely her professional success, is made possible due to Zionism and modernity. But there is an authorial ambivalence toward this would-be liberation because Rachel's success as a television personality is yoked to her failures in her personal life (her inability to communicate with her autistic daughter, and the unaccounted-for absence of her husband from her life). In *Les Silences du Palais*, women's liberation is presented as an oppression within an oppression. Tunisian patriarchal colonialism operates within the larger framework of French colonialism. In *Shchur* and *Les Silences* women achieve their liberation through a profession affiliated with show and performance (a television career in *Shchur* and a singing career in *Les Silences*). Yet, in *Shchur* professional success is presented as doomed to be counterpointed by failure in personal relationships, because, according to the film's logic, professional success (associated with Ashkenaziation and Westernization) implies sacrificing one's primary cultural identity. It is not surprising, therefore, that Rachel's sister Penina, whose name is the metonymy of traditional Jewish Moroccan culture, is, in the last instance, represented as potentially more subversive than the official rebel Rachel. Indeed, as Bilu observes, evil spirit disease (which is what Penina suffers from) is a form of female protest and might be understood "as a cathartic acting-out of the conflict between the sexes in a traditional society."[45]

Autobiography, the Road Metaphor, and Hybrid Identity

As Michael Fischer observes, "[E]thnic autobiography and autobiographical fiction can perhaps serve as key forms for exploration of pluralist, post-industrial, late twentieth-century society."[46] It is therefore probably no coincidence that, as Trin T. Minh-ha comments, "It is often said that writers of color, including anglophone and francophone Third World writers of the diaspora, are condemned to write only autobiographical works."[47] Recent developments in postcolonial film theory have focused on the notion of hybrid cinema "in which autobiography mediates a mixture of documentary, fiction, and experimental genres, characterizes the film production of people in transition and cultures in the process of creating identities."[48] As an example of hybrid cinema *Shchur* assimilates into its ethnic autobiography the point of view of a woman (author, actress, and protagonist) whose search for identity and liberation is not only ethnic but also feminist. As Miller argues: "The claim for this difference in women's self-representation—'the definition of identity by way of alterity'—has played an essential role in constituting a genealogy of women's life—writing."[49] As an ethnic, feminist autobiography *Shchur* occupies a unique place in the history of Israeli cinema through its double search for Israeli identity and new representational forms. Furthermore, its personal, almost confessional tone links it to the postmodern genre that, according to Alice Jardine, adopts "feminine writing"[50] as an instance of postmodern thought. Because the autobiographical elements involved in Azulay Hasfari's film were so personal and painful, she showed her brothers the text and gave them the right of veto. Her elder brother (Shlomo in the film) told the journalist Orna Kadosh, "We gathered the whole family and discussed it. She [Azulay Hasfari] was quite surprised when she got our okay. She was really tormented by her right to expose intimate family life."[51]

Azulay Hasfari chose as the narrative frame for her ethnic melodramatic autobiography the road film genre. Cinema, travel, and identity are thus inextricably linked in her film. Exile and travel become in *Shchur* overdetermined: they represent, in the very act of revolt against the family, a return to its nurturing functions. The theme of a search for lost identity appears in many road films, such as Peter Fonda's *Easy Rider* (1969), Michelangelo Antonioni's *Passenger* (1975), and Wim Wenders's *Paris, Texas* (1984). The last uses the landscape of the American desert as a backdrop and geographic metaphor for the protagonist who literally lost his identity. Cheli's (the surrogate of Azulay Hasfari) trip to her father's funeral becomes a journey to repressed childhood memories. Like most films in the genre[52] *Shchur* acquires its dramatic force, its pedagogy, through unexpected confrontations that occur along the way. Yet, Cheli/Azulay Hasfari's life as a road film transcends the boundaries of personal memory and becomes an allegory for a collective search by second-generation Moroccan youth for their lost identity. As Minh-ha argues, what Third World, colored, and exilic writers "chose to recount no longer belongs to them as individuals. Writing from a representative space that is always politically marked (as 'colored' or as 'Third World'), they do not so much remember for themselves as they remember in order to tell."[53] These writers thus become the folk storytellers of their ethnic communities in a postmodern age.

Shchur can be read as an allegory of the current, almost obsessive search of Israeli second-generation youth for the lost identity buried in their diasporic roots. Indeed, the actual search for identity currently practiced by both Ashkenazi and Moroccan second-generation youth often takes the actual form of travel, of going on the road. Since the warming of the relations between Israel and Morocco, many second-generation Israeli descendants of Jewish Moroccan parents have traveled to Morocco in search of their identity, a trend paralleling the Ashkenazi "Holocaust tourism" discussed in the previous chapter.

Shchur, with its unique blend of the realistic and the fantastic, is an experimental diasporic film using basically Western film forms to speak from non-

Western culture to a mixed audience. As a hybrid film *Shchur* performs the disjunction typical of ethnics in a state of cultural transition, and reveals the process of exclusion by which nations and identities are formed. Moreover, as an ethnic film *Shchur* is also a diasporic film, a form of "otherness" that poses cultural and political challenges to the hegemony and homogeneity claimed by the Israeli nation-state. *Shchur* demonstrates that without accepting the "Orient within," the struggle over Israeli identity is not over yet.

CHAPTER FIVE

In the Land of Oz

Orientalist Discourse in *My Michael*

The writing of Amos Oz's novel *My Michael* was completed, as noted in the Hebrew edition, in May 1967, a month before the outbreak of the 1967 war. *My Michael* was the best-selling novel of the 1968–69 period, and its extraordinary success, as well as the heated controversy it elicited, was due, as Amos Elon observes, to much more than "pure literary merit."[1] That *My Michael* scandalized some reviewers who blamed it for being politically subversive suggests, as Elon points out, that Oz touched a raw nerve.[2] This chapter examines the defining features of this "raw nerve" by comparing the novel to Dan Wolman's film adaptation of the literary original. Furthermore, unlike more traditional analyses of the novel and the film, this chapter, written from a feminist perspective, locates the two texts within the context of colonial and Orientalist discourse. Through an analysis of the possible conflation of feminist/colonialist discourses in *My Michael*, as well as its location in the context of other "colonial" texts (some of which have also been adapted into "colonial/postcolonial" films), this chapter suggests a new reading of one of the "canonical" texts of Israeli literature and cinema.

Evidence for the conceptual kinship of the fields of feminist and colonial studies can be found in the degree to which they draw upon a common nomenclature; both critical approaches to culture make use of terms such as fetishization, difference, ambivalence, Manichaeism, mimicry, masquerade, and the other. Moreover, recent developments in feminist critique stress how the dominant colonial discourse reproduces a system of textual practices used to conceptualize "femininity" through the notions of "conquer," "penetration," "terra incognita," "exploration," "dark continent," "exoticism," "travel," "tourism," "expedition," and other related terms used to describe the colonial/imperialist enterprise. After all, "picturing the colony as female," Judith Williamson observes, "makes it so much more conquerable and receptive."[3] Furthermore, at a metatheoretical level, as Robert Young suggests in his critique of Edward Said's conceptualization of "Orientalism," the difficulties invoked by the logic of Said's own arguments regarding the automatic reproduction of essentialism by any account of discursive "Orientalism" "could be compared to those encountered in feminism: if 'woman' is the constructed category of a patriarchal society, how do you posit an alternative without simply repeating the category in question or asserting a transhistorical essence that the representation travesties?"[4]

The present exploration, conceived more than thirty years after the completion of the writing of the novel, allows for some historical perspective. In light of the proximity of the novel to the outbreak of the June 1967 war, the political dimension of the novel (epitomized by the metaphor of the Arab twins) can be seen as almost prophetic—in particular regarding the Palestinian Intifada.[5] It is also worth noting in this context that Dan Wolman's filmic adaptation of the book was released in 1974 after the 1973 war. Israeli reality at that time was, as it is now, a reality defined by the occupation that issued from the June 1967 war. Within the context of the history of Israeli cinema, *My Michael* was made toward the close of a period that came to be known as "Israeli Personal Cinema," a cinema characterized by the conscious desire to deal with "private-marginal" issues and to avoid both the "grand issues" of the heroic-nationalist films and the "vulgarity" of the *bourekas* films.[6] Yet, as I suggest in this chapter, Wolman's flight into inwardness and privatization in the form of "family melodrama" did not completely "redeem" his film from the charges against, and ambivalence of, Orientalist discourse.

Oz's work, too, is not impervious to critique despite his liberalism. Oz is the most celebrated and translated Israeli writer abroad (Bertelsmann, the German publishing enterprise, chose Oz as one of the greatest novelists of the twentieth century), and to a large extent he projects to the international community what it regards as Israeli political conscience and moral voice. He is usually given a special stage by prestigious American, British, and French newspapers to express his opinions regarding major political events, such as the assassination of Israeli prime minister Yitzhak Rabin, Israel's 1996 Operation Grapes of Wrath in Lebanon, and so on. Oz also has won many prestigious Israeli and international literary prizes, and frequently, as in the case of his being awarded the Israeli prize for literature in 1998, he has become the focus of political controversies and target of attacks, in particular by the Israeli Right.[7] Yet, Oz's work is not lacking in Orientalist discourse.

The novel's protagonist and narrator is Hannah Gonen, a young woman married to a Ph.D. student in geology at the Hebrew University of Jerusalem. Through her narration, the reader learns the story of her marriage, a marriage

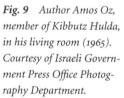

Fig. 9 *Author Amos Oz, member of Kibbutz Hulda, in his living room (1965). Courtesy of Israeli Government Press Office Photography Department.*

perceived by her to be dull and flat. In order to escape her uninspiring life, she indulges in fantasies composed of early memories, imaginary adventures with the heroes of juvenile travel and adventure literature (Michael Strogoff and Captain Nemo), and semisuppressed sexual fantasies centered around her memories of a pair of Arab twins, Khalil and Aziz, with whom she used to play as a child in Jerusalem during the British mandate.

My Michael, like Oz's other works, is characterized by extensive use of binary oppositions—strategy typical of the "meta-Zionist narrative."[8] The major binary opposition is constituted through the characters of Hannah and Michael Gonen. Whereas Michael, the male scientist, represents rationality and pragmatism, Hannah, a former student of Hebrew literature, represents irrationality and impracticality. Oz thus maintains the traditional patriarchal binarism of male/culture/reality versus female/nature/fantasy. It is not an accident that Michael was born in Holon, a new and ahistorical suburb of Tel Aviv,[9] whereas Hannah is a native of Jerusalem, the historical city associated with mysticism, suffering, and religious and nationalistic "madness." Indeed, as Amos Elon points out, it was Amos Oz who claimed that Jerusalem is a city where everybody is at once yearning to crucify his adversary for his opinions and, at the same time, to be crucified for his own.[10] When Hannah and Michael first meet, Michael immediately identifies Hannah as a Jerusalemite. Thus, Jerusalem's mystical and poetic aura is intended to invoke a polar opposition to the secular and prosaic atmosphere of Holon. The cultural and ideological dichotomy invoked by Jerusalem and Holon, the two antithetical metaphors, is carried over into the personas of the protagonists themselves.

The film, unlike the novel, ignores binarism and emphasizes instead the text's melodramatic aspect, which is rendered, primarily, through the mise-en-scène. Hannah, like the heroines of the woman's picture (Douglas Sirk's and Werner-Rainer Fassbinder's melodramas in particular),[11] is frequently shot looking through the window trapped in her own home/prison. The horizontal and vertical lines of her "framed" setting give the spectator a claustrophobic sense of her restricted existence. Wolman's use of frames within frames (doors, windows) becomes a visual expression of repression and confinement. The typically small Israeli apartment becomes visually analogous to the larger Israeli "state of siege." Hannah is also often photographed walking in Jerusalem's narrow lanes, an image that renders the psychological suffocation felt in the city as a metaphor for the greater Israeli "ghetto."

Imaginary Orientals

There is a tendency in Hebrew literature, much like in colonial discourse, to associate the other (the Sephardi and the Arab) with sexual potency and virility. In A. B. Yehoshua's novel *The Lover,* which epitomizes the logic of Israeli discourse on the other, both the mother and the daughter, sexually, "surrender" to the other. The young Arab boy seduces his boss's daughter and the Sephardi religious deserter seduces the mother, the man's wife. In colonial discourse, the romantic nostalgia for a "pure" civilization—that is, one anterior to Western contamination—has been inherited from nineteenth-century Orientalism. This nostalgia is joined with the hope of discovering in the "uncontaminated" regions of the East a "free" sexuality devoid of the repression typical of industrialized Western societies. The fact that Orientalism constructs a concept of the "Orient," and in particular a concept of "liberated Oriental sexuality" emphasizes the function of the East as the desired imaginary of the West. The hypersexualization of the East—its promise of, to use Said's words, "excessive freedom of intercourse" and "freedom of licentious sex"[12]—is a European invention whose cinematic expression in the 1970s and 1980s can be found in works of directors such as Pasolini and Fassbinder.[13] Pasolini's celebration of imaginary Oriental sexuality, as well as of violent sexual encounters—in his cinema and life alike—was intimately related to his proclaimed beliefs in the purity of the Third World and the world-historical victory of "the agricultural subproletariat of the Third World (and the Italian South) over Europe's weakening and thoroughly compromised bourgeois civilization."[14] A similar view is expressed by many colonial narratives of which *My Michael* is an Israeli echo.

It is quite amazing to see how, for example, Paul Bowles's novel *The Sheltering Sky* (1949)—an interesting example of colonial narrative—resembles Oz's novel in its treatment of the Orient and femininity.[15] *The Sheltering Sky* tells the story of a couple, Port and Kit Moresby, who leave America in 1947 in order to travel in North Africa. In the course of their journey in the Sahara Port dies and Kit is "kidnapped" and "raped" by Tuareg nomads. Kit develops an erotic obsession with the Tuareg Belqassim, an obsession that can be read as analogous to the West's confrontation with the violent and vital sexual vigor of the Third World. However, instead of being rejuvenated by the more virile other, Kit, like Hannah in *My Michael*, is physically and mentally destroyed. Her loss of control over her own mind signifies the victory of the dark-skinned races over white decadence.

Paul Bowles's *Sheltering Sky*, like Oz's *My Michael*, embodies all the old colonialist projections concerning imaginary Arab sexuality. The second part of *The Sheltering Sky*, beginning with Port's death, takes the form of a rape narrative rife with white male fantasies concerning the sexual energies of dark-skinned peoples. At the beginning of the novel, as Millicent Dillon observes, "Kit Moresby is the observer, while her husband Port is the protagonist. . . . But by the end of the novel, Kit is no longer the spectator outside the action. After Port's death, she goes deeper and deeper into the Sahara and descends into darkness and madness."[16] The penetration into the Sahara and Africa, with its "inevitable" fall into madness, engages the tradition of colonial travel literature exemplified by Joseph Conrad's *Heart of Darkness*. Kit's "rape" in the novel by the imaginary Tuareg Belqassim follows the normative colonial Orientalist discourse in its representation of the other's sexual prowess: "There was an animal-like quality in the firmness with which he held her, affectionate, sensuous, wholly irrational—gentle but of a determination that only death could gainsay. . . . In his behavior there was a perfect balance between gentleness and violence that gave her particular delight . . . but she knew beforehand that it was hopeless, that even had they a language in common, he never could understand her."[17] Some of Hannah Gonen's sado-masochist sexual fantasies involving the Arab twins bear a striking similarity to the male fantasies that Bowles displaced onto his heroine's consciousness.[18] Whereas in her fantasies of domination Hannah feels an "exquisite thrill,"[19] in her fantasies of submissiveness she feels horror. The Arab twins in *My Michael*, like Belqassim in *The Sheltering Sky*, have the sexual vigor of wild animals.[20]

Indeed, the notion of "the savage body," as Rana Kabbani points out, is typical of nineteenth-century European myths of the Orient that saw the "savage man" as "a creature of instinct, controlled by sexual passions." The native, according to this perception, "was more like an animal" and Richard Burton, like other European writers, "often spoke of African and Arab man and beast in one breath."[21] As the examples of Bowles and Oz show, this nineteenth-century colonial view of the body of the non-European other as a "savage" was carried over more or less intact into twentieth-century literature. A more salient twentieth-century demonstration of this tendency to fetishize and hypersexualize the "savage body" can be traced through Isak Dinesen's writing in which "African natives can be collapsed into African animals and mystified still further as some magical essence of the continent."[22]

The Western association of Belqassim in *The Sheltering Sky* and the Arab twins in *My Michael*, with transgression of conventional morality and Western inhibitions follows the colonial discourse in its depiction of the Orient as a place that "seems to have offended sexual propriety" and suggests "untiring sensuality, unlimited desire, deep generative energies" and the "escapism of sexual fantasy."[23] Hence, as Said suggests, the Orient becomes "a place where one could look for sexual experience unobtainable in Europe."[24]

It should be noted, however, that the issue of Orientalism within the *Yishuv* (the Zionist settlement prior to the establishment of the State of Israel) and contemporary Israeli society is related to the question of the perception of the Middle East and the Arabs in Zionist ideology. The Zionist and Israeli perception of the East is in constant flux, reflecting, as it must, changes in Israeli self-identity as well as traumatic political conflicts with the East. In the visual arts, as well as in literature, different schools also offered a panoply of

Fig. 10 *Two antithetical metaphors: the Jerusalemite Hannah (Efrat Lavi) and Holon-born Michael (Oded Kotler) in Dan Wolman's* My Michael. *Photograph by Ya'acov Agor. Courtesy of Dan Wolman.*

opposing views of the East. For teachers at the Bezalel Academy (the first art college in Palestine) during the 1920s, for example, "the East was the foundry in which the Jewish nation had been forged."[25]

The Bezalel artists' approach was manifested through a romantic biblical iconography depicting the East as a primeval Eden, its inhabitants in harmony with nature. Representation of the Arab, the son of the East, is avoided by the Bezalel artists. When Oriental types are shown dressed as Arabs, they represent biblical figures and not "local natives." For their rivals, the modernists, "the acculturation of the Jewish people in the East" was seen "as one of the main goals of Zionism,"[26] and the Arab was the prototype of the new Jew. The early modernist painters like Gutman, Shemi, and Rubin painted, as Yigal Zalmona observes, "sensual, powerful and physical Arabs. They are the paradigm of rootedness and connection with nature, the absolute opposite of the stereotypical frail, ethereal diaspora Jew. As in the Hebrew literature of that period, here too the Arab was the incarnation of the sensual, earthy Gentile of diaspora literature. The Arab as a mythical figure attracts, intrigues and arouses envy."[27] In some cases the meeting with the Arab at the beginning of the century aroused, as in the case of the writer and critic Yosef Haim Brenner, who influenced Oz's writing,[28] curiosity and admiration mingled with fear and revulsion—"the embodiment of 'otherness.'"[29] The charm of indigenous Orientalism was called into question early in the history of the Yishuv following the 1929 Arab uprising and the massacre of Jews in Hebron. Hence, the Arab in the Yishuv art scene became "an amalgam of ambivalence."[30] It is

Fig. 11 *Two colonial travelers: Kit (Debra Winger) and Port (John Malkovich) in Bernardo Bertolucci's* The Sheltering Sky. *Photograph from the author's private collection. Courtesy of Bernardo Bertolucci.*

also apparent that the East, within this cultural and ideological framework, was seen, as it had been by romantic artists in Europe, "as unfettered and sexually permissive, a place of freewheeling corporeal vitality."[31]

In Oz's novel the Orientalist sexual fantasies are reserved for the Arab twins, who are used as, to quote Amos Elon, "meta-political symbols of primeval vitality."[32] Still, Hannah Gonen's sadomasochist sexual fantasies involving the Arab twins open a space for an Orientalist as well as a non-Orientalist reading. On the one hand, Hannah's fantasies are clearly fantasies of sexual debasement; but on the other hand, they constitute visions of Dionysiac release that, when translated into political terms, can be read as the revenge of the oppressed and repressed.

Significantly, in Oz's writing, as Alter observes, "the violent forces locked up in nature are linked with wild sexuality," but nature "has itself become the invading threat . . . and the Arabs when they are imagined directly are merely extensions, embodiments, of an inimical yet seductive nature."[33] Oz's interest, to again use Alter's imploded language, in the "erotic underworld" is in line with the interest of Orientalist discourse in the East as the id of Western civilization.[34]

The ambiguity of the metaphor of the twins in regard to colonial discourse is strengthened by the fact that it is evident, as Alter suggests, that Hannah "is far more fascinated than frightened by them."[35] Despite the hypersexualization of the other and the prominence of Orientalist presuppositions in the representation of the Arab twins, there remains a certain ambiguity. The fascination with the other/Arab, within the conceptual framework of the novel, can in its historical context also be read as subversive. This reading might explain both the heated polemics surrounding the publication of the book, and the hostile reception of the novel by some reviewers who accused it of being subversive and dangerous.

Ethno-Porno: Interracial Erotica

What was perceived by some readers and critics as the novel's subversive dimension has to do with its transgression of Israeli/Zionist/Jewish taboos regarding interracial (Jewish/Arab) sexual relationships. In "colonial discourse" the quest for the non-Western other involves as well a quest for "another" sexuality. Indeed, the two quests are one and the same in the sense that the allure of the other is, presumably, grounded in his/her promise of "different body/ different skin color" inviting "different sexuality." In fact, the most significant formal manifestation of what Abdul R. JanMohamed calls "the Manichean allegory" in colonialist literature is the racial romance. Racial romances can vary "from pristine fantasy versions to more mixed and problematic ones. . . . In all cases, however, they pit civilized societies against the barbaric aberrations of an Other."[36] In *My Michael* as in Forster's *Passage to India* the interracial erotica is confined to the boundaries of the fantasized other, and racial/national borders are never transgressed in "reality."

In Paul Bowles's *Sheltering Sky*, on the other hand, sexual and racial boundaries are transgressed in the form of interracial erotica. Nevertheless, neither Bowles's nor Bertolucci's sexual politics (in the film adaptation of the novel) transgress Western ethnocentrism. The American married couple Kit and Port Moresby are trying to resolve marital problems through a travel expedition through North Africa. Both of them have sexual encounters with natives. Port has an encounter with an Arab prostitute, and Kit lives out a voluptuous affair with Belqassim, a Tuareg tribal chief. The novel's as well as the film's narrative focalization is the white couple; the natives (Arab, African, and Tuareg) are used as an "ethnic backdrop" aimed at magnifying and sanctifying "white *angst*."

A deconstruction of the design of the major sexual encounters in *The Sheltering Sky* reveals that Bertolucci's sexual politics in this movie are heavily laced with traces of colonial discourse. Port has a one-night stand with a Moroccan prostitute. Thus, her character is colonized twice: first as a subject of a colonized country under the French protectorate, and second as a prostitute whose body has been "colonized" by her pimp and clients. In contrast to Port's "other woman," Kit becomes the lover of a free subject. Tuareg nomadic culture resisted the Arabization of the Islamic crusades and France's attempts to colonize the Maghreb. Furthermore, Belqassim is the chief of a Tuareg tribe; his status as a young Sahara desert prince counterbalances, to some extent, the "inferiority" implied by his racial difference. In Oz's *My Michael* Hannah also talks about Khalil and Aziz as her "twin princes." This view of the other as a "noble savage" is not far from the romantic utopian view of the Arab fighter typical of the first Zionist settlers who even adopted his "Orientalist paraphernalia" (the kaffiyeh, *abaya,* and *shaberia*) as the attire of the fighters of Hashomer (the first Jewish military organization in Palestine). It should be pointed out, however, that within the economy of desire in the filmic *My Michael,* this Orientalist romanticism (which in the 1970s no longer had a grip on the Israeli collective imagination) was replaced by the fetishization of "low-class" (both Arabs and Oriental Jews) "objects of desire."

In *The Sheltering Sky*, Port's desire to escape the fate of the American "lost generation" through fusion with Mother Nature ("Mama Africa") epitomized by the "dark African continent" climaxes with his actual death. This view of Africa (and the "territorial zone" of the non-European other in general) as an alluring, destructive woman is a recurrent motif in colonialist literature. It can be found in such novels as Graham Greene's *Heart of the Matter* as well as in Joseph Conrad's much discussed *Heart of Darkness* with its portrayal of Kurtz's fixation on the dark, satanic woman.

Questions raised by "colonial discourse" assume a greater urgency when discussed in relation to filmic representations of the other. The "perverse pleasures" of cinema and its potential for pornographic exploitation have been studied exhaustively by feminist film theorists. Issues of color—"the epidermic schema," to use Frantz Fanon's suggestive phrase[37]—become all the more "visible" in a visually oriented medium based on a creative play of light and darkness, the two binary elements that constitute the Manichean allegory of colonial discourse. Bertolucci is thus able to utilize the pornographic potential of cinema to comment on the exploitative nature of all colonial relations. When Port, the husband, returns home from the Arab prostitute to his waiting white wife, he is not portrayed as an adulterer. Instead he is granted the status of "primal explorer"—just back from a fresh/flesh trek through exotic sexual otherness.

Bertolucci's poetics of sexual indeterminacy in *The Sheltering Sky* subliminally suggest an ethno-porno iconography. Kit's "mimicry" (her disguise as a Tuareg boy) allows her to enter Tuareg society. In the private chamber where she is kept and confined, both sexual partners unwrap the traditional male indigo turban. Kit, by now, has been transvested, her skin blackened. All this "camouflage" occurs so that Belqassim can enjoy her being sexually other (female) and racially different (white). The ritualistic, worshiping manner in which the African sexual partner tenderly undresses and reverently wipes the desert dust off Kit's body conjures forth an image of the American partner as a sex goddess rather than a sexual slave. This fantasy of master and slave is not far from Oz's Hannah, who fantasizes about herself as a cold queen lording over dark submissive slaves. In *The Sheltering Sky*, Kit's cage/castle provides the couple, temporarily, with an intimate isolation free of the colonial outside world with its racial segregation. However, as in Bertolucci's *Last Tango in Paris*, the moment the door of this artificially constructed "private space" opens to the "public space" marked by racial separation, the couple's private Eden collapses, recalling Albert Memmi's comment about the illusions of exogamy: there is no "space" free of sociocultural contingencies.[38] It should also be stressed that the fact that Belqassim is stunningly beautiful and delicate fetishistically assuages the transgression that overlies the text. Indeed, fetishism structures the whole scene, giving to Kit her white skin and racial "supremacy."

The potentially anxiety-inducing idea regarding contact between black manhood and white womanhood is soothed in the film by giving the Western partner an ego-reinforcing focus. Only the white male enjoys orgasm (as in the encounter between Port and the Moroccan woman), and the spectator is kept ignorant about the black male's subjectivity. Is he ravished by the delights of sexual difference, or by the discovery of Kit's white skin? Furthermore, Bertolucci's mise-en-scène reproduces cultural codes of mastery and submission taken from popular erotica, thereby establishing white racial "supremacy." This is most notable in the scene in the private chamber in which Kit is standing on the bed while Belqassim, sitting and kneeling, performs oral sex with her.

Both Kit's and Port's respective encounters with the exotic other lead to sexual practices quite rare in mainstream cinema. These practices allow the Western man to be nurtured while not "virily" performing, and for the Western white woman to enjoy sexuality that does not require phallic penetration. A feminist reading would gladly welcome this less phallocentric representation of human sexuality. However, the fact that, unwittingly or not, this reduction of phallocracy requires the recourse to an exotic other as a flight from Western alienation is disturbing.

Bertolucci, just like Bowles four decades earlier, is a kind of "colonial traveller" in Said's sense of "displaced percipient."[39] Said describes colonial texts as "encapsulations" of the encounters between Europe and "primitivity" where a "vacillation" between the foreign and the familiar occurs. In *The Sheltering Sky* Port experiences precisely this kind of vacillation. He enjoys the delights of cultural differences as a freshly arrived American in Tangier, while simultaneously disavowing these differences by affixing universalist rules governing prostitution to his first North African experience. Homi Bhabha's analysis of colonial discourse may suggest a better insight into Bertolucci's fetishization of the other along lines of race and sex. Bhabha reminds us that skin, "unlike the sexual fetish, is not a secret; it is the most visible of fetishes which plays a public part in the racial drama which is enacted everyday in colonial societies."[40] In *The Sheltering Sky* the "blackening" of Kit's skin (her newly acquired suntan) metamorphoses the white skin of the Western female from a "visible fetish playing a public part in racial drama" into a "secret" fetish playing a private part in sexual drama. Not only does the scopic economy of the mise-en-scène of the sexual drama enacted in the hidden room between Kit and Belqassim establish the idolization of white skin, but also the fetishistic textual regime of this scene leads to the sexualization of what Frantz Fanon refers to as the "epidermal schema."

In the same thrust, Bhabha underlines the parallelism between sexual fetish and the fetish of colonial discourse (or of racial stereotypes): the first facilitates sexual relations ("It is the prop which makes the whole object desirable and lovable");[41] the second facilitates colonial or interracial relations. In *The Sheltering Sky* the scene between Port and the North African young woman demonstrates how the sexual fetish (signified by the Arab woman's dazzling erotic paraphernalia) facilitates colonial relations by simulating a pornographically familiar haremlike eroticism. Similarly, the erotic scenes between Kit and Belqassim illustrate how the skin, the "key signifier of cultural and racial difference,"[42] facilitates and intensifies sexual relations. Bertolucci's exploitation of racial difference through the revitalization of tired libido (Port) or the investment of libidinal excess (Kit) seems to follow a prevalent tendency of our age of postmodern postcolonialism regarding the representation of sexual/racial relations.[43] It can be argued that this trend is triggered by the epidermal fetish, which due to its "visibility" offers a tremendous voyeuristic potential to the scopophilic cinematic apparatus by injecting into the sexual fetish a new vitality.

Bhabha argues that colonial discourse is characterized by the holding of multiple contradictory beliefs. Bertolucci's *Sheltering Sky* cultivates countless contradictory endemic beliefs about Africa and Africans/Arabs. Africa is both convivial and hostile, hospitable and rejecting, unpolluted and fly infested. Africans are both ravishingly winsome and grotesquely repulsive. They have healthy, sculpted bodies or degenerate, demonized ones. They are capable of gratuitous, altruistic behavior or can reveal themselves as money-grubbing and easily corruptible. In short, Arab/African culture, within the economy of Bertolucci's quest for the other, is both utopian and dystopian. A similar double vision has been discovered, as Emily C. Bartels observes (in her discussion of the imperialist construction of Africa by Richard Hakluyt), by Christopher Miller, a leading scholar of "Africanist discourse," in French texts of the nineteenth century. This ambiguity, Miller claims, "exposes Europe's longstanding ambivalence about Africa."[44] Hakluyt himself in his representations produced an Africa "which is at once familiar and unfamiliar, civil and savage, full of promise and full of threat."[45]

Bhabha's and other critics' view of ambivalence and ambiguity as the salient features of colonial discourse is challenged by others. Thus, for example, according to JanMohamed colonialist fiction is generated predominantly by the ideological machinery of the Manichean allegory and not by "ambivalence." In fact, JanMohamed claims that the Manichean allegory is so strong that "even a writer who is reluctant to acknowledge it and who may indeed be highly critical of imperialist exploitation is drawn into its vortex."[46] Vijay Mishra and Bob Hodge, in their attempt to define "what is post(-)colonialism?" claim: "Those writers who use forms of 'appropriation' recognize that colonial discourse itself is a complex, contradictory mode of representation which implicates both the colonizer and the colonized."[47] And nowhere according to them is this tendency more evident than in the works of V. S. Naipaul.

Imaginary Women

Interlinked with the Oriental other is the view of women as other. Women in *My Michael* are seen as susceptible to madness and hysteria. This vision expresses the notion of feminization of the Orient suggested by colonial narratives. Although, for example, Kit in *The Sheltering Sky* is portrayed as a sophisticated twentieth-century woman, her being "swept away" into irrational sexual adventure with Belqassim recalls the sexual fantasies of the heroine in *A Passage to India* whose encounter with the "sensuality" of India engages her (actually her male narrator-creator) in fantasies of being raped. Nor is it an accident that the name of one of the Arab twins in *My Michael* is Aziz, like the name of the Indian hero of *A Passage to India* who is arrested on a charge of attempted assault.

In the novel Oz chose to render his vision through the eyes of a first-person narrator, a young woman. Her stream-of-consciousness controls the narrative and conveys her obsession with sex, violence, and death. The choice of a woman as a protagonist and narrator by a male author raises an interesting question that has already been raised in regard to other male authors and Flaubert in particular. Flaubert's famous claim "Madame Bovary, c'est moi" has been discussed at great lengths by critics who, as Andreas Huyssen suggests, have tried "to show what Flaubert had in common with Emma Bovary— mostly in order to show how he transcended aesthetically the dilemma on which she foundered in 'real life.'" In such arguments, Huyssen stresses, "the question of gender usually remains submerged, thereby asserting itself all the more powerfully."[48] As Huyssen observes, the question of Flaubert's "imaginary femininity" was also raised by Jean-Paul Sartre. Sartre says: "Our problem then . . . is to ask ourselves why the author . . . was able to metamorphose himself into a woman, what signification the metamorphosis *possesses* in *itself* . . . just what this woman is (of whom Baudelaire said that she possesses at once the folly and the will of a man), what the artistic transformation of male into female means in the nineteenth century . . . and finally, just who Gustav Flaubert *must have been* in order to have within the field of his possibles the possibility of portraying himself as a woman." [49] Huyssen's claim, however, is that "the imaginary femininity of male authors, which often grounds their oppositional stance vis-à-vis bourgeois society, can easily go hand in hand . . . with the misogyny of bourgeois patriarchy itself." [50] In the novel Oz describes Michael Gonen, the career-oriented, practical-minded husband, as a representative of a new type of Jerusalemite bourgeoisie whose numbers are increasing and whose origins are in the *Shephela* (the Tel Aviv area).

The problematics associated with Flaubert's "imaginary femininity," as well as Huyssen's claim, correspond faithfully to the problematics provoked by Oz's imaginary femininity. In Oz's novel Hannah Gonen is deliberately portrayed as an Israeli Madame Bovary caught between the delusions of an internal fantasy world and the realities of a prototypical Jerusalemite provincial life during the fifties. Like Madame Bovary, who escapes to the delusions of the sentimental romantic narrative in order to "transcend" her bourgeois, provincial life, so Hannah Gonen escapes to the sensual world of fantasy and daydreaming in an attempt to break from her petit bourgeois claustrophobic existence.

In the novel Hannah's "imaginary femininity" is portrayed as indeterminate in its sexual identity. Indeed, Hannah is represented as a woman who in her childhood and youth wanted to be a man: "When I was a child I adored the books my brother had by Jules Verne and Fenimore Cooper. I thought that if I wrestled and climbed trees and read boys' books I'd grow up to be a boy. I hated being a girl. I regarded grown-up women with loathing and disgust." [51] In the novel Hannah is represented as a self-hating woman who rejects her femininity and especially her maternal role. She is portrayed as a "bad mother" who is completely indifferent to her son. Her hobbies and fantasies as a child and adolescent were clearly masculine. She liked travel and adventure literature and despised (unlike Madame Bovary but like Flaubert himself) women's literature.

Both Genia, Michael's aunt, and the "crazy" elderly neighbor, Duba Glick, incarnate the image of the old woman Hannah despised as a child. To a certain extent, they are also both Hannah's doubles, or rather, the materialization of her childish fears. Genia is a man-like character, a distorted caricature of Hannah's youthful fantasy about becoming a male. She has a small mustache, and a masculine "bad" face. She is a physician (ironically a pediatrician, not unlike Hannah, who works with children in a kindergarten) who tries to convince Hannah to have an abortion (an act signifying rejection of the maternal role). Mrs. Glick, on the other hand, is an older version of Hannah herself. She is the grown-up "madwoman" Hannah always feared becoming: "When I was a girl of eight I believed that if I behaved exactly like a boy I would grow up to be a man instead of a woman. What a wasted effort. I do not have to rush up panting like a mad-woman."[52] Oz's "poetics of sexual indeterminacy," rendered through the oscillation of his heroine between male and female sexual identity/desire, conveys the male writer's ambivalence toward the "imaginary femininity" he himself created.[53]

Themes of bisexuality and sexual disguise are common in colonial discourse. Von Sternberg's *Morocco*, for example, tells the love story of a vaudeville singer and a foreign legionnaire. The ship's captain who brings the vaudeville actresses to Marrakech calls them "suicide passengers," alluding to his knowledge that there will be no return journey. As in *The Sheltering Sky* and other colonial narratives (for example, Conrad's *Heart of Darkness* and Forster's *Passage to India*), the text suggests that the alluring fascination of the other and the desire it invokes culminate in madness. In *Morocco* Amy Jolly (Marlene Dietrich) follows her lover Tom Brown (Gary Cooper), the legionnaire, into the heart of the Sahara. The last shot shows her kicking off her high-heeled gold sandals as she vanishes in the desert sand dunes. Amy Jolly, like Kit in *The Sheltering Sky*, immerses herself (literally) in the sands of the desert. Hence, the power of the desert/Orient, the film suggests, causes women to transgress social conventions, to surrender to archaic forces (the id). The image of the Sahara becomes an image of madness, uncontrollable passion, and the irrationality that leads to the destruction of the white race.

The trope of geographic "otherness" in colonial discourse is significant. In many colonial and postcolonial fictions the landscape is formally invested with markers of "cultural" strangeness in order to allow the "colonizer" to apply a different cultural code when "decoding" the other, as well as to provide the colonizer with a "justification" for his/her own "strange" behavior on being confronted with geographic/cultural "otherness." In *A Passage to India*, to give one prominent example, the landscapes of India, and in particular the Marabar caves, much like the desert in *The Sheltering Sky* and *Morocco*, "represent the fundamental, unconscious identity from which all natural and social differences emanate and to which they all return when they can escape their phenomenal manifestation."[54] The unconscious realm of the caves mirrors the repressed sexuality of Adela Quested, much as the desert in *The Sheltering Sky* and *Morocco* invokes the "return of the repressed."

Paul Bowles's choice of the Orient as an "elective center" followed, to invoke Said, a long and established tradition of nineteenth-century French pilgrims who "did not seek a scientific so much as an exotic yet especially attractive reality. This is obviously true of the literary pilgrims, beginning with Chateaubriand, who found in the Orient a locale sympathetic to their private myths, obsessions and requirements. Here we notice how all the pilgrims, but especially the French, exploit the Orient in their work so as in some urgent way to justify their existential vocation."[55] Bowles, the existential traveler-tourist according to Robert Briatte, the author of the only authorized biography on Paul Bowles, had on a May night in 1947 a dream of Tangier, the "white city." In Briatte's interpretive description, "in the labyrinth of the unconscious the images of his dreams delineated a landscape of quite startling precision: narrow little alleys designed to make one lose one's way, terraces looking out over the ocean, staircases ascending nowhere."[56] As a result of this "vocational" dream, Briatte observes, Bowles decided to spend the summer in Morocco and to write. He left his wife, Jane, in the United States, and that August in Fez he began writing *The Sheltering Sky*. Bowles's delirious moment of "unconscious epiphany" and hallucinatory vision of the labyrinthine Tangier as a chaotic and mysterious city invoke the archaeological and geographic metaphors prevalent in colonial discourse on the Orient. Bertolucci used a similar vocabulary to describe Port and Kit's journey into the Sahara: "[T]hey go back into the past of North Africa. To reach the truth they have to go deeper into the Sahara, they have to pass through the ruins of the Kasbah and the abandoned ksour that takes them into the labyrinth of tunnels . . . somewhere very obscure and somewhere very big. There isn't anything in the world that gives you a sense of timelessness like the desert. Port and Kit's trip to the desert is parallel to their trip into the past."[57] The Oriental desert in both Bowles's and Bertolucci's discourses becomes the id of Western civilization. Here colonial, anthropological, archaeological, and psychoanalytic discourses are clearly interwoven. The trip to the desert is the quest for the past—that of the individuals Kit and Port, as well as that of Western civilization in search of its Eastern roots.

In *My Michael* the city of Jerusalem (a historical meeting point of East and West) functions as an emblem for the realm of the unconscious. Yet, the expulsion of Hannah's objects of fantasy, Khalil and Aziz, from the city as a result of the 1948 war has pushed the repressed beyond the border, the symbolic wall between us and them, good and bad. Hence, the repression and demonization of the other/enemy is emblematized by the border. And indeed *My Michael* ends with Hannah's fantasy of the "return of the repressed," with Khalil and Aziz as a pair of armed Palestinian "terrorists" crossing the border and "penetrating" into an Israeli-Jewish landscape.

The novel portrays Hannah's sexual desires as deviant. She shifts between sadomasochist fantasies involving her imaginary "Orientals"—the Arab twins, Khalil and Aziz—and pedophiliac longings for Yoram, a young boy whom she tutors. Her sexual fantasies switch from degradation to seduction, and from submissiveness to domination and vice versa. Thus, she gives expression to the traditional "male" as well as "female" principle. Following the tradition of melodrama, Hannah seeks sexual fulfillment outside of her home/prison. The possibility of pedophiliac adulterous sex and the private world of sexual fantasies are presented as the only avenues of escape from the prison of the family.

Woman's desire in the novel is also linked to madness, a recurrent motif in melodrama. Madness in *My Michael* is, in fact, represented as an exclusively feminine trait. Hannah's madness is mirrored by that of Mrs. Glick, the neighbor whose hysterical attacks, like those of Hannah herself, incite her to "terrorize" in return her good and patient husband. The novel, following a long cultural tradition of misogyny, thus links the notion of femininity to madness, fantasy, and escapism.[58] Oz seems to be implying that in Israel where everybody is constantly required to express strong political opinions, only a "deviant" and "crazy" woman can afford the luxury of being uninvolved, of indulging, narcissistically, in an unabashedly private world. As much as Flaubert, according to Huyssen, could express his passion for the inferior romances only through the "inferior" character of a woman, so could Oz provide an alternative/utopian vision of nonengagement in Israeli political reality only through a "madwoman."

It is not surprising that the Israeli popular, but prestigious, semiscientific periodical *Mahshavot* (*Thoughts*) chose to interview the Israeli poet Dalia Rabikovitch to comment on *My Michael*. At the time of the interview Rabikovitch was associated with poets and writers of the 1960s and 1970s such as Nathan Zach, David Avidan, and Yehuda Amichai, who argued for more personal writing and for art for art's sake, against the view held by the Palmach generation. Only after the Israeli invasion of Lebanon in 1982 did Rabikovitch, like other Israeli artists, become politically involved through the Peace Now movement. In her personal life and writing Dalia Rabikovitch, like Oz himself, incarnates the tension between the private and the political. The assumption behind this interview was that Hannah Gonen (who as a fictional character completely rejects the political and escapes into madness) is a character with whom Rabikovitch—the sensitive, beautiful, and vulnerable poet—could identify. In the short introduction to the interview the editor says: "Hannah Gonen is a very special woman, who lives in a very personal world, yet her suffering is very universal. Therefore we decided to talk to the poet Dalia Rabikovitch and not to an erudite literary scholar."[59]

In the novel *My Michael* Flaubert's claim ("Madame Bovary, c'est moi") is echoed through its presumably autobiographical component. Dan Wolman, the director of the filmic adaptation, however, said quite blatantly—although he was completely unconscious of the resonance carried by his remark vis-à-vis Flaubert—"I made the film because I felt very close to Hannah Gonen."[60] In Oz's novel even the indulgence in a private world has a metapolitical function. It is presented as subversive in relation to Israeli reality and the general population's preoccupation, verging on obsession, with the "big issues" traditionally associated with the public sphere. In Wolman's film, however, the metapolitical realm receives less emphasis. As one of the prominent directors of Israeli personal cinema, Wolman prefers subtlety to contrived symbolism à la Oz. His restrained and realistic, almost impressionist style renders "politics" through the representation of "personal stories," and never through thick symbolism. Wolman's narrative solution to the problem of the novel's "central consciousness" was to adopt Hannah's subjective point of view as the controlling perspective of the film. As in the woman's picture, woman's subjective point of view organizes the economy of the film's gaze. Unlike in most mainstream films, and in Israeli cinema in general, Wolman's heroine activates, instead of absorbing, the gaze. The filmic Hannah (Efrat Lavi) is an active gazer; in some scenes she is even a voyeur.

In one of the most memorable scenes of the film, as Hannah is watching the crazy neighbor Mrs. Glick through the window frame, Wolman dissolves the faces of the young and old woman into a single face embodying an image of feminine madness. This subjective point of view visualizes the heroine's "data of consciousness" and provides the spectator with a vivid glimpse into her private fears and anxieties. Although Wolman sometimes uses a voice-over narration quoting from the film's literary source, the spectator's (unlike the reader's) access to the heroine's consciousness is limited. This restricted access is compensated for in the film through the privilege accorded to Hannah's gaze.

Hannah's gaze is utilized deliberately for erotic ends. Here, female desire is expressed unequivocally and emphatically. Given Wolman's well-known sympathetic treatment of homosexual themes, the desire of the filmic Hannah, like the desire of the literary Hannah, is not without ambivalence. In the film *My Michael* there is an interesting role reversal in regard to the gaze-choreography common to mainstream cinema. In most of the erotic scenes Hannah, and not the man, is the one who activates the gaze. Such, for example, is the situation in the wedding-night scene when Hannah watches Michael undressing. Unlike as in the passionate lovemaking of her fantasies, her husband is seen slowly and meticulously taking off his clothes and pedantically putting each piece of clothing in its proper place.

In another scene (which does not exist in the novel) Hannah is shown gazing with a yearning look at some muscular, half-naked porters. In still another scene she is seen walking in *Mahane Yehuda,* Jerusalem's open-air market (associated in particular with Mizrahim, and more generally with religious Jews, Palestinian workers, and working-class people), sending seductive looks toward the low-class, mostly Oriental men. In other scenes she is seen gazing at Arab workers who remind her of "her" twins. Hannah's "objects of desire" are both Jewish and Arab Orientals, and they are always associated with low-life sensuality. They are the opposites of her Ashkenazi, nonsensual husband/ scholar. The only exception is Yoram, her pedophiliac love object, whose innocent, Ashkenazi, sensitive adolescence (he is a dreamy type and likes travel literature) is a narcissistic projection of herself as a young girl wishing to be a boy.

Hannah is also depicted as a voyeur in two scenes in which her husband is being seduced by Yardena, a woman with whom he carries on a light flirtation. The positioning of Hannah as the voyeur has a psychological dimension as well. Hannah observes life but cannot participate in it. Her real life is the life of the imagination. She is fully alive only in her fantasies and daydreams. In one of the more memorable scenes of the film[61] Hannah asks Michael, "What do you live for?" Michael looks straight into Hannah's eyes and answers: "People don't ask what they live for. People just live, period." The scene is a minidramatic climax for Hannah and Michael, two people with different life philosophies. In contrast to Hannah's existential search for meaning (a paradigmatic search prominent in Israeli personal cinema), Michael is advocating a pragmatic attitude.

The film emphasizes the novel's "poetics of sexual indeterminacy" through visual trompe l'oeil. As Hannah's mental state is deteriorating, she cuts her hair so short that she looks almost like a boy (the cutting of the hair is obviously loaded with Freudian connotations of self-castration).[62] When Michael arrives home he looks with shock at his wife's very short hair; the composition of the shot, from behind Michael, for a brief confusing moment makes the two look like male twins. In another scene Hannah is seen taking a shower and hallucinating on participating in an orgy with the Arab twins. The tomboy Hannah with her short hair and flat bosom looks like a young man, and the hallucinatory mènage à trois is heavily laden with latent homosexuality. Sexual ambiguity is evident also in Hannah's neglect of the traditional maternal role, which is taken over by Michael, who is seen feeding, playing with, and teaching their child.

From Imaginary Orientals to Imaginary Women

It is interesting, but also disturbing, that Oz chose to metaphorize and embody Israeli fears through imaginary Arabs and imaginary women. In the work of Oz, as Gila Ramras-Rauch observes, "the Arab's sociopolitical existence is internalized in the Israeli, and the Arab becomes the focus of libidinal dreams and fantasies."[63] Ultimately Oz's "binarist" and patriarchal writing distills to a projection of fears, neuroses, and fantasies, to the "other" side of Israeli society: Arabs and women. It is not surprising, therefore, that these others were selected to convey Oz's vision of the existential situation of Israel. Wolman's film, on the other hand, subverts the comforting solution of the binary opposition by preferring "realism" to "symbolism" and expressing latent homosexuality through the film's economy of the gaze.[64] Although Oz's novel is permeated with images of bisexuality, gay sexuality has never been the central concern of any of his works. Oz, in particular in *My Michael*, seems to be interested in sexual ambivalence rather than in "pure" and determinate sexual identity. In fact, *My Michael* is the only of Oz's works that concerns itself with questions of sexual identity. This is due, perhaps, to the choice of a woman to generate the narrative's "central consciousness," thus creating tension between the voice of the narrator and the voice of the author. The autobiographical aspect involved in this tension and the problems of identification it may have raised may explain Oz's poetic "politics of sexual indeterminacy." By contrast, Wolman's engagement with homosexual subjects, an almost taboo topic in Israeli literature and cinema,[65] is well known. In *Hide and Seek* (1981), for example, set in Jerusalem in 1946, he portrays a homosexual relationship between a young Jew and Arab, a sensitive issue in Israel, let alone in 1946.

The "rescue" of melodrama, during the last fifteen years or so, from its traditional "low" status to its "high" criticism has been grounded, as Wimal Dissanayke wrote, "upon a retheorizing of such questions as the nature of representation in cinema, the role of ideology, and female subjectivity in films." [66] These questions, though mainly theorized in relation to American melodrama, have even greater ramifications in non-Western societies where the separation between the public and private spheres, as well as the confinement of women within each of them, is more pronounced. Paradoxically, in Israeli society, despite this separation and the traditional exclusion of women from the political centers of power, the dichotomy of political/personal is, as many critics have observed, problematic. In some respects the dichotomy is in fact almost impossible to maintain. Wolman's preference of melodrama over Oz's metapolitical symbolism thus seems to promote an open-ended reading that makes room for the expression of female subjectivity.

Yet, it should be emphasized that Wolman's "political correctness" does not make his film more interesting than the novel. Perhaps the opposite is true. The interest of the novel, what some reviewers perceived as its subversive and dangerous message, lies, to the contrary, in its ability to disturb and stir. Despite what I read as the misogynist representation of women in the novel (their proneness to madness, their irrationality, their "deviant" sexual life, and so on) one cannot but conclude that, in the last instance, the women in Oz's novel are more "interesting" than the men. Hannah is not only the negation of her "uninteresting" husband, but also the negation of "dull normalcy." The paradox, of course, is that in his political positions and public pronouncements Oz, like A. B. Yehoshua, is the advocate of nonfanaticism, what came to be known in Israeli public discourse affiliated with the Left as "sane Zionism." [67] Yet, in his writing (both in his fiction as well as in his polemical essays) Oz, as Gertz points out, indirectly celebrates madness (both personal and political) mainly through his use of poetically charged and excessive language that makes madness look more "interesting" than sanity. One may gauge the evolving sense of Israeli personal and political identity in this tension between madness and normalcy. After all, as Edward Said observes: "If in a Jewish state, normality is defined by Jewishness, abnormality is the normal condition of the non-Jew. The logic extends itself to history and society more generally considered." [68] Hannah's fantasies, which attempt to disrupt this "logic of normalcy" by hybridizing Israeli Jews with Palestinians through the metaphor of sexual union, will materialize as "real acts" in the cinematic narratives about forbidden love that are the focus of the last two chapters in this book.

CHAPTER SIX

Forbidden Love in the Holy Land

Transgressing the Israeli-Palestinian Conflict

■ The provocation is a love story.

Nissim Dayan, director of *On a Narrow Bridge*

■ If you think that we are going to be Romeo and
Juliet, then forget it. I don't believe in those stories.
They are only good for the movies.

Nadia, the female Palestinian protagonist of *Nadia,*
to Ronen, an Israeli Jewish boy

■ In essence the story seems banal. We know over
thousands of versions of love stories between a Jewish woman and Arab man in the context of the
conflict that end in the doom of the woman. There
are many ways to do that; the question is which one
you choose.

Benny Barabash, scriptwriter of Gideon Ganani's
Crossfire

■ It could have worked if an Arab man had fallen in
love with an Israeli woman. We have already seen
this in *Hamsin* and *Hannah K.* But an Israeli man
falling for an Arab woman? Give me a break.

Potential financier to Nissim Dayan

Israeli new historian Ilan Pappe claims that "most Israeli filmmakers . . . feel
the need to use the sexual and romantic bridge as a way to understand the
other side. Most of the films that courageously deal with Arab-Jewish relationships choose the medium of a love story, which is usually tragic (for example in *Hamsin, The Lover* and *On a Narrow Bridge*)." According to Pappe,
this need is "a way to avoid and evade rational recognition of the arguments

and feelings of the other side. Nevertheless, these films reflect impressive progress relative to the films made before 1967, in which collaboration with Arabs was possible only given unconditional support of the Zionist project."[1] Pappe, however, does not forget to mention that there is one salient difference between "the attitude of Israeli cinema and the new Israeli historiography toward the topic of friendship and cooperation: Whereas the historians draw optimistic conclusions from these attempts at collaboration, Israeli cinema, by contrast, chooses the model of Greek tragedy in order to convey a pessimistic message about the impossibility of overcoming the mutual hatred, as in the film *Hamsin*."[2]

Stories of "forbidden love," dealing mainly with interracial romances, are a recurring theme in Western culture. European colonizers and their settler descendants have always been terrified by the prospect of miscegenation. "The fear of mixing blood stems from a desire to maintain the separation between the colonizer and the colonized, the 'civilized' and the 'savage,' yet that binary masks a profound longing, occluding the idea of the inevitable dependence of one on the existence of the other."[3] Similar fears of mixing blood exist in Jewish Israeli society. They were vividly described by Daniel Wachsmann, the director of *Hamsin*: "We screened *Hamsin* at a Hashomer Hatzair kibbutz (the most left-wing youth movement in the Zionist Left). Some of the members, liberals of European origin, were as disturbed by the subject matter as Jews from Arab countries who are very vocal about their anti-Arab bias. They were apparently less upset by the thought that young women from the kibbutz have affairs with Scandinavian volunteers than that one might sleep with an Arab."[4]

"Real" (nonreel) stories of forbidden love between Jews and Arabs in Israel usually exist far from the public eye. When they are exposed to public attention, it is because they have a criminal component or because the lovers have been subject to extreme social hardship as a result. The displacement, taking place in Israeli cinema, of the Israeli-Palestinian conflict to the territory of forbidden love, makes it easier for the Israeli audience, as Pappe rightly observes, to encounter the conflict whose roots are complex and painful. Furthermore, the transfer of the conflict to the intimacy of the private space "loosens," and sometimes even disarms, the defense mechanism erected by many Israelis when confronted with "*the* conflict." It is easier to face the "big" conflict when it is broken down into "small" conflicts that aim to negotiate its meaning on the microlevel. Hence, the shifting of the conflict onto the terrain of forbidden love is used in Israeli cinema as a distanciation device. Ultimately the tautologous nature of these cinematic tales is that the end of the forbidden love story, and by implication of the conflict, is a chronicle of a death well foretold.

In what follows I shall discuss the fears of "forbidden love" between Israeli Jews and Palestinians as they are expressed, criticized, and transgressed in the relatively large group of Israeli films that deal with the issue. The analysis attempts to trace chronologically the reflection and construction of Israel's political, social and cultural reality in Israeli cinema. It also strives to understand and expose the sexual economy and ideology embedded in the deep structure of these stories of forbidden romance.

Hide and Seek (1981), Dani Wolman

"Queer" moments of latent homosexual desire that only surface in *My Michael* become overt in Wolman's following film, *Hide and Seek*. *Hide and Seek* is set in Jerusalem of 1946, as Jewish resistance against the British mandate and the Palestinian Arab population is growing. With his mother (Gila Almagor) engaged in rescuing Holocaust survivor children in Europe and bringing them to Palestine, and his father operating abroad with the Ha'pala organization, twelve-year-old Uri (Chaim Hadaya) is entrusted to the care of his gentle, intellectual, stereotypically Yekke (German Jewish) grandfather (Binyamin Armon).[5] Much like the character of Michael in *My Michael*, the grandfather functions as a mother and father, carrying out both "maternal" and "paternal" traditional duties. Much of the boy's days are spent with his young friends who pass the time playing war games. As the frustrated Uri falls behind in his studies, the grandfather brings in Balaban (Doron Tavori), a young and sensitive biology student, to tutor the child. The first part of the film is devoted to an exploration of the relationship between the two, which evolves from an initial period of distrust and resentment to friendship and respect. But when Uri and his pals find the tutor exchanging letters with a young Arab man, their friendship is threatened because they begin to suspect that Balaban may be a spy. Toward the end of the film Uri is seen peeping into a room in an Arab neighborhood of Jerusalem where Balaban and the young Arab, half-naked, are gently caressing each other. The erotic and tender primal scene is violently disrupted by a gang of Jews from the Haganah, dressed like Arabs, who break into the room and beat Balaban and his Arab lover with clubs.

Balaban's love relationship with the Arab youngster is represented in *Hide and Seek* as the ultimate transgression of interethnic romance between Arabs and Jews not only because it violates gender, national, and ethnic boundaries but because it takes place in the midst of a national struggle, the 1948 war, which according to the Israeli ethos expresses the greatest moment in the history not only of the Zionist movement but also of the Jewish people. Balaban's sin, according to the Haganah's view, is not only his violation of the sexual taboo, but his evident skepticism, if not indifference, toward what the Jewish side sees as its absolute right to the land. Within this context, homosexuality as a manifestation of human contact with the Arab "enemy" is thus portrayed as a betrayal of the national cause. Intimacy with the "enemy" threatens the cohesion of the collective and casts doubt on its exclusive right. The same homophobic ultranationalist view was also present in *Exodus*, in Dov's initiation ceremony into the Irgun (see chapter 1). But whereas *Exodus* presents homophobia uncritically and unquestionably as a manifestation of Jewish pride, *Hide and Seek*, on the other hand, takes a critical stance toward nationalistic zeal associated with homophobia. Like *My Michael*, which depicts the blurring of boundaries between private and public in Israeli reality, *Hide and Seek* criticizes the nationalization of personal intimate spaces and their subordination to the so called national cause.

The film, belonging to the youth film genre, subjects the spectator to the perspective of the young boy who is his or her mediator into the experience of Jewish life in Palestine during the end of the British mandate. As in *My Michael*, the Arabs in *Hide and Seek* are associated with a world of Oriental sensuality and otherness. The Arab lover first "penetrates" the viewer's space of desire seated upon a white horse with his dark upper body naked while Balaban, constrained by the codes of behavior in a public space, caresses the horse in an affectionate gesture of displaced eroticism. The spectator knows nothing about the Arab lover, who remains a backdrop object of desire confined to the realm of the senses only. The spectator, whose gaze at the Arab and Balaban is mediated through the gaze of the young, curious boys, is left to speculate as much as they as to whether the handsome young man is an Arab or not. Yet, enjoying the advantage of "superior ethnic knowledge," the spectator more so than the "naive" boys is likely to recognize the young man as other and different, namely as an Arab.

This sensitive film is, like *My Michael*, tainted by some Orientalist touches; nevertheless, it provides a very subtle and thought-provoking criticism on the political and ideological meaning of the taboo on homosexual interethnic love. Balaban, the gentle human teacher, could have become a real role model for the sensitive and inquisitive Uri, and a superior substitute for his absent

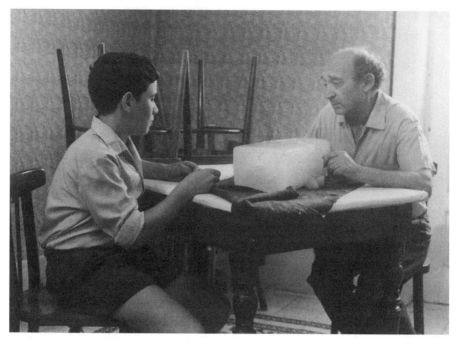

Fig. 12   *The twelve-year-old Uri (Chaim Hadaya) and the gentle grandfather (Binyamin Armon) in Dan Wolman's* Hide and Seek. *Photograph by Eyal Yitzhar. Courtesy of Dan Wolman.*

father, whom we never see in the film. Yet, the humanistic tutoring of Balaban (and of the gentle, intellectual Yekke grandfather) is destined to fail in a nationalistic, homophobic, and racist context that suffocates the individual and forces him into ideological and sexual conformity. Despite his sensitivity, Uri, therefore, is destined like the other iconic Uris that preceded him in the cultural history of the mythological Sabra to carry on the Sabra's "tradition" of homophobic and xenophobic militaristic collectivism.

Hamsin (1982), Daniel Wachsmann

The interracial relationship that in *My Michael*, both in its literary and film manifestations, was confined to the realm of fantasy, materialized as a "real" taboo-shattering event in Daniel Wachsmann's *Hamsin*,[6] which in 1989 was selected "best film of the decade" by the Israeli Academy of Motion Pictures. The film depicts an erotic relationship between Khaled, a Palestinian man,

Fig. 13 *A Zionist Western in the Wild East: Hava (Hemda Levi) and Gedalia (Shlomo Tarshish) in Daniel Wachsmann's* Hamsin. *Courtesy of Daniel Wachsmann.*

and Hava, a Jewish woman. Perhaps more than any other Israeli film, *Hamsin* touches upon the core of the Israeli-Palestinian conflict. Not only does it deal with a politically taboo topic (the ongoing expropriation of Arab land by Israel inside the green line, Israel's border prior to the 1967 war) but it also deals with the ultimate taboo of interracial love. To a certain extent the film not only anticipated the Palestinian Intifada, which broke out five years after its release, but has provided a critical and pessimistic look at the deep structure of the Israeli-Palestinian conflict. *Hamsin* demonstrates that there are some borders that still cannot be crossed even by ostensibly liberal Israelis.

The film focuses on a family of Jewish landowners in a Jewish moshava (agricultural village) in Galilee.[7] Gedalia (Shlomo Tarshish) is a farmer who, compared to the other settlers in the moshava, holds liberal political views. He is the employer of Khaled, an Arab worker (Yassin Shoaf) from an adjacent Arab village. When Gedalia learns that the government is going to begin confiscation of lands belonging to an Arab family with whom he is on good terms, he offers to buy the land from its owners. Since his own resources are meager, he proposes a profit-sharing plan to the owners, whereby both can reap the benefits of the land. This offer angers the other Jewish settlers in the moshava—many of whom have their own plans for the land—as well as some of the young Arabs, who oppose any land dealings with the Jews. Eventually, the family, pressured by Palestinian "nationalists," rejects his offers, claiming that they prefer that the land be taken by force rather than sold to Jews. When Gedalia discovers that his sister Hava (Hemda Levy) is having an affair with Khaled, he kills him by releasing his largest mating bull to fatally wound the Arab lover.

The power of *Hamsin* derives from its politics of representation, which employs two parallel plots: one Palestinian and the other Jewish. *Hamsin* is perhaps the first Israeli film that, while predominantly presenting the conflict from within the Israeli perspective, also tries to penetrate sympathetically into the consciousness of the other side, as if to speak through it. The film uses Palestinian actors who speak Arabic, and part of it takes place in a purely Palestinian territory, "uncontaminated" by Israeli Jewish presence. In this respect the film not only accords literal and symbolic space and voice to the Palestinians but also attempts to represent their point of view. *Hamsin* is also perhaps the first Israeli film that activates the mechanism of spectatorship to generate identification with the Palestinians. Although the members of the Israeli Jewish family are the protagonists of the film, in many of the scenes there are only Palestinians; the spectators become witnesses, "political voyeurs" of sorts to their conversations, discussions, and internal conflicts. Despite the film's overwhelming naturalism (its use of Arabic language and nonprofessional actors, its attention to details, its grasp of the landscape, etc.) the film operates simultaneously on the mythic level as well. It invokes the classical biblical theme of quarrels over the land, thus implying that the archaic, mythic nature of the conflict over Canaan between colonizers and colonized has not changed over the centuries. Zionism, within this ideological perspective, is seen as the tragic repetition of this mythic structure. If *Exodus* provided a celebratory version of this conflict, then *Hamsin*'s deep pessimism presents the tragic side.

Generically speaking, *Hamsin* is structured like a Western dislocated to the East. The film uses some of the components of the classical Western and adapts them to the specific local and political situation. As in the classical Western, the mother, in this case Malka, Gedalia and Hava's mother (Ruth Geler), is the representative and agent of civilization. She confesses to Hava that she hates the farm life to which her husband has subjected her. By "expelling" Hava from the "paradise lost" of her grandfather's home on the farm in Galilee and sending her to study music in Jerusalem, she hopes to acculturate and civilize her wild tomboy daughter and save her from the brutality and dangers of the wilderness.[8] Hava's brother Gedalia, on the other hand, is the Zionist version of the American pioneer rancher. Like the hero of the classical Western he is tough, individualistic (he is in conflict with the rest of the moshava), and unattached to any woman except for his mother and sister, whose relationships with him bear the Oedipal mark. Gedalia confesses to his mother that he is most comfortable in the fields with his herds and bulls. The conflict with the Palestinians over land invokes the conflict of the white American settlers with the Native Americans, and the atmosphere of the moshava recalls that of the frontier settlements in the American West. Even the local provincial kiosk where the people of the moshava meet at night for drink and conversation recalls the atmosphere of the frontier saloon in the classical Western.

Hamsin is rich in sexual metaphors intimately tied to the conflict over the land. Indeed, from its inception the Zionist project of settling Palestine, as well as Arab resistance to it, were portrayed using sexual imagery. The Zionist project was described in terms of both military and sexual conquest: "Kibbush HaAdamah" (conquest of the land), "Kibbush HaSafa" (conquest of the Hebrew language), "Kibbush HaAvoda" (the conquest of labor). As David Biale suggests, "Zionism meant both the physical rooting of the 'people of the air' (*Luftmenschen*) in the soil of Palestine and the reclamation of the body."[9] In the final analysis, he claims "the ambiguities of Zionism as an erotic revolution prefigured the larger political question, which remains to this day, of how to constitute a Jewish national body in the modern world."[10] Essential for this revolution was the cultivation of the "knowledge of the land (place)" in an attempt to re-create the connection with the geography of the ancient homeland.[11] Hence the phrase *LiKhbosh et HaAdama BaRaglyim* (to conquer the land by foot) has become a propagating motto of the Zionist project embedded within the rhetoric of colonial/patriarchal discourse.

Yet, this possessive, libidinally invested attitude toward the land has not been exclusive to the Zionist project. "Erotic geography" is recurrent in many Palestinian literary works, especially in what came to be known as the Palestinian "resistance literature." In this literature (epitomized perhaps by the poetry of Mahmud Darwish), poetic images of Arab Palestinians living off the land in organic harmony with nature are contrasted with dehumanized images both of destruction, brutality, and militarism associated with the Zionist enterprise and of the Israeli occupation, signified by the bulldozer, which violates the integrity of the Palestinian pastoral landscape and rapes its soil.

In the film *Hamsin* Gedalia is portrayed as obsessed with his ranch where he employs Palestinian workers. A descendant of Jewish Zionist settlers who lived the ideal of "Avodah Ivrit" (Hebrew labor) in the 1930s, in the 1980s he ironically employs Palestinian workers from the nearby Arab village whose land was confiscated by Israel. In the film's sexual economy Khaled, the Palestinian worker whose nationalist and sexual awakening begins as a result of his work at Gedalia's ranch, is compared to the bull that finally kills him. As in *My Michael*, repressed Palestinian nationalism is symbolized through sexual desire, the desire of Jewish women to be inseminated by Palestinian men, ending with the destruction of the inseminator. The raging bull, released by the Zionist settler, thus becomes an icon of repressed Palestinian nationalism. Gedalia's anger at the transgression of the sexual taboo by Khaled and his displaced incestuous libidinal desire for his sister are metamorphosed into the image of the raging, uncontrollable bull, which paradoxically becomes a symbol of the explosive frustration felt by the two sides to the conflict.

The Palestinians in *Hamsin* are portrayed as connected to and loyal to their land. They prefer that it be taken by force rather than voluntarily sold. Practicing the ideology of the Tsumud (the stubborn clinging to the land), they believe that selling the land is tantamount to betrayal.[12] The rootedness of the Palestinians is visually established throughout the film by their always being seen literally sitting on the land. By contrast the Jews always sit at home on chairs. They are physically distant from the land. Unlike the Palestinians, whose attachment to the land is based on their emotional view of it as home, the Jewish settlers of the moshava relate to the land as real estate. The members of Gedalia's generation, the sons of the moshava's founders, have become greedy and racist land dealers. The idealistic motivation of their pioneer fathers to become new Jews rooted in their land has been lost on their sons, who, like the stereotype of the old diasporic rootless Jew, buy and sell their land and houses for profit.

The failure to create a new Jew rooted in his land continues the theme of Wachsmann's first feature film, *Transit* (1980), which dealt with the unadaptability of European Jews to life in Israel. The new breed of Jewish farmers is enticed by money and bereft of idealism. They engage in shady business deals and black market sales. Their operations are always carried out at night under cover of darkness, and are followed by criminal and racist activities like the beating of Khaled and the Arab watermelon sellers, or the intimidation of the

Palestinians in the local cinema.[13] Within this context of greed, racism, and hatred Gedalia seems to be different. Unlike other members of the moshava, he is attached to his land. When he brings Abu Yusuf the money with which he wants to buy this land in order to save it from confiscation, he tells him: "People are crazy here. You and I are different," referring to their shared love of and special commitment to each other (Gedalia's father saved Abu Yusuf's life in the 1930s). Yet, during his visit, Gedalia sees slaughtered doves in Abu Yusuf's courtyard, indicating betrayal by destruction of the symbol of peace and coexistence. In this scene, for the first time in the film, the Palestinians are shot above the Jews, intimating the moral superiority reflected in their refusal to treat their land as an exchange commodity. Immediately after this scene we see the actual act of confiscation. Paradoxically, the image of the bulldozer, which within the Zionist iconography has become the positive signifier of building the new Jewish homeland, for the Palestinians signifies the Zionist passion to expand and demolish traditional, agrarian, rural Palestine.

To further reinforce the sense of isolation felt by Gedalia, the landscape, and especially the boundaries of his ranch, are framed by barbed-wire fences. The landscape of the Jewish cowboy is imprisoned and imprisoning. It is as oppressive as the scorching *hamsin* (heat wave). As if given the impossibility of revenge, the Palestinian landscape, traumatized by the conflict, imprisons the people trapped in the struggle. The landscape, now part of the conflict, becomes threatening and menacing, as in the end of the novel *My Michael*. Wounded by Israeli bulldozers, it awaits the return of the repressed. Although Gedalia is attached to the soil in this scene, the film conveys a sense of alienation from the Palestinian nativist landscape. The long tracking shot of Gedalia's drive in his military-style Jeep through the narrow lanes of the Palestinian village with the money for Abu Yusuf in his pocket conveys the impression of penetration into an alien territory. The accompanying soundtrack is the Muslim call to prayer chanted in Arabic by the muezzin. An uncanny feeling of alienation, fear, and menace seems to overcome Gedalia and likewise the (non-Muslim Arab?) spectator.

Hava is similar to the Palestinians in her attachment to the soil. Like Abu Yusuf's family, she refuses to sell her grandfather's house, and with the assistance of Khaled she renovates and reconstructs it. She separates from her family and prefers to live in the old house with Khaled as her lover. The willingness of the mother and Gedalia to sell the house to the people of the moshava who plan to turn it into a museum signifies a process whereby time and history are commodified. The Zionist enterprise, embodied by the house of Hava's pioneer grandfather, is designated to become a museum displaying the history of the moshava and the early Jewish settlements in Galilee. As a museum that freezes and reifies time and history, it signifies the death of old-style Zionism and the rise of the new commodified Zionism. Hava opposes turning her grandfather's house into a dead relic of the past and instead, living up to her name, which derives from the Hebrew cognate meaning life, tries to revive and relive the past in the present. As the new/old Israeli, Hava is tied to her pioneer grandfather (the past), who is the negation of the old Jew, and yet she is very "modern."

The name Hava (Eve), the "mother of all living" according to the Bible, emphasizes her intimate connection to the land and nature. Although her name indicates that she is mother earth, the primordial woman, there is actually an androgynous quality about her. She has short hair (like Hannah Gonen in *My Michael* after she goes crazy), rides a horse,[14] drives a Jeep, smokes, and drinks beer. Hava is positioned between culture and nature. She is expelled to the city by her castrating mother, who hopes that her music studies will turn her into a cultured lady. As an agent of civilization the mother suppresses Hava's libido and her adventure-seeking nature. The mother tries to model her tomboy daughter after the ideal of the daughters of the Bilu colonies[15] who received a European bourgeois education that included French and piano lessons.

Hava is represented as a hybrid—a bridge between culture and nature, man and woman, past and present, Jew and Palestinian. She lives in temporal, spatial, and sexual liminal zones. Like her biblical predecessor she is the temptress in her relationship with Khaled. The Sabra, the prickly fruit appropriated by the Zionists to represent the new "native" Jew, ironically becomes Hava's "apple" delivered to her by the courting Khaled. Hava's androgyny and liminality are echoed by the frog in the scene where she is spying on the half-naked, washing Khaled. The frog, an amphibian, can live both in water and on land. As a creature that can change its sex, the frog represents sexual liminality. Hava's sexuality, too, is ambiguous. As the radicalized ("Galilized") version of the Jerusalemite Hannah of *My Michael*, she is almost the young man Hannah always wanted to be. Hava is perhaps the only ray of hope in the pessimistic scenario of the Israeli-Palestinian conflict as represented by *Hamsin*. Immersed in two cultures yet not fully of either, she is "on a narrow bridge" between the two peoples in conflict.

The grandfather's house is used in this context as a metaphor for a possible home shared by Jews and Palestinians. Hava wants home, "paradise regained," and not a museum. She tells Khaled: "You can't imagine what kind of garden there used to be. Do you think that it can become home again?" To which

Khaled laconically responds, "Yes. It's possible but it will take a lot of work." This short dialogue summarizes, to a certain extent, the political "message" of the film. Construction of a Garden of Eden, a common home for the two peoples, requires extensive labor. *Hamsin*, however, suggests that hard work is perhaps not enough. Khaled's and Hava's dream to enjoy love in their Eden is not to be realized, as Khaled (in an ironic twist to his name, which means eternity in Arabic) is killed in a premeditated murder disguised as a "work accident." The model for coexistence, established by Hava's father, who saved the life of the Abu Yusuf family in 1939, is brutally ruptured by her brother, who, consumed by incestuous envy and unconfined racism, murders Khaled.

Despite the Edenic, utopian tones set by the love story between Khaled and Hava, the power dynamics between the two are clear. Hava is the white lady/master while Khaled is the dark slave who relinquishes his own desires to hers. After they kiss for the first time while Hava is driving the Jeep and Khaled is sitting next to her, she orders him like one orders a child or a servant, "Get off now, Khaled!" Hava assumes the role of a tyrannical lady, like Hannah in *My Michael* who dominates the twin Arabs in her fantasies. The relationship between Gedalia, the Jewish landlord, and his Arab employees also assumes a master-slave pattern. Although they work the same long hours at the same job, the Arabs, not fit to enter the landlord's house, sleep in a shed or in the tool shack and eat by themselves. Gedalia's rage at Khaled for having sex with his sister is directed toward the crossing of national, spatial, and class boundaries of the power relationship that this romance implies. The Arabs are not supposed to enter Jews' homes, let alone lie there with their masters' women.

In the context of the violent and brutal relations between the local people, Hava and Khaled's master-slave relationship is a milder and more liberal replica; thus, paradoxically, it contains the utopian promise of subverting this very pattern. After the kissing scene in the Jeep, the upset Khaled opens the gate of the master bull's cage and the bull charges violently while Gedalia yells at Khaled, "What is the matter with you?" The bull thus becomes a symbol of frustrated masculinity yearning for libidinal release. It is the projection of suppressed libido, hatred, violence, and sex. This raging bull (the representative of a traditional, agrarian, "subaltern" society) becomes fixed in Gedalia's mind as an image of Palestinian rage, much as the bulldozer (the representative of modernized, technological, and dehumanized society) has become a fixed icon of Israeli aggression for the Palestinians.

Water also plays a major role in the sexual economy of the film, as suggested indirectly by the name of the film, *Hamsin*. The *hamsin* that plagues the landscape and its inhabitants during the course of the film is invested with sexual imagery. Water, as a primary source of life, is also laden with sexual meaning. Hava's gaze, directed toward Khaled, is always associated with water. Both characters drink water throughout the film, sucking the water sensually from a bottle rather than from glasses or cups. They transfer bottles of water from one to another, and in one of the scenes Gedalia transfers the water bottle to Khaled. It is as if Khaled symbolizes for Hava a source of water, of life. Hava is thirsty for Khaled's fertile touch, for his love.

The ritual of drinking water and transferring the bottles from one to another invokes an aura of the Native American peace pipe ritual, which also bears sexual connotations. It connects Hava, Gedalia, and Khaled in a triangle of forbidden love generated by repressed desires. Gedalia, who is unmarried and lives with his mother, is erotically attracted to both Khaled and Hava, while Hava and Khaled are overtly attracted to each other and latently to Gedalia (when Hava returns home from Jerusalem, when greeting her family she only touches and kisses Gedalia). Hava and Khaled are the only characters in this triangle who actually practice "forbidden love."

In one of the more memorable scenes in the film, Gedalia and Khaled sprinkle water over each other from phallic pipes while washing themselves in the yard of the ranch. This is the only scene in which Gedalia is seen smiling and the two men playfully exhibit their homoerotic attraction, constituting one of the rare moments of grace in the film. The playful shower scene takes place in the morning after Khaled sees Hava half-naked, and she, conscious of his gaze, returns her own.[16] Other moments of harmony and reconciliation mediated through water occur when Khaled and Hava, working together on the renovation of Hava's grandfather's home, drink for the first time from the same jar.

Gedalia is an ascetic type who lives a hermitlike existence with his castrating mother. He sleeps in a narrow bed in the living room where he can enjoy neither intimacy nor privacy. He is isolated and not on good terms with the people of the moshava. Reserved and isolated, he does not initiate eye contact when communicating with others. He is obsessed with his ranch, his ultimate desire being fusion, unification with the land, with mother earth. The heat wave of *Hamsin* thus assumes the role of a symbolic thirst for sex, of unsatisfied eroticism and self-denial of pleasure and gratification.

The culmination of the film, with its break in the *hamsin*, is also an orgasmic culmination releasing the characters' repressed desires. The film is structured around the desire for relief from the heat, from the oppressive force of the heat wave, that elicits the release of uncontrolled drives, instincts of sex and death, Eros and Thanatos. If the film is paced to the rhythm of a slow sexual intercourse progressing toward powerful orgasm, the murder of Khaled is not only an expression of Gedalia's fear of his own repressed desires toward Khaled and his sister, but also a release of libidinal energies culminating in a violent orgasmic murder. The primal scene, in which Gedalia watches his sister making love with Khaled, is a sort of a voyeuristic primary scene (recalling a similar voyeuristic incident in *Hide and Seek*). Punctuated by strong red and yellow colors, the scene recalls the intrauterine condition. Red and yellow are also the symbolic colors of birth and death. In the morning after this primal scene, Gedalia looks at the bull and releases him to kill Khaled in the narrow vaginal tunnel through which the bull passes to inseminate the cows on Gedalia's ranch. The bull kills Khaled as he stampedes through the tunnel to the cows.

Wachsmann accentuates the Oedipal tensions in both the primal scene and the murder scene through plays on looking and action, spectator and film. The question of the gaze in *Hamsin* assumes political meaning. The mother, who pushes Gedalia to see what really is going on in their old house, awakens him and orders in a commanding voice: "Open your eyes, Gedalia!" The sleepy Gedalia rushes to the old house and peeping and "zooming" into the lovers' nest, which they built together, he sees Khaled lying on top of the apparently excited Hava and penetrating her. Gedalia's reaction is to close his eyes in horror as if to expel this transgressive image from his sight, to avoid the shocking truth. His symbolic act of closing his eyes is repeated and intensified in the film's closing scene. After the murder, Gedalia is seen sitting in the cabin of his pickup truck, as if frozen in an anxiety dream, wearing sunglasses and breathing heavily, as rain begins to fall, breaking the heavy *hamsin*. The dark glasses are used by Gedalia as shutters to the literal and metaphoric penetrating light of truth that ultimately, as in the original tragedy of Oedipus, is sheer horror. Because of the Oedipal dimensions of this murder, the dark glasses also hint at the dialectic of blindness and seeing that dominates the Sophoclean text and relates it to issues of self-knowledge and identity. The focus of the camera gaze on Gedalia's symbolic act of blinding himself suggests that the sexual is ultimately political and vice versa, and that the Israeli-Palestinian conflict is inherently structured like a Greek tragedy.

As a peace-seeking Arab, a "Palestinian Uncle Tom," Khaled's growing political and national consciousness is developing against Jewish racism and aggression. The film portrays Khaled as a shy "good boy" who does not drink and smoke, suggesting that until he got involved with Hava he was an inexperienced virgin. Khaled's growing into sexual maturity thus parallels and echoes his emerging political maturity, both triggered and achieved through the Jews. Khaled's search for identity as a Palestinian and a man is accelerated

125

by his growing involvement with Gedalia and Hava, the Jewish masters. In fact, the story of Khaled addresses the conception, common among Israeli scholars with the noticeable exception of Baruch Kimmerling and Joel S. Migdal, that the rise of Palestinian national consciousness and identity has been historically shaped amidst the conflict with Zionism.[17]

The generational tensions evident in *Hamsin* also have played a major role in shaping national consciousness for both Jews and Palestinians. Among Israeli Jews the difference between the pioneers' generation and the second generation is, as was previously discussed, a tension between old-style Zionism (idealistic, ascetic, heroic) and "real estate" new Zionism. Among the Palestinians the tension is between the Nakba generation who have reluctantly collaborated with the Jews in order to survive and their children who have refused to collaborate and instead prefer to assert their national feelings and rights.

The violent murder, assumed to be carried out under the influence of the oppressive heat wave, alludes to Albert Camus's *L'Etranger* (*The Stranger*). Traditional criticism of Camus's novel has referred to the "Mediterranean experience" of the murder (the glittering sun, the sea, and the dazzling heat) as partially responsible for the otherwise inexplicable and absurd act committed by Meursault, the protagonist, to whose field of vision the narrative is restricted. This type of criticism, which according to Edward Said has "imputed to *L'Etranger* the universality of a liberated existential humanity facing cosmic indifference and human cruelty with impudent stoicism,"[18] suppresses the racist element involved in the murder. After all, Meursault's "inexplicable" aggression was directed toward an Arab and committed in a French colony. By contrast, in *Hamsin*, the murder of Khaled, though clearly motivated by racism, is dominated by mythic overtones as the Palestinian-Israeli conflict assumes the "grandeur" of an existential struggle whose metaphor is the *hamsin*. The pessimistic scenario of this political conflict, as represented by *Hamsin*, suggests that the conflict is threatening to become an existential problem with no political solution.

The irony associated with the murder is that although it is related to "family honor," it is nevertheless carried out by a liberal Jew of European descent. Indeed, the film implicitly suggests that Israeli society, which likes to see itself as "Western" and enlightened, is no less "primitive" than the East, which practices blood revenge for the violation of "family honor." So-called liberal Israel is not free of "primitive," Oriental tribalism.

This was Wachsmann's own position, which he described as follows: "I built the story so that it would lead towards Khaled's death, because deep inside me I felt that the situation is hopeless. I suffered from a deep fear deriving from my awareness that we live within a ring of violence that is closing in on us. Our course—as dictated by the regime, the education and the prevalent way of thinking—is leading towards a solution which can be nothing but tragic. I felt lonely, consumed by my fears of what is happening here." [19]

On a Narrow Bridge (1985), Nissim Dayan

Among the films about forbidden love between Jews and Arabs, *On a Narrow Bridge* is the first Israeli film to invert the traditional interracial romance between an Arab man and Israeli Jewish woman. The film revolves around a love story between a reserve military prosecutor in Ramallah (in the West Bank) and a female Christian Palestinian school librarian. The prosecutor, Tel Aviv attorney Benny Taggar (Aharon Ipale), is divorcing Ilana, his Ashkenazi, Peace Now wife, an architect who is designing a youth center in the West Bank, played by Dayan's wife, Rachel Dayan. Stoned by a group of children while driving through the city, Taggar leaps out of his car and pursues them into their school. Upon opening the door of the school library he comes face-to-face with the librarian, Laila Mansour (Salwa Nakra-Haddad), who tells him to keep his hands off the boys. It is love/hate at first sight. Laila is the widowed daughter-in-law of Anwar Mansour (Torcel Kurtiz), a wealthy local man who collaborates with the occupiers. Benny courts Laila, defying all conventions, and she responds, earning the disapproval of almost everyone. When Anwar learns of the romance, he calls on Laila's brother Tony (Yussuf Abu Warda) to end the love affair by killing his sister. Tony, a PLO fighter, does not murder his sister but tells her to escape to Jordan. Laila takes the bus from the Allenby Bridge to Jordan.

The name of the film derives from the saying of Rabbi Nahman of Bratslav: "The whole world is on a narrow bridge, and the main thing is not to be afraid at all." The script is based on "The Woman from Ramallah," a short story written in 1971 by Haim Hefer, one of Israel's most well known writers of the Palmach generation. The story is based on an Arabic folktale, "Kays and Laila," whose origin is probably an ancient Indian legend about an impossible romance between two innocent young lovers from hostile tribes. Some scholars speculate that the Arabic version inspired Shakespeare's *Romeo and Juliet*, and that the name Juliet derives from the Arabic name Laila. The film was also the first Israeli feature to be shot in the occupied territories. Originally, Dayan planned to shoot the film in Bethlehem, which at the time had the reputation of being a more active town than the peaceful Ramallah. Very soon, however, he realized that Bethlehem was too touristy, and the shooting moved to Ramallah, where Dayan discovered very lively political activity beneath the city's calm surface.

The story of the film's production deserves special attention since it mirrors and emphasizes the contradictions inherent in such an explosive situation: an Israeli film sponsored in part by a grant from the Ministry of Industry and Trade's Council for the Encouragement of Quality Films, making it off-limits for Palestinians, with a mixed Israeli-Arab cast of actors and a mixed film crew, shooting in the occupied territories under the protection of the Israeli Border Guards, and with a film plot that deals with interracial love flourishing under the Israeli occupation—a taboo topic for Jews and Palestinians alike.[20] Indeed, this situation, pregnant with tensions, attracted Dina Tzvi-Riklis, an Israeli Jewish woman filmmaker, to make a documentary on the shooting of the film titled *View from on a Narrow Bridge* (1985). Tzvi-Riklis's documentary demonstrates the ironic and tragic blurring of fiction and reality in Dayan's film. At one point in her film the siren sounds and loudspeakers announce a curfew. The "real" residents of Ramallah simply respond as they usually respond to a curfew and go inside their houses. Dayan realized they could have filmed the scene without staging anything.

The unintentional parallelism between the story of the production and the film plot is echoed in the intentionally ironic casting. Benny Taggar is played by Aharon Ipale, an Israeli Oriental Jew who left Israel to work as an actor in Los Angeles. Salwa Nakra-Haddad, who plays Laila Mansour, is in reality a Palestinian living in Israel who acts in the Israeli theater (she also plays in Amnon Rubinstein's *Nada*). Makhram Khouri, a Palestinian actor also living in Israel, plays the Jewish military governor of Ramallah—with a kippa on his head (in Michel Khleifi's *Wedding in Galilee* [1987] he also plays the role of the military governor of the Galilee area). Yussuf Abu Warda, another Palestinian actor and citizen of Israel, plays Laila's brother Tony Hilo, a PLO fighter who has been expelled to Jordan for "terrorist activity" and is called back by Anwar Mansour to avenge the family honor. Gregorious, the Greek Orthodox priest, is a Jewish actor, Victor Attar, and the young stone thrower from Ramallah is Shahar Cohen, son of religious Jews from Jerusalem. Anwar Mansour, who collaborates with the Israelis, is played by the only actor with no connection in reality to the conflict—Torcel Kurtiz, a Turkish political exile who played in *Yole* and *The Herd* (directed by Turkish filmmaker Yilmaz Guney). Kurtiz also played in *The Smile of the Lamb* (1986), directed by Shimon Dotan and based on David Grossman's novel. Dayan selected Kurtiz because he wanted to downplay ethnic affiliations and emphasize that the people of the region share a common background. Kurtiz, Dayan said in many interviews, was not selected because of his Turkishness but because of his facial features, voice, and the relative anonymity of his presence. There was another explanation according to Dayan. Some of the aristocratic families in the occupied territories were "planted" by the Ottoman Turks. These families of the nouveau riche have become part of the local aristocracy, and there are still Turkish characteristics in their behavior.

Dayan's cross-casting of Arab and Jewish actors was consciously directed not only by professional but also by political considerations. Dayan, himself an Oriental Jew, does not see any difference between Palestinians and Oriental Jews. "If I had the political prisoners who populate Israeli prisons because of people like Benny Taggar in IDF uniforms and put Benny Taggar in a refugee camp, no one would notice the difference," he said.[21] In the first scene when Taggar and Laila make love, Laila rips apart his IDF uniform, reprimanding him with, "You come to me like that?" As he tears her black widow's garment in retaliation, the physical struggle between them turns into a passionate embrace. This scene (which to most Israeli film critics looked quite ridiculous) embodies the ambivalence of the relationship. Regarding this undressing scene, Dayan said: "All the actors brought something of themselves to the film and Salwa more than anyone, because she is a Palestinian woman. For example, in the original script the Jew breaks into her place at night, dressed in civilian clothes, and the romance begins then. Salwa came to me and told me: 'This is not written the way it should be. I need to love him, but also to hate what he represents. With civilian clothes he has no meaning for me. Dress him in an IDF uniform, otherwise I won't be able to play this scene. I will not be able to kiss him, and he will not be able to tear off my widow clothes.'"[22] Nakra-Haddad's and Dayan's statements suggest, perhaps unconsciously, not only the ambivalence embedded in this relationship but also the "perverse" dynamic of the relationship between the master and the slave, the tormentor and the tormented, the occupier and the occupied, a trope so ubiquitous in popular culture. The statement also suggests the erotic power of the military uniform, a topic too taboo perhaps even for Nakra-Haddad and Dayan.[23]

Perhaps more than any other film in the group of films dealing with love between Israeli Jews and Palestinians, *On a Narrow Bridge* addresses the overlap between the position of Oriental Jews in Israel and Israeli views of the Orient (what Dayan prefers to call the Byzantine world). Dayan's own ethnic background is a natural starting point. His parents were born in Haleb, Syria, while he grew up in Tel Aviv in a mostly Oriental neighborhood and later in life moved to Ashkenazi-dominated circles. It is possible, as Israeli film critic Meir Schnitzer suggests, to see a development in Dayan's film career that is linked to his own biography as he moves out of his original context into wider Israeli society, and struggles to maintain an Oriental identity in the Ashkenazi hegemonic context.

Dayan's first film was *Light out of Nowhere* (*Or min haHefker*, 1973), a social film about the life of Shaul, an adolescent from an Oriental background who grows up in a poor Tel Aviv neighborhood.[24] In *The End of Milton Levi* (*Soffo shel Milton Levi*, 1981) this adolescent becomes a tired, married Oriental adult. Dayan's television saga, *Michel Ezra Safra and His Sons* (*Michel Ezra Safra veBanav*, 1983), based on Amnon Shamush's novel about the Jewish community in Syria before the establishment of the State of Israel, is an attempt to explore the Oriental roots of Dayan's protagonists before they began their journey to the "West."

On a Narrow Bridge is the continuation of the television serial drama. Here the hero is supposedly one of Michel's sons, an Oriental Jew born in the "West" who begins to head back east.[25] It is even possible to see Benny Taggar as the same Shaul from Dayan's first feature film, *Light out of Nowhere*. His name is now Benny Taggar and he is a successful lawyer cut off from his Oriental roots. He has even changed his name from Turgeman to the more Israeli-sounding Taggar. Taggar is presented as a social climber. His family lives in Jerusalem, but he has moved to Ramat Hasharon, one of the wealthiest communities in Israel. He is married to an Ashkenazi woman and lives in a nouveau riche–style home. His reserve service as a military prosecutor in Ramallah assumes the function of a journey in search of roots. It is an intense encounter with Oriental reality: the Arab population as well as the Israeli military government, whose personnel is composed of Oriental Jews only. In this schizophrenic reality of split Orient in which Oriental Jews become the oppressors of Oriental Arabs, Benny also confronts Aharon Abadi, a childhood friend who is the military governor of Ramallah, played by the Palestinian actor Makhram Khouri.

Benny Taggar's romance with Laila is the manifestation of the crisis of an Oriental Jew who realizes that his constructed Ashkenazi identity is a sham. His romance with Laila is a story of love for a repressed Orient, a discovery of lost roots, and an attempt to retain his whole self through his other half: Laila, daughter of the Orient. Taggar's love story is an attempt to recuperate from the trauma of the schizophrenic self by discovering an "authentic" Orient. The encounter with Laila forces Benny Taggar to explore his artificial, Ashkenazified, Westernized identity and to come to terms with his Oriental roots. Throughout the film Taggar is forced to reexamine his life and his identity, and to discover his "essential" core, his "authentic" identity, which has been suppressed and repressed by his marriage and his adoption of a Western-Ashkenazi lifestyle. Alienated from his Oriental Jerusalemite family, from his childhood world, and from his Ramat Hasharon home and family, Taggar is trying to rediscover his real self through his love affair with Laila, who becomes the catalyst for his identity crisis.

By choosing an Oriental Jew as "the lover," Dayan draws attention to the schizophrenia inherent in the "psyche" of a contemporary Israeli Oriental Jew who is required to repress and suppress his own self in order to be included in the so-called Israeli collective. Paradoxically, the film suggests that Taggar's confrontation with his repressed self through his meeting of Laila enables him to recover his lost roots and regain a wholeness of identity. Taggar's journey to his lost and buried identity contains the promise that the Oriental Jews are the very narrow bridge to peace, despite their image as Arab-haters. A similar suggestion is offered by the film *Beyond the Walls,* which presents a united coalition of Orientals: Jews and Palestinians who fight together against the prison's corrupt management despite its strategy of divide and conquer. Taggar, the Oriental Jew, is heir to the mythological Sabra who dominated Israeli cinema up to the 1980s. Unlike the "sensitive," self-tormented heroes created during the 1980s by many left-wing Ashkenazi Israeli filmmakers, Dayan's hero is tough, and presumably antileftist. His sensitivity is expressed only through his love of Laila, who returns to him as the Oriental object of nostalgia, longing and fascination. The film deconstructs the stereotypical images that prevailed in Israeli society in the 1980s: on the one hand, of the Oriental "chakhchakh" (a derogatory name for Oriental Jew) as a violent right-wing Levantine; and on the other, of the stereotypical Ashkenazi "Vozvoz" (a derogatory term for Ashkenazi) as a bleeding-heart left-winger. In Dayan's film, Taggar is a successful liberal lawyer, whereas his Ashkenazi, Peace Now wife is represented as hypocritical. The search for ethnic identity and the pursuit of a new collective identity based on the one that was repressed by the hegemonic, absorbing Ashkenazi culture are fulfilled through the restoration of the divided Oriental self. This self not only rejects the dominant culture and exposes its lost original roots but it also tries to achieve wholeness through identification with the "enemy."

Dayan's deconstruction and reconstruction of the Oriental self in *On a Narrow Bridge* is influenced by his subscription to the belief in what he calls the Byzant, or the Byzantine world. Dayan presents an Arab world far removed from the stereotypes that most Israelis have about the Palestinian occupied territories. It is a refined and rich world, ornamentalist, Byzantine, aristocratic, Christian Greek Orthodox, and mysterious. The type of religion that Dayan portrays through the characters in Laila's family is also different. It is Christianity stuffed with a Byzantinism, which Dayan also sees in the Jewish side in Sephardic Judaism.[26] Thus, for example, the scene shot in the Sephardi synagogue in Jerusalem is supposed to visually echo the scene that takes place in the Orthodox church in Ramallah. The Byzantine atmosphere is invoked by icons that recur throughout the film. Laila's family is Greek Orthodox, and she volunteers to restore icons for the church. She confides her love for Taggar to the priest Gregorious, with whom she works, and he, contrary to stereotypes, is sympathetic. Dayan has also pointed out in many interviews that he framed shots to resemble the aura of Byzantine icons.[27] Dayan believes that Byzantinism is responsible for the underdevelopment of the region and the stagnation of its culture. The Israeli Jews' real war is not to fight the Arabs, Dayan has proclaimed, but to fight the stifling Byzantine worldview that is present in both Arab and Jewish culture. According to Dayan, the aristocratic patriarch Anwar Mansour, who collaborates with the Israelis, is the most Byzantine of all. The struggle against the Byzantine world, Dayan maintains, should be fought together with the new proud Palestinians, represented in *On a Narrow Bridge* by Laila's brother, the PLO exile Tony Hilo. Tony is not a collaborator, and he therefore does not conduct a dialogue from a position of subordination. He rejects the old ways, and instead of killing his sister for reasons of family honor, he kills Azulai, the Shabak (Israeli secret internal security service) agent.[28]

In response to Israeli film critic Meir Shnitzer's question regarding the relationship between the Byzant and the West Bank, Dayan said: "The whole East suffers from the Byzantine disease. . . . My film expresses the longing to return to the Bedouin tent, something like Lawrence of Arabia, and from my point of view it is like someone who has tasted from the tree of knowledge and wants to go back to Paradise lost. There is total chaos in our society because we have not decided yet where we are positioned, and in the West Bank this chaos is even more salient because the occupiers are Oriental Jews who under different circumstances would have been under Arab control."[29]

According to Dayan, since Saladin crossed the Yarmouk, no significant cultural, social, or political development has occurred in the region. The Israeli-Palestinian conflict, according to him, is in effect a tribal rivalry based upon the ancient practice of blood revenge. It is therefore not accidental that all the important Jewish characters in *On a Narrow Bridge* are of Eastern extraction: Abadi, the governor, is a cousin of Safra's sons from Dayan's television drama, *Michel Safra and His Sons*, probably a descendant of Jews from Aleppo; Taggar/Turgeman is a "Samech Tet" (Sephardi Tahor, or pure Sephardi) from an old Jerusalem family, who moved to Tel Aviv; and Auzulai, the Shabak agent, is a Moroccan Jew. Against this group of Oriental men Dayan posits one Ashkenazi woman, Taggar's estranged wife, Ilana. Unlike Ilana, Laila, Dayan says, is Turgeman's natural mate, whose double he could have found in his childhood Jerusalem neighborhood of Nahlaot. But instead he changed his name to Taggar and married an Ashkenazi woman. "I, too, married this way," Dayan says, "and I think that all of us Oriental intellectuals are traitors." [30] In the same breath, however, Dayan adds that it is impossible to return to past traditions; he is happy that Israel is a European island in the East,[31] and he feels no nostalgia toward the Orient.

The question then arises as to why Dayan chose the love-story formula to deal with what he perceives to be the heart of the Israeli-Palestinian conflict, namely Byzantinism. According to Dayan, he was interested first and foremost in telling a melodramatic story through which he could present the occupation and whose materials (e.g., the original Romeo and Juliet legend) were borrowed from the Orient.[32] In an interview for a publication issued by Jewish settlers in Israel's occupied territories, Dayan explained the Palestinian objection to his film as connected to the specific formula of the love story that he used:

> If we had told the opposite love story in which the man is Arab and the woman is Jewish, we would not have had problems. For example: If the defendant's counsel, modeled after Leah Tzemel,[33] had fallen in love with one of her Palestinian clients, an Arab fighter, a real man in Arab terms, nobody would have been offended. But here, we are dealing with a paradox on all levels, despite the fact that we tried to decrease the tension by choosing a Christian Arab woman as the protagonist. I do not want even to imagine what would have happened if the woman had been a Muslim teacher in a refugee camp.[34]

While the melodramatic formula used in Dayan's film is not pushed to its maximum possible realization, Dayan did push one of the elements to its extreme: Taggar is clearly presented as a tough prosecutor. He inflicts very harsh sentences on Arabs who throw stones at Jews, and as mentioned, he first encounters Laila because he runs after a boy who throws stones at Israeli Jews. Taggar is presented as very persistent in chasing the boy. When Taggar goes looking for his wife in a Tel Aviv pub, he sees her with her Peace Now friends who tease him: "We heard that you gave ten years to a kid who threw stones. How much would an Israeli kid get for the same offense?" In an added ironic touch, the first time that Laila yields to him is in the hospital after one of the boys from the school where she works is killed by an Israeli soldier.

In one of the many interviews he gave to the Israeli press, Dayan said: "Before he touches the forbidden fruit, Taggar is consumed by a longing for dark skin, black eyes and his mother tongue, all lost when he chooses to succeed in what he perceives as prestigious and glamorous white Israel." [35] Dayan recalls a real tragic love story reported in the news during the time of shooting in which an Arab woman was forced to marry a sheikh in Kuwait to escape the wrath of her family over her forbidden romance with a Jewish Israeli man. Her lover, married and the father of four, committed suicide. [36] The choice of Ramallah as the backdrop for the love story is also related to Dayan's attempt to soften the melodramatic components of the forbidden love–story formula. Dayan explained why he chose Ramallah: "First, because it is a Christian town, and it was clear that a story in which a Palestinian woman falls in love with a Jew could not have happened in a Muslim town. And second, because of its shocking beauty most evident in the winter, its conservative character and its British-Mandate architecture." [37] In the same interview Dayan also said that throughout his six-month research period in Ramallah, he learned of five other cases of Israeli men who fell in love with Palestinian women from the West Bank. Most of these stories ended tragically. To film critic Rachel Ne'eman, Dayan said that he is a feminist, and he therefore considers the conquest of woman a symbol of perversion. "The essence of the Byzantine is to hide the woman behind the window. The Renaissance is first and foremost the liberation of woman, it is Venus de Milo." [38]

The use of the love-story formula is intimately related to the politics and ethics of representing the Israeli occupation. In the final scene of the film Benny Taggar cries to Laila before she alights the bus crossing the Allenby Bridge into Jordan: "I have nowhere to go." Ironically, then, the occupier within this ideological framework is represented as the victim. Dayan himself said regarding this scene: "In the final scene at the Allenby Bridge they both are victims. She is very miserable, he is standing facing the east, but cannot cross the bridge to Jordan. He has no place to go back to. The military has expelled him, he has no home, he has nothing, and now his love is also being taken away. And then she tells him: I'll come back to you. As if this is at all possible." [39] Laila's disappearance from Taggar's life returns him to chaos. He becomes dis-Oriented again, lost between East and "West," a liminal hero who lives between cultures. To a certain extent it can be argued that Taggar is feminized by his contact with the East. Like the liminal figures of women in the group of films dealing with forbidden love between Jews and Arabs who become narrow bridges in the dialogue between the Palestinian and Jewish cultures, so is the new, "feminized" Taggar transformed from a tough military prosecutor into a desperate lover.

It is curious that the Palestinian leadership is presented in the film as reactionary. The Intifada, which broke out a year after the release of the film, demonstrated that the picture portrayed by Dayan was not only distorted, but unjust toward the real political forces that operated in the occupied territories under the leadership of a young and energetic local Palestinian cadre. *On a Narrow Bridge* is a fantasized version of the Israeli occupation that implicitly suggests that even the toughest oppressor has a human face, and that *l'amour fou* can transcend political reality. The choice to work with Palestinian collaborator Khalil Janho, who was used as a special consultant for the film, conforms to this fantasy. Dayan said that he was even willing to collaborate with the devil in order to make this film.[40]

Zyad Fahoum, assistant director of Constantin Costa-Gavras's *Hanna K* (1983) and a Palestinian from Nazareth, wrote:

> The character of the Arab woman 'trapped' in powerful sensuality, as she is portrayed in Nissim Dayan's film *On a Narrow Bridge*, projects the repressed dreams and fantasies of the Israeli macho occupier. She is a Madonna of purity and white beauty in a world of fanatic and degraded Oriental men. Namely, a white shadow or a spot on the sun that blackens its natural environment. With her clichéd portrayal, she is used as a moral justification for the deep-rooted and total hatred of the macho Israeli, Dayan-Taggar, toward the world of Oriental men—of which he himself is part. They are all retarded, collaborators, fanatics, murderers, and anonymous stone-throwers stuck in the Byzantine age. The conclusion one derives from the film is that the struggle of the Arab men against the occupation derives among other things from their objection to the liberation or the kidnapping of their women by the Israeli occupier.

In his review Fahoum mentions the findings of an American researcher, Riki Sherwer Marcuse, who in the 1990s conducted a comparative study between racism in Israel and the United States. Marcuse found that racism was always related to sex, as in the case of Israeli soldiers who served in the West Bank for whom a stereotypical attitude was complemented by hatred and contempt toward Arab men. Contrary to the soldiers' fear of Arab men, Marcuse also found a passion for Arab women reflected in a prevailing opinion among Israeli soldiers that their largest reward for army service is to successfully seduce Arab women, who present the challenge of attaining the unattainable because they are so restricted by the oppressive vigilance of their own society. The Israeli soldiers were most attracted to what they called "white" Arab women— namely, those with fair complexion and light hair.[41] Fahoum asks:

> Is this perhaps another resistant Palestinian territory that has not yet surrendered to total occupation and therefore calls for the completion of the conquest, or perhaps, forced liberation? And how did it happen that a film that comes to preach tolerance and love between the Israeli and Palestinian people, East and West, or for that matter between the East and itself, as Dayan sees it, ends up forcing upon us a racist and distorted picture of the East? Does not the act of preaching itself constitute an act of occupation? Does not the interference in others' business—even for their forced liberation—constitute none other than imposition or occupation?[42]

The story of *On a Narrow Bridge* is told from the point of view of Benny Taggar, the occupier, and the camera constantly follows him. From a postcolonial perspective the love story can be seen as an expression of the relationship between the occupier and the occupied, the colonizer and the colonized. The Zionist Israeli occupier colonizes not only the land but the natives as well by entering their women. Yet, Benny Taggar, not satisfied with sexual and emotional conquest alone, tries to colonize Laila's worldview and values as well. He takes her to Tel Aviv, the fortress and capital of Western Zionism, and forces her to show him affection in public despite the fact that the codes of her society prohibit it. He even invites her to move in with him in Tel Aviv. His attitude toward Laila epitomizes the contradictions inherent in the ideology of "enlightened occupation." He encourages her to liberate herself from the two principles that dominate the patriarchal codes of Arab society: the family honor, which needs to be maintained by the woman, and the modesty that symbolizes the purity of the woman. The film, therefore, despite its call for tolerance and love between the two peoples, fixes the woman in a double state of occupation. She is colonized not only by the colonizer, but also by her own society and family, which expel her. The bridge between the lovers, the Palestinian and the Israeli people, occupation and liberation, Western modernity and Byzantine Orientalism, the individual and the collective, Orientals and Ashkenazim, Oriental Jews and Palestinians, the Byzantine past and

Figs. 14 and 15 *A schizophrenic Orient: Benny Taggar (Aharon Ipale) and Laila Mansour (Salwa Nakra-Haddad) in Nissim Dayan's* On a Narrow Bridge. *Courtesy of Nissim Dayan.*

the postmodern world is indeed very narrow. The only hope is the meeting point on the narrow bridge between Oriental Jews and Oriental Palestinians. Although ultimately Laila is the one who crosses the bridge to Jordan, Benny Taggar finally realizes that the ethnic boundaries of his identity have been reshaped as a result of his encounter with Laila. The film can thus be seen as a self-reflexive attempt by Dayan to expand the boundaries of his own identity through his quasi alter ego Benny Taggar.

The Lover (1986), Michal Bat Adam

The Lover, made by Michal Bat Adam, one of the very few Israeli women directors, is based on A. B. Yehoshua's novel by the same name.[43] The fact that the film was made by a woman who also plays the role of the mother and is known for her sensitive treatment of women's sexuality in her films creates a certain set of expectations regarding the representation of the theme of forbidden love in the film. Like Wolman, Bat Adam used the melodrama genre to adapt the novel to film. *The Lover* is the story of Adam (Yehoram Gaon), a garage owner; his teacher wife, Asya (Michal Bat Adam); and their adolescent daughter Daffi (Avigail Arieli). In his garage Adam meets Gabriel Arditi (Roberto Pollack), a strange man from Argentina who returns to Israel after living for fifteen years in Spain to collect an inheritance from his dying grandmother (Fanny Lubitch), who is not quick about dying. Deciding to repair her old car, he takes it to Adam's garage but realizes that he has no money to pay him. Adam suggests that he reimburse him by helping Asya with Spanish translations for her Ph.D. dissertation. Asya and Gabriel fall in love and do not bother to hide it from Adam and Daffi. When the 1973 war breaks out, Adam forces Gabriel to get drafted, but when he disappears during the war he goes to look for him out of pity for his worried wife. Finally he finds Gabriel disguised as an ultra-Orthodox man living in a religious Jerusalem neighborhood. In the meantime Daffi is having a romance with Naim (Aous Khatib), her father's young Arab assistant, and Adam enters a forbidden affair with Daffi's friend Tali (Noa Eisek). The father, who finds Daffi and Naim in bed together, beats the boy and returns him to his small village in the mountains.

The Lover is constructed around a series of forbidden loves: Asya's love for Gabriel, Adam's love affair with his daughter's friend, and Daffi's love for Naim. Yet, the romance between Naim and Daffi is represented as the most transgressive and is also the only affair that ends in the actual punishment of the violator, despite the fact that it is Daffi who takes the initiative in their relationship. When Adam invites Naim to spend the night because he needs his help breaking into Gabriel's grandmother's home, Daffi's "curious erotic gaze" (in fact, she cannot see through the door) is directed toward Naim as he takes a bath in their home. "Why is it taking him so long?" Daffi asks her father while standing at the bathroom door. In yet another scene, when Gabriel's grandmother tells Naim (after catching him breaking into her apartment) to go and take a shower, he responds ironically: "Why is it that each time I go to a Jew's home I'm told to take a shower?"—thus alluding to racist and xenophobic fears regarding the smell of Arabs, their hygiene habits, and the obsessive compulsion to "clean" and "wash" them every time they "penetrate" a Jewish territory.

Recalling the murder of Khaled by Gedalia in *Hamsin*, in *The Lover*, the young Naim is "expelled" to his village. "I can also have you deported," the angry father tells Naim after he beats him and takes him away. "What have I done?" Naim asks, "Did I murder, steal? She [Daffi] is the one who wanted it." Yet, the father, consumed by reverse Oedipal desire that fuels his racism, remains determined to punish Naim. In a humiliating act of compassion he gives him a sum of money, a sum that he believes would enable the young Palestinian to finish his education. Yet, Naim, aware of the injustice that has been inflicted on him, returns the money, glares accusingly at Adam, and disappears along the narrow road that takes him deeper into the landscape, to his home village. This act of expulsion restores the boundaries of ethnic and national segregation upheld in Israeli society. Naim has learned his lesson: Jewish women are forbidden to Palestinian men. And indeed the film, much like the novel, ends with a scene devoted to the expulsion of all the threatening others: Gabriel the Argentinian/Sephardi/Haredi, Tali the juvenile seducer, and Naim the young Palestinian. In agreement with the ideological economy of the novel and the film, and despite their liberal edge, this expulsion promises the restoration of normalcy. When Adam returns from the expulsion scene, Asya tells him that while he took Naim away she told her lover Gabriel not to come back again. In the last scene we see Adam, Asya, and Daffi reunited. The reunification of the family, the resumption of harmony and normalcy, the film suggests, can be achieved only by the expulsion of the others whose very presence poses a threat to the repressed sexuality of the Jewish protagonists and their "sane" Zionist Israeli identity.

Nadia (1986), Amnon Rubinstein

Nadia is about Nadia (Hanna Azulay Hasfari), a sixteen-year-old Palestinian Israeli girl and citizen of Israel who dreams of becoming her village's doctor.

To fulfill her ambition she enrolls in a Jewish boarding school far from her home. Her decision is met with opposition on the part of family and friends for whom this ambition seems to go against tradition. Neither is her social absorption into the class easy, and Nadia finds herself trapped between two worlds. Complications are added when she becomes romantically attracted to a classmate, Ronen (Yuval Banai). The delicate balance topples as a "terrorist" attack arouses emotional response from her classmates. Her silence is interpreted as identification with the act, and Nadia feels compelled to return to her village. But her classmates, who had earlier promised to conduct a soccer game with Nadia's local village team, decide to fulfill their promise to her despite the charged emotions following the terrorist act, and Nadia's relieved smile at seeing them entering her village promises reconciliation between her and her Jewish classmates. The film is based on a short story by Galila Ron-Feder, a writer with a reputation for youth-oriented novels. The story was commissioned by the Jerusalem Van Leer Institute, which asked Ron-Feder to write a novel on the theme of conflict resolution.

Although the film does not deal directly with a love story, part of the difficulty experienced by Nadia in her attempt to integrate into Israeli Jewish youth culture is presented through her response to the attempts of Ronen, the most desired boy in the school, to court her in typical Israeli fashion. Nadia finds those attempts not only embarrassing but also doomed to fail. "If you think that we are going to be Romeo and Juliet, then forget it. I don't believe in those stories. They are only good for the movies," she scoffs. Nadia's response not only expresses ideological resistance to her potential loss of identity through the melting pot of Israeli youth culture but also functions as a metatextual commentary on the forbidden love films that preceded *Nadia*. It is as if the film wanted to signal to its viewers that it is not going to fall into this trap again. The film, with what Israeli film critic Dan Fainaru calls its "Disney spirit,"[44] suggests that the Israeli-Palestinian conflict can be easily resolved. Its "message" is that a Palestinian, if she is determined and ambitious enough, can both integrate in Israeli society and still maintain her Arab identity and intimate ties with her ethno-national community.

The two Palestinian actors Yussuf Abu Warda and Salwa Nakra-Haddad to a certain extent continue the roles that they played in *On a Narrow Bridge*. Both play "enlightened" Arabs. Abu Warda is the progressive father who, not in keeping with the stereotypical behavior of a Palestinian farmer, supports his daughter's decision to study and encourages her to overcome the difficulties she is facing in the Jewish boarding school. Nakra-Haddad plays the role of Nadia's educated cousin who works as the village physician and serves as

Nadia's role model. Nadia herself is presented as being very serious about her studies. Her extreme desire to become a physician is presented in the film not as personal ambition but as motivated by communal ideals. She is driven by the desire to raise the quality of life in her Arab village to that common in the Israeli Jewish sector. Unlike Nadia, a bookish and ambitious pupil who, ironically, recalls the stereotype of the diasporic Jewish social climber, her Jewish classmates are consumed by frivolities: infatuations, car theft, fighting, and so on. Whereas Nadia is adult and serious, they are portrayed as conforming to the "universal" (Western) codes of teenage culture. The Arabs in the film (like in many other films of the "Palestinian Wave" in Israeli cinema) are more cultured, refined, and noble than the Jews.

The fact that a Jewish actress (Hanna Azulay Hasfari) was chosen to play the role of the Arab heroine raises speculations that Rubinstein was attempting to "Judaize" Nadia by making her less "other" to an Israeli audience. Rubinstein denied these allegations. The reason, according to him, was the difficulty of finding a good Arab actress of the right age, and the excellent screen test of Azulay Hasfari convinced him that she was the ideal choice. Azulay Hasfari was neither sixteen years old when she played the role (she was actually twenty-five years old) nor did she know a word of Arabic. She admitted that "[t]he idea of playing an Arab girl was very difficult for me at the beginning. . . . I did not try to play an Arab. I thought of her as a religious Jew and this was the source of the character's modesty."[45] Like in *Shchur* (which signifies Azulay Hasfari's growing political consciousness), so in *Nadia* the heroine attends a boarding school, the springboard offered to the "elite" of the minority groups (Palestinians and Mizrahim) in order to guarantee their socioeconomic mobility in Israeli society. *Nadia*'s use of the genre of youth film, which was very popular in Israel during the 1970s, assured its didactic representation of a sanitized version of the "Palestinian problem" inside the "green line." A beautiful, industrious, and ambitious heroine driven by a desire to integrate into Jewish society and to advance her own community, encouraged by an enlightened and open-minded father, and surrounded by apolitical Arabs, is indeed "good only for the movies." Nadia, who refuses to play Juliet, eventually plays into the hands of the Israeli Jews who construct for her the identity of the "good Arab."

Streets of Yesterday (1989), Judd Ne'eman

In *Streets of Yesterday*, Israeli law student Yosef Raz (Paul McGann) escapes to Germany after having aided a Palestinian friend, Amin Khalidi (Alon Abut-

Fig. 16 A "Disney version" of the Israeli-Palestinian love story: Ronen (Yuval Banay) and Nadia (Hanna Azulay Hasfari) in Amnon Rubinstein's Nadia. Courtesy of Amnon Rubinstein.

bul), who had been wounded in an attempted terrorist operation against the Israeli foreign minister. The minister was in fact murdered by an extremist anti-Arab Shin Bet agent, who objected to his calls for conducting peace talks with the Palestinians. In this rather prophetic film (with regard to the murder of Yitzhak Rabin),[46] a love story between Yosef and Nidal (Susan Silvester),[47] Amin's sister, is flourishing. The motto of the film—"All a man can betray is his conscience," borrowed from Joseph Conrad—underpins the message of the film. The question of betrayal, in this highly convoluted plot, becomes an ethical question of interpersonal relations rather than a question of faithfulness to a narrow notion of nationalism (or patriotism).[48] The theme of betrayal[49] emphasizes the fragility of the borders erected between these two national groups and the moral burden "forced upon" the conscientious Israeli with a still fresh memory of the Jewish Holocaust, who finds it difficult to play the role of the victimizer of the Palestinian.

Streets of Yesterday, like Ne'eman's previous film, *Fellow Travellers* (1983) (in Hebrew "Magash HaKesef"—literally The Silver Platter), deals with the themes of the Holocaust and the Palestinian question, interestingly juxtaposing them in a number of suggestive ways. The film's plot takes place both in Jerusalem and in Berlin, two divided cities. When Yosef Raz is arrested by the German secret service upon boarding a train in West Berlin, an elderly passerby comments, "We've seen this before," alluding to the historical resonance between the persecution of the Jews in the Holocaust and the present. The film constantly alludes to the Nazi past. The motives of both the Israeli anti-Arab members of the Israeli secret services and the pro-Palestinian Yosef are explained as deriving from the "lessons" of the Holocaust. The film's final scene takes place in the Olympic stadium of Berlin (a reference to Leni Rifensthal's *Olympia*) and is loaded with iconography reminiscent of the Nazi period. The lynching of the Jewish Mossad agent by the Palestinians in this particular location invokes traumatic memories of the German-Jewish past and causes Yosef, who together with Nidal is watching the lynching scene, to cross the border again, this time back to his "blood group": the Jews.[50] Fixing an accusing look at Nidal, who like himself observed the scene without interfering in the brutal violence inflicted on the Jewish Mossad agent, Yosef is seen leaving the murder scene with an expression of disgust and resentment on his face. Yosef's affair with Nidal was an attempt on his part to cross a border in order to merge completely with the Palestinians through identification with them. Yet, the memory of the Holocaust and Jewish victimization invoked by the lynching scene brings to an end his attachment to his Palestinian lover. Yosef realizes that he cannot "betray" the collective memory of his people. Although the film does not support the position (held by the extremist Mossad agent) that the memory of the Holocaust justifies the oppression of the Palestinians, it nevertheless acknowledges its power in the formation and consolidation of Jewish Israeli identity, including Jewish sympathy for the suffering and victimization of the Palestinians. Consequently, former and contemporary victims blend in *Streets of Yesterday* in a hopeless cycle of violence.

In this English-language thriller that emulates Hollywood and European codes of the genre in its attempt to appeal to an international audience (unlike *Exodus*), Ne'eman casts Paul McGann in the role of the Israeli leading male, Yosef Raz. To an Israeli eye McGann definitely does not look, act, or speak like the type of Israeli man that he is supposed to play. His body language, facial features, and style of dress all speak "Europeanness." The film is also designed to be palatable to a wide Israeli audience. The fact that Nidal lives in Germany and is married to a German "Jew-lover," a professor of archaeology who works for the Israeli secret service, renders her semi-European, a Palestinian "in disguise," making the romance between the two less "forbidden." The couple's "otherness" with respect to both Jewish Israeli and Palestinian stereotypes results in a milder version of the forbidden love story and makes it, perhaps, less "disturbing" and more palatable to both Israeli Jews and Palestinians. This is so despite the plot's explosive ingredients: terrorism, betrayal, forbidden love, and negative portrayal of the Israeli Secret Services—one of the more sacred and revered institutions in Israel. The geographic displacement of the plot (a large portion of which takes place in Germany) and the "Europeanization" of the protagonists, as well as the linguistic shift from Hebrew, Arabic, and German to the "universal" language, English—all are responsible for creating a distance (mental and ethical) between the spectators and the screen.

Crossfire (1989), Gideon Ganani

Crossfire is a film based on a real story that took place in Tel Aviv and Jaffa in 1947 at the height of the struggle of the Jewish underground organizations against the British mandate. The Jews, close to obtaining statehood, are on the

Fig. 17 A story of betrayal: Nidal (Susan Silvester) and Israeli law student Yosef Raz (Paul McGann) in Yehuda (Judd) Ne'eman's Streets of Yesterday. *Photograph by Nicole de Castro. Courtesy of Judd Ne'eman and Nicole de Castro.*

verge of war with the Arabs. At a British border post two youths in their twenties—Miriam Zeidman (Sharon HaCohen), a Jewish woman from Tel Aviv, and George Khouri (Dan Turgeman), an Arab from Jaffa—accidentally meet and become romantically involved. George's friends, Miriam's family, and in particular her Haganah member brother (Sinai Peter) all object to the romance. The young couple continues to meet despite the objections and their awareness that they are being followed by members of the Jewish underground. As a result of the United Nations resolution in November 1947 on the partition of Palestine, political tension turns into open war and a wall is built between Jaffa and Tel Aviv. Narrowly evading the Arab marksmen posted along the wall, Miriam arrives at George's house. However, she does not manage to escape the notice of a Jewish underground member, who begins to follow her. While George is making final preparations for the couple's escape abroad, Miriam is captured by the Lehi underground and executed on charges of treason.[51]

The execution is not portrayed in the film, raising the question as to why the spectator is spared a view of horror. Why does it take place outside the frame? Why does the director not make the spectators collaborators or at least complicit observers of this crime, witnesses to the fear on Miriam's face? The answers to these questions derive from the schematic ideological formula by which the film is organized: two attractive young people belonging to hostile camps, surrounded by pragmatists and fanatics. George has "extremist" friends who try to recruit him to the war against the Jews, and Miriam has a fanatic, possessive, and jealous brother. "Extremism" within this formula is perceived as bad.

Despite this criticism it is important not to overlook the progress achieved by this film with regard to the representation of the Palestinian-Israeli conflict. The film contains more fights, quarrels, and conflicts than love scenes. The hatred between the two peoples seems to overcome them, and the violence that it breeds is exercised mainly by Jews and targeted against Palestinians. Shraga beats his sister, Miriam, for her involvement with George, while the Lehi members kill British soldiers in a beach café and attack Arabs in Jaffa. After the café attack George criticizes this act of terrorism and calls the Lehi members murderers. Miriam refuses to accept his accusation claiming "they are not murderers—it is revenge." George tries to break the cycle of violence and revenge by taking the bomb, given to him by his Palestinian friends to avenge the murder of his friend Pierre by the Jewish underground, and throwing it into the sea, and tries to escape abroad with Miriam. But the cycle of revenge is continued by the Jews who murder Miriam just before the couple manages to run away.

The motif of "Don't touch my sister,"[52] prominent in *Hamsin*, is at work here as well. But whereas in *Hamsin* it was a conscious and organic part of the psychopolitical fabric of the film, in *Crossfire* it is present as an unconscious theme, suggesting perhaps the director's fear of a more explicit statement about Jewish racism. As in *Nadia*, the male protagonist is played by a Jewish actor (Dan Turgeman), thus recalling the practice of earlier Israeli cinema of using Ashkenazi actors to play Oriental Jews and Oriental Jews to play Arabs.

As in *Streets of Yesterday*, the cultural and national gap between the two lovers is softened through their class differences. George's upper-class upbringing, his polished English, elegant clothes, and fancy car stand out against the brutal and dull backdrop of the khaki-clad Haganah members with whom Miriam associates. George is a gentleman in the European colonial tradition. He is the antithesis of the macho and violent hooligans associated with the Jewish undergrounds.

The scriptwriter, Benny Barabash, claimed that the character of George was based on his meetings with Palestinians as a Peace Now activist and on his work on *Beyond the Walls* (which he cowrote with his brother Uri Barabash). Barabash also said that *Crossfire* is the first film in Israeli cinema to portray the night of the United Nations vote also from an Arab perspective. The film shifts from the family of the Jewish woman sitting around the radio to hear the results of the vote, to the family of the Arab man, also sitting by the radio. The attempt to present the conflict prior to the 1948 war from different points of view provides the dramatic backdrop to the melodrama.[53]

The ideological core of the film is expressed by the scene where Miriam and George elect to commemorate their love on film. They shoot one another while on a picnic framed by a typical Palestinian landscape with Sabra bushes in the background. They ask an Arab shepherd who happens by to take their picture together. The developed picture, however, shows their feet only. While the depressed Miriam, prohibited from seeing George, is lying on her bed crying, her younger brother, an amateur photographer who wants to comfort her, reconstructs the picture using photomontage, to show both Miriam and George together. The brother's model of inspiration is the famous photomontage of Hertzl and Kaiser Wilhelm. Benny Barabash commented on this: "In my opinion this is the best thing in the script . . . the idea and what stands behind it is a metaphor of Zionism, which is a phantom and a photomontage."[54] The photographic manipulation is also a self-reflexive statement on the power of the visual image to reconstruct history, to create fiction on the basis of historical reality. Predictably, then, after seeing this photomontage Miriam decides to run away to her lover.

Crossfire, like *Hide and Seek*, provides a retrospective look from the late 1980s back to the British mandate period. The elegant Tel Aviv beach cafés provide George and Miriam the only sphere of freedom from both Jews and Arabs where they can dance and openly express their love. "Neither Jews nor Arabs frequent this place," George comments. "This is a neutral zone." Yet, an attack on one of the cafés by the Lehi, carried out a few minutes after George's remark, reminds the couple of the inescapable presence of the conflict. Politics invades their private space, and their love is again contaminated. On the allegorical level George and Miriam's love is also a forbidden love story between Tel Aviv and Jaffa in which Miriam becomes a victim of paranoia and political fanaticism. In the scene when she runs away to George under the fire of marksmen on both sides, her neck is wrapped in a luxurious scarf, reminiscent of the Arab kaffiyeh that George gave her as a present. In this scene Miriam becomes a liminal figure who literally and symbolically crosses the boundaries erected between the two "cities" and the two nations. This crossing assumes the metaphoric status of the woman as a narrow bridge. Miriam is crossing the no-man's-land between Tel Aviv and Jaffa. Like Hava in *Hamsin*, Miriam is a liminal character who tries to cross boundaries, to live in both worlds. However, like the other women in the forbidden love stories in Israeli cinema, she is headed for a tragic fate.[55]

Observation Point (1990), Dina Tzvi-Riklis

Observation Point is a short film structured almost like a filmic exercise on the power of the gaze. The uniqueness of this film, however, derives from its conscious entangling of the erotic with military and oppressive power. In other words, the power of the gaze "literalized" in the film is stripped of its symbolic power and reinvested with its "real" power, the divine power of sustaining or destroying life. In the reality of occupation and oppression that characterizes the Palestinian-Israeli conflict, this power is reserved for the Israeli occupying soldier. Appropriately the film revolves around a reserve soldier positioned on a rooftop observation point in an occupied Palestinian town. The soldier surveys his surroundings through binoculars (recalling Jimmy Stewart in Alfred Hitchcock's *Rear Window*) through which much of the film is viewed. Through his observation the soldier becomes a witness to different

Fig. 18 Love and partition: George Khouri (Dan Turgeman) and Miriam Zeidman (Sharon HaCohen) in Crossfire. Photograph by Nicole de Castro. Courtesy of Nicole de Castro.

events taking place in the life of the Palestinians who live under the mercy of his gaze. As a distant observer, the soldier is not directly involved in the events he observes. His detachment is enhanced by the earphones of his portable radio, which literally block out the Palestinian voice and leave the surveillance experience to the realm of the eye alone. His radio is tuned to the IDF radio station popular in particular among Israeli youth, which provides the ironic soundtrack of the film. The irony is enhanced through the tension between the often silly and infantile content of the programs and the visible reality of the occupation. This tension also exposes the distance, physical and mental, between the reality of civilian Israel and the occupied territories.

The curious gaze of the soldier is focused mainly on the daily life of one Palestinian family, particularly on the beautiful young daughter whose marriage is also viewed by the soldier. He also focuses on her little brother who grows pigeons on the roof of the family house. The boy eventually becomes entangled in subversive activity against the Israelis in which he finds his death. Similarly to *Ricochets* (1986),[56] where the seductive gaze of the beautiful Shiite young woman becomes a deadly trap, so in *Observation Point* the Palestinian woman who traps the Israeli soldier's gaze is involved with acts of violence and death. The arresting images of beautiful Arab women function as lethal weapons in these two films. These images of Oriental feminine beauty threaten the occupier and weaken his power (and perhaps his prowess as well). Although most of the time the soldier observes the woman from his observation point, at one point his penetrating look is returned by the woman. Feeling ashamed, the soldier removes his binoculars, thus acknowledging the power relationship (sexual, political and military) existing between the occupier and the occupied. Twice the soldier is seen crossing the line that separates his observation point from the reality projected on the Palestinian "screen" facing him. In these scenes the soldier physically approaches the young woman and the little boy. After the incident in which the soldier kills the young woman's husband for having given her brother some explosives, the scene changes and we see a new soldier in the observation point and the young newly married woman holding a baby.[57]

Day after Day (1998), Amos Gitai

It is quite interesting that the wave of forbidden love stories almost disappeared during the Intifada with the exception of *Crossfire*, *Streets of Yesterday*, and *Observation Point*. It was left to Amos Gitai, the returning Israeli exile, to bring full circle the story of forbidden love. The forbidden love theme was neglected and forgotten during the 1990s, the decade that witnessed the end of the Intifada, the beginning of the peace process, the signing of the Oslo Accords, the murder of Prime Minister Yitzhak Rabin, and the rise to power six months after his assassination of Binyamin Netanyahu and his Likud-dominated government. Gitai's *Day after Day* (in Hebrew Yom-Yom), produced at the end of this tumultuous decade, is the first to deal with the aftermath, the "fruits" of the forbidden love story.[58] *Day after Day* is about the relationships between Mosh (Moshe Ivgi) and his Jewish mother, Hannah (Hannah Meron);[59] his Palestinian father, Muka (Yussuf Abu Warda); his wife, Didi (Dalit Kahan); his lover, Grisha; his doctor; and his best friend, Joel (Juliano Merr).[60]

The restless Mosh, who refuses to have children and is caught up in an identity crisis, is the first hybrid of Israeli cinema, the son of a mixed couple living in a mixed Jewish-Arab city. As in *Observation Point* there is a main observer in the film, Mimi (Karen Mor), a traffic controller who follows the action on large screens and enters the plot only to ask questions about what is happening. Mimi, as Israeli film critic Uri Kleine observes, "is also us, who find ourselves in the film and at the same time view it from the outside."[61] In a series of situations all taking place in Haifa (one of the few still-mixed cities in Israel) the spectators observe the life of these people while Mosh is "flaneuring" around. The forty-year-old Mosh is a hypochondriac in the midst of a midlife crisis, including a collapsing marriage. Rushing back and forth from one place to another, from his wife to his lover and from her to his friend, he does not even slow down to hear the news, which he finds too depressing. He is always restless, anxious, and nervous. After his beloved mother dies, Mosh's identity crisis intensifies, and yet it seems to reach some kind of "solution." Mosh is the cinematic "son" of Amos Gitai, perhaps the most politicized Israeli director, who during the 1980s lived as a voluntary exile in Europe.[62] Mosh's restlessness, his obsession with death, and his midlife crisis not only reflect Gitai's own uncomfortable homecoming during one of the most difficult periods for the Israeli Left; they also are a metaphor for the difficulty of coexistence, and the need to overcome this difficulty. Mosh's drifting in endless circles represents the state of contemporary Israel itself.

Mosh/Mussa, played by Moshe Ivgi, a Mizrahi Jew considered by many to be one of Israel's leading actors, represents the new antihero of Israeli cinema, the answer to the mythological Sabra of the national-heroic genre. Hypochondriacal, "kvetcher," impotent, and childless, he is a "*nebekh*" (nebbish), the Israeli version of the diasporic "schlemiel."[63] While on army reserve duty (which is presented as a complete farce) he complains incessantly, acting like a not-so-brave Israeli echo to the classical caricature of militarism as portrayed in the figure of Schweik in Jaroslav Hašek, *The Good Soldier Svejk and His Fortunes in the World War* (first published in English in 1973). As Palestinian-Jewish, diasporic-nativist hybrid, Mosh/Mussa—despite his hypochondria, sterility, and impotence (he is unable to have sex with his "sexy" lover)—is an appealing hero. The feminized Mussa/Mosh no longer corresponds to stereotypes that have existed in the Israeli imagination. His binational hybridity signifies a transgressive boundary crossing that is capable of destabilizing the ethnic and national hegemony claimed by the Israeli nation-state. The paradox is that his friend Joel, played by the real "hybrid" Juliano Merr, is the real macho in the film (recalling Merr's "real-life machoism").

The lovers in this film, unlike in the other films dealing with love between Palestinians and Israeli Jews, are neither young nor beautiful. The film's spectator observes a mature relationship of two elderly people whose love stood a test of fifty years (the age of the State of Israel at the time of the film's release) and furthermore "produced" a son, a living testimony of this love. In contrast to all the films in the forbidden love genre, the moment of falling in love is not seen on-screen. It is only recounted later by Yussuf to his son after Hannah's death. The relationship between Yussuf and Hannah is a given, and does not go through the process of validation of "authenticity" that characterizes all the other films in this genre. The film marginalizes the forbidden love story, thus preventing the spectators from discussing the viability of Palestinian-Jewish coexistence. The film assumes Hannah and Yussuf's relationship to be real, reflecting Gitai's own pragmatic attitude toward the repressed binational character of Israel to negotiate, talk, and love in order to attain normalcy.

Many of the characters in *Day after Day* sleep with each other, yet only Yussuf and Hannah love each other. The scene in which Hannah and Yussuf are seen sitting on the bed in their apartment looking affectionately at each other and embracing just before Hannah's death is a rare and unique love scene in Israeli cinema, and according to Palestinian director Elia Suleiman, the most beautiful and touching yet. Hannah and Yussuf do not talk, they just look and gently touch each other. This image of grace, harmony, and peace contains a utopian dimension in the midst of the chaotic reality that the film depicts. Within the forbidden love genre Yussuf and Hannah are the only couple that transcend the Israeli-Palestinian conflict through their love, rather than relive and intensify it.

Yet, the ideal love that exists between Hannah and Yussuf, which suggests an idyllic model of coexistence between the two peoples, is not continued by the "product" of their love: Mussa/Mosh, their son. Mussa/Mosh's love life is as chaotic as Israeli life is. With his friend Joel he shares both his wife and his lover, thus symbolically displacing the dispute between the Jews and the Palestinians over the same land into the familial-sexual arena. Mussa's hypochondria and sterility signify the impasse Israel had reached during the time of the film's production and the dead end of the peace talks with the Palestinians after Yitzhak Rabin's assassination. His sterility, viewed in this context, signifies the end to a potential "dynasty" of hybrid offspring. Yet, the vagueness surrounding the causes of his sterility (his wife claims that he is biologically sterile, while he claims that he does not want to bring children into this "fucked-up retarded country") leaves room for hope. After his mother's death, Mosh draws closer to his father, who tells him, for the first time, the full story of his relationship with Hannah, offering another hint that things might yet change.

Fig. 19 *Caricature of Israeli militarism: The two Israeli Schweiks Joel (Juliano Merr) and Mosh/Mussa (Moshe Ivgi) in Amos Gitai's* Day after Day. *Courtesy of Ilan Moscovitch.*

Fig. 20 *The childless couple Mosh/Mussa and Didi (Dalit Kahan) in Amos Gitai's* Day after Day *represent the state of contemporary Israel itself. Courtesy of Ilan Moscovitch.*

One of the most memorable scenes in the film is Hannah's funeral. In the backseat of a car we see Nadiv, the Jewish contractor; a rabbi; and Yussuf's brother. In the front seat we see Yussuf, Mosh, and Didi. The rabbi then says the Kaddish and when he finishes, Nadim, Yussuf's brother, reads a Muslim prayer in Arabic from the Qur'an. This bireligious funeral, inconceivable in contemporary Israel, recalls the funeral scene in *Exodus* (see chapter 1). Through this utopian scene the film again conveys the hope for religious and cultural pluralism in the "Jewish State."

Gitai was born and lives in the same city where the film takes place. "I wanted to make a film that took place in Haifa that would be part of a trilogy of portraits of the three large cities—Tel Aviv, which I dealt with in my last film *Zichron Devarim* (*Past Continuous*), present-day Haifa, and Jerusalem, in my next film. Despite their geographic proximity, each of these cities represents a completely different Israeli way of life. It is my hope that the three films will together sketch a broader picture of the present Israeli reality," Gitai told Kleine.[64] Haifa, he explains, is a complex city. "This is a happy-go-lucky city detached to a certain extent from the tumult around it. It is, in my opinion, the most modern city in the country, despite the detachment and the Mediterranean tranquillity in which it exists, because it is made up of minorities, and creates a dialogue between the different peoples that manage to live here with a certain degree of coexistence."[65]

In *Day after Day*, with its mixture of the melancholia of the Left and the restrained optimism of the returning exile, Amos Gitai turns Mosh into the hybrid hope of unforbidden love. Mosh's (Mussa's) identity crisis thus manifests, perhaps, the (hopeless?) struggle for shaping a multicultural binational identity in Israel/Palestine.

CHAPTER SEVEN

The Day After

The Sexual Economy of the Israeli-Palestinian Conflict

■ But every mythology begins with creeping things
that emerge from the ground and devour one another,
until a holy marriage mends the rent in the universe.

Aharon Shabtai, "Lotem Abd al Shafi" (a poem
translated by Vivian Eden)

The Jewish Victim

The framing of many of the stories of forbidden love in the Israeli genre is
based on legends or famous themes and tales borrowed from Greek mythology. The use of the Romeo and Juliet story is most evident in *Hamsin* and *The
Lover*. The murder scene of *Hamsin* uses the mythological bull (the Minotaur
of Greek mythology) to signify the cathartic release of libidinal energies. The
Keis and Laila legend, which according to some scholars is the origin of the
Romeo and Juliet story, is the inspiration for *On a Narrow Bridge*. The Andromeda legend constitutes the organizing principle of *Crossfire*,[1] the legend
of Pygmalion and Galatea is assimilated into *Fictitious Marriage*,[2] and the sav-
ing of the damsel in distress by the prince/knight is the dominant motif in
Hannah Gonen's fantasies in *My Michael*. This type of framing displaces the
patterns of relationships portrayed in these films from reality to the world of
legend and mythology.[3]

The use of mythological and legendary framing for these films dictates their
tragic endings as well as their dialectics of sacrifice. In most cases the actual or
implied victim is a Jewish character. In *Hamsin*, despite the barbaric murder
of Khaled, Gedalia, the movie implies, is no less a sacrifice on the altar of the
conflict. It is Gedalia who suffers from Hava's choice of Khaled, which he perceives as an absolute violation of the natural order (although the other two
forbidden loves suggested by the triangle, between Gedalia and Khaled or be-

tween brother and sister, are even more transgressive). The barbaric murder, disguised as accident, is presented through Gedalia's point of view, hence internalizing the intense emotionalism of this dramatic scene and suppressing the release of the spectator's anger at the "liberal" Jewish protagonist.

In *On a Narrow Bridge*, although Laila is sent into exile by her brother, who tries to save her life, the film, as I previously showed, presents Taggar as the ultimate victim, a sacrifice of the schizophrenic Oriental self. In *My Michael* Hannah's fantasies about her Arab princes are one sided. She plays with her obedient princes, but eventually they rebel against her domination and return to take revenge as all the repressed do. Hannah becomes a victim of her own fantasies. She loses her sanity and experiences an emotional death. Hannah thus becomes another victim of the Orientalist fantasy. In *Crossfire* Miriam is also represented as a sacrifice in the drama of the conflict. The one exception to the Jewish monopoly on victimhood in these films is *The Lover*. The Palestinian protagonist in *The Lover* is not punished by death; yet, like many heroes in Greek mythology, he is sent into exile, paradoxically in his home village.

The positioning of the Jew in these narratives in the traditional role of the victim raises some questions. From the 1980s on the authentic representation of Palestinian actors became a norm in Israeli cinema. Yet, this progress in terms of casting did not drastically change the authentic representation of the Palestinian point of view in Israeli cinema, what Shohat calls the politics of focalization. In most of the films made in the 1980s, as Shohat observes, the Israeli leftist point of view mediated the Palestinian one.[4] *My Michael* leaves no opening for a Palestinian perspective. Hannah's fantasy is one-sided, and the Palestinian twins are devoid of any voice. The Palestinian stonemasons in the film are repeatedly conjured on the film's screen, as well as in Hannah's memory, joined by Oriental music on the soundtrack. These characters, always positioned in a pastoral, rural, holy land–type landscape, remind Hannah of "her" twins and are the object of her desiring, longing, and nostalgic gaze. The Palestinians remain in the realm of fantasy as a repressed and disavowed memory of past existence. *Hide and Seek* does not represent the Palestinian point of view either. The relationship between the Jewish and the Palestinian youngsters takes place behind and beyond the spectator's gaze. Throughout the film the spectator is subjected to either Uri's or Balaban's point of view. The Palestinian youth has no distinct identity. He has neither name nor voice and certainly no point of view in the film. The only character who speaks on behalf of the Palestinians is Balaban. When Uri attacks Balaban for not taking part in the struggle for independence, Balaban challenges him saying, "Against whom is the struggle?" to which Uri replies "against the British, the Arabs, against everybody . . ." Balaban persists, asking if all the Arabs are enemies and if he knows any Arab personally. Uri angrily replies that he does not and does not want to either.

The final point of view in the film also belongs to the Jew. The film ends with a chance encounter between Uri and Balaban after the violent incident with the Haganah members. Balaban is seen walking with his bicycle, which he carries like a cross. He fixes an accusing gaze at Uri and continues to ascend the mountain, one of the hills around Jerusalem. The focus of the film at this privileged moment on the image of the Jewish Jesus, carrying his cross along the Via Dolorosa "paved" by the traitor Judas (Uri), posits the icon of the suffering Jew as the ultimate victim. Balaban, and not his Palestinian lover who was murdered by the Jewish underground, is the victim, the sacrificial lamb. Whereas *Hide and Seek* ends with the inquisitive, accusing gaze of Balaban, *Crossfire* ends with the shot of the orange grove where Miriam was secretly executed by the Jewish underground. Again, the non-Jewish victim— in this case George—is not acknowledged. The spectator of this film is spared the gaze of this character, who like Balaban is a suffering lover left alone.

In *On a Narrow Bridge* and *Hamsin,* both political films dealing with contemporary issues related to the conflict, treatment of the Palestinians is more salient. *Hamsin,* although implying a Jewish victim, is the first Israeli film to give a stronger voice to the Palestinian point of view, and there are scenes in the film shot from Khaled's point of view. The character of the sensitive Khaled conducts close and intimate relationships with Gedalia and his sister. Khaled is a peace-seeking Palestinian, an industrious and devoted worker torn between his loyalty to his Jewish employers and his people. His character is shaped as positive—humanist but passive. The open ending of the film reflects the stagnant political situation as a continuing tragedy for both parties. Situating the conflict in the realm of high emotional psychological drama personalizes the political. The Jewish and Palestinian lovers who are tempted to taste the forbidden fruit are the victims of this tragedy. Yet, the narrative is controlled by Israeli Jew Gedalia Berman, whose point of view dominates the film, and the Palestinian voice is mediated through the "extremist" Palestinian youths who are presented as violent and ultranationalist. As in *Hide and Seek,* so in *Hamsin* the film privileges the Jewish protagonist's gaze. The camera, whose gaze rests on Gedalia's tortured face after he commits the crime, turns him into a victim rather than a repulsive murderer. The rain that breaks the *hamsin* washes the blood and leaves no traces at the scene of the crime.

On a Narrow Bridge, which was shot in a Palestinian town, signifies a spatial shift in the representation of the Palestinians. After all, they are shot in their territory. Yet, as I previously showed, the representation of the Palestinian perspective in this film is problematic to say the least. Taggar, who mediates between the Palestinians and the Israelis, is a tough prosecutor who represents the Israeli occupier. Laila, who is supposed to represent the authentic Palestinian voice, becomes more and more submissive and completely loses her voice as the narrative progresses. Furthermore, Taggar becomes tougher with her people the more romantically involved she becomes. Dayan thus represents a perverted version of the oppressor-oppressed relationship that, from a Palestinian point of view, is degrading. In this film, too, the final privileged gaze of the camera is left to the Jewish protagonist, whose tragic facial expression when his Palestinian lover "deserts" him constitutes the Jewish lover, and not the Palestinian, as the victim of the conflict in the spectator's mind.

In *The Lover*, as in *Hamsin*, the interface between Israeli and Palestinian society is mediated through work relations—in this case, the Palestinian employees of Adam, the garage's owner. Naim, an "assimilated" Palestinian, who can recite the poetry of Bialik and insists on speaking in Hebrew even when approached in Arabic (by Gabriel's eccentric grandmother), is only an accidental visitor from the Israeli family's point of view. Although the film seems to criticize Israeli society, portraying it as willing to tolerate Naim as long as he does not transgress the boundaries erected by it, the question still remains whether the young "Uncle Tom," Naim (who echoes the character of Khaled in *Hamsin*), indeed faithfully represents the Palestinian Israeli. "This 'small Arab' type belongs to the 1970s," said Kamal Khativ, who plays the role of Naim. Even his name, Naim, which means pleasant in Hebrew, signifies his "smallness" in the film.[5]

In *Fictitious Marriage* the point of view that motivates the narrative is that of an Israeli protagonist, an impostor of a Palestinian worker from Gaza. The negotiation between Palestinians and Israelis is conducted through the mediation of an Israeli impostor who, presumably, has sexual relations with a Jewish Israeli woman. The privilege accorded in all these films to the Israeli point of view shows that the space they open to Palestinian self-representation is ultimately, as Shohat suggests, subjugated to the Israeli perspective, and even the transgressive force of love fails to challenge it.

Sexual Economy of Fear

The analysis of the underlying sexual economy of the cinematic narratives on forbidden love between Jews and Arabs reveals a love formula that is a further expression of the dominant Jewish voice, namely the voice of fear. African-American director Spike Lee once said: "I've never seen black men with beautiful white women. Usually they (the white women) are ugly and unattractive. By contrast, one always sees white men with gorgeous black women." This statement, despite its arguable factual accuracy, provides an important interpretation of the economy and ideology of the trope of forbidden love and the type of power relationship that it both reflects and constructs. Lee suggests that the white man can get the "best," namely the most beautiful and desired women of the oppressed group, while the "best" that the black man (who is most powerful in his own group) can aspire to get from his oppressors is its most rejected, least-valued commodity—the ugly and undesirable women. Obviously, Lee's position reflects a patriarchal bias that perceives and conceptualizes racial power relationships exclusively based on how much a male can attain in a given racist social order. Within this patriarchal perspective women are perceived as exchange objects for consumption by the superior or dominant race. The colonizer, the oppressor, and the "superior," therefore, have a better chance of acquiring the better "commodity."

Contrary to what Lee's interpretation suggests, in most of the films discussed here, it is the Palestinian man (and not the Palestinian woman) and the Israeli Jewish woman (and not the Israeli Jewish man) who are portrayed as objects of sexual fantasy and desire. This may be a reflection of the fact that all these films (except for *The Lover*) were made by men, saying more about the "psyche" of the Israeli Jewish man and his secret neuroses and anxieties than about the "psyche" of Israeli Jewish women. What is most evident about this object choice, however, is that the Palestinian poses a threatening presence. There is a fear, to use Meir Kahana's language, echoing Nazi racism targeted against the Jews, that "he will steal our women." The "stealing" of women, and in particular young women ("our daughters" in Kahana's language), whose young bodies symbolize the "national womb" and the promise of the genetic reproduction and perpetuation of the national-ethnic group, is perceived within the ideological economy of these films as revenge of the oppressed for the stealing of their land and houses. It should be pointed out, however, as my analysis shows, that some of these films, *Hamsin* in particular, rather than reflect these racist tenets, consciously use them in order critically to expose their hidden mechanism.

An interesting answer to the question of why Palestinian men constitute the "threat" in the forbidden love genre is provided by Dayan, the director of *On a Narrow Bridge*: "The whole East suffers from masochism and the Jews fit in quite well, even though some are of European origin. European anti-Semitism was also along those lines: Watch out, the Jew will screw our daughters. The legend says that the Jew has a bigger prick, and this is anti-Semitism, this is racism. And what is the American white male's hatred of the Black? It is the fear of 'what will he do to our daughters.'" In response to the Israeli film critic Meir Schnitzer's comment that the opposite (Jewish women sleeping with Arab men) has already occurred in Israeli cinema, Dayan replied: "Yes, but the Jewish women who did it with the Arabs from the outset had an image of whores or loose women. The scripts saw to it."

Fear of the presence of the Palestinian Arab man in the midst of "our" (Jewish) towns is perhaps most evident in Ram Levi's film *I Am Ahmed* (*Ani Ahmed*, 1966), one of the earliest emphatic documentaries made by Israeli directors on Palestinians. The film revolves around Ahmed, a Palestinian from the village Arara, who migrated to Tel Aviv in order to find work in the big city.[6] Despite the sensitivity that the film shows in its treatment of the Palestinian protagonist and his difficult experience of displacement, exile from his home village, and the alienation that he feels in the big Jewish city, the film is, nevertheless, trapped by latent Orientalist conceptions. The ideological incongruity in *I Am Ahmed* is revealed through the juxtaposition of the audio and the visual dimensions of the film. While Ahmed, like a curious tourist, is seen sympathetically—strolling alone in the big city of Tel Aviv (big by Israeli standards in the 1960s), his eyes hungrily consuming shop windows, neon lights, night clubs' billboards and embracing, happy couples—the voice-over narration is conducting a sort of dialogue related to the Orientalist conception of Arab men as driven by their passion to conquer, possess, and violate Western women. On one hand, Ahmed's voice accompanying these images says that "the Israelis don't like to see us walking around in their streets, near their homes and their women," thus revealing to the spectators his full awareness of Israeli Jewish racism. Yet, the images that we, the spectators, see implicitly enforce Western men's fears because they show Ahmed following (almost spying on) an embracing couple, staring at them with what we might interpret as disturbing voyeurism. The camera, which persistently observes Ahmed in his lonely wandering along the city's streets, shows him stopping by a shop window with naked female mannequins, smiling a "dirty smile." These sequences of double voyeurism (the camera's voyeurism directed toward Ahmed, and Ahmed's presumed voyeurism directed toward Jewish women) are disturbing. They create dissonance between the "progressive" narration that acknowledges and exposes Jewish xenophobic feelings, and the visuals that, paradoxically or not, reinforce these same racist assumptions.

Despite the film's sincere attempt (very atypical of Israeli cinema of these years) to portray its Arab protagonist as a complex and multidimensional person, and in spite of Levi's effort to represent Ahmed's point of view and give him literal and symbolic voice by listening to his narrative, it is ultimately the Israeli Jewish point of view that prevails. This perspective, mediated through the visuals, tries to reconcile between two conflicting identities, each attempting to define itself against the other. Ahmed's wandering through the city maze and his fascination with the glamour and progress that it offers posit him as a new species of the flaneur. Unlike Walter Benjamin's flaneur, the icon of the modern city—which is the biggest attraction of the twentieth century according to him—Ahmed is an involuntary ethnic flaneur whose flanerie is the result of racism rather than urban "free floating." Ahmed's flanerie oscillates between "innocent lookism" and voyeurism. His gaze does not reside in the realm of perversion because his solitary strolling does not derive from unsociability but rather from isolation imposed on him by Israeli Jewish racism. Although Ahmed's gaze turns the Jewish women walking in the street into objects "receptive" for scopophilic penetration, and although it positions them as props similar to the female mannequins in the shop windows, its roots are not morbid. Ahmed's voyeurism derives from a sense of displacement and rootlessness, the origin of which is not only the anomaly characterizing modernity and urban alienation but also and mainly Zionist Orientalism that views the Palestinian man as a menacing presence threatening to steal, possess, and dominate Jewish women. Ahmed is not Benjamin's "urban native" but rather the "rural native" lost in the city jungle. As a detective of street life in Tel Aviv, he projects both isolation and alienation expressing the tragedy of the Palestinians who live in Israel as strangers in their own homeland.

The patterns evinced in the portrayal of Palestinian men break down in the portrayal of women. Male chauvinism neutralizes national chauvinism as the Palestinian woman is portrayed as less of an other than the men in these films. The female love objects in On a Narrow Bridge and Nadia are associated with the world of books, knowledge, and national idealism. Laila is a school librarian and Nadia, the object of curiosity for Ronen, is a bookish, industrious, and ambitious girl. Both seem to be intellectually superior to the Israeli men who desire them. They are also very dignified and aristocratic in their appearance, much like the wife of Issam in Beyond the Walls whose noble bearing is so different from the character of Uri's daughter, a stereotype of the working-class Oriental woman. The Palestinian women in these movies are also associated with national struggle, and therefore, from an Israeli point of view, with "terrorist" activities. To a certain extent the bookishness of these women recalls the stereotype of the diasporic male Jew. It should also be pointed out that the woman in *On a Narrow Bridge* is Christian, a fact that makes her less of an other because the Christian community is considered to be more open, progressive, and economically better off than the Muslim. Furthermore, Laila's aristocratic background makes her less of an "inferior" in relation to the occupier male. In *Nadia* the young woman is an Israeli Palestinian played by a Jewish actress whose acting style is modeled after young religious Jewish women. All these attributes turn her into a more familiar and likable character.

Alternate Coalitions

To a certain extent it can be argued that the linking between the Israeli Jewish woman and the Palestinian man is a linking of two minorities represented as other in Israeli cinema. Viewed from this vantage, this linking can be read as a consolidation of a coalition of minorities against the dominance of the Israeli man. This is most evident in *Hamsin,* where Khaled's search for national and sexual identity and Hava's rebellion against her family meet through sexual union and not through an assertion of political position. Using the house they renovated together as their lovers' nest, Hava and Khaled become objects for the gaze and control of the Israeli man. Without their knowledge and consent they become objects for Gedalia's voyeurism. The primal scene is also the first time in the film that both, and particularly the rebellious Hava, cannot return the gaze as would sovereign subjects who are in control of their life. For Gedalia, who until the revelation of the romance acted reasonably, the primal scene is his breaking point. Even in *On a Narrow Bridge,* where the link is between a Palestinian woman and an Israeli man, the coalition is still one of minorities since the man is a Mizrahi whose love for Laila is represented as his rebellion against Ashkenazi domination and his lifelong suppression of the Orient within. Yet, what might be seen as a coalition of the oppressed has its own logic. After all, Taggar is the oppressor and Laila is the oppressed. Furthermore Laila's love annihilates her political existence. The "woman in love" wins over the rebellious nationalist. Unlike thousands of Palestinians who were expelled to Jordan by the Israelis, Laila is forced to leave her homeland because her love for an Israeli officer who plays a major role in the Israeli occupying apparatus is not acceptable to her family and community. The major criticism against the film, thus, is its choice of a love story as the medium for discussing the conflict. The reduction of Laila from a proud Palestinian to a woman in love denies and disavows her national identity and her right to liberate herself and her people from the oppressor.

Homosexual love between Jewish and Palestinian men is rare in these films, overtly addressed only in *Hide and Seek*.[7] Only latent homoerotic love is quite pervasive in the "Palestinian Wave" in Israeli cinema and in particular in *Hamsin*, *Beyond the Walls*, *The Smile of the Lamb*, *Streets of Yesterday*, and others. The seeds of this theme were already planted in *Exodus* in the brotherly love between Ari and Taha, who even literally mix their blood as a sign of brotherhood and camaraderie.

Beyond the Walls (1984) by Uri Barabash best epitomizes this dimension in the forbidden love story between Israeli Jews and Palestinians. Although the film is not overtly about sexual love between the Oriental Jew Uri Mizrahi (Arnon Tzadok)[8] and the Palestinian Issam Jabarin (Muhammad Bakri), who are manipulated into a conflict by the Ashkenazi prison management in order to control both groups, they, as Shohat observes, "end up striking together" against the prison management "and symbolically 'win' over their oppressors." Hence, as she suggests, "[t]he pride and courage expressed through the emotionalism of Arnon Tzadok, and the quieter, almost saintly, presence projected by Muhammad Bakri, as well as the film's cinematic structuring of identification with the Palestinian and the Oriental Jew, forge a powerful image of the alliance of two oppressed groups."[9]

The inevitable end of Issam and Uri's symbolic love is overused in *Beyond the Walls 2* (1991), an exploitation film[10] that tried to capitalize on the commercial and critical success of its predecessor.[11] The sequel visually and thematically strengthens this love through the handcuffs that literally tie them together and therefore force them to share the same destiny. This not-so-subtle device—in the film Issam explains to Uri that "the handcuff is a symbol of our shared destiny"—transforms the two into a living metaphor of the Palestinian-Israeli conflict: two people who are forced to live together and, according to this film, also to die together.[12] The film uses many self-reflexive devices to enhance this theme including a theatrical musical written and performed by the prisoners themselves that, in a *mise-en-abyme* style, is based on the plot of the first *Beyond the Walls*. In this musical the two actors reverse their roles, with Uri playing the Palestinian and Issam the Israeli.[13]

The film ends with the killing (or murder) of Uri and Issam by the IDF. The two, after a long and slow dance of death with their bodies entangled in what can be seen as both an embrace and a fight, finally unite into one inseparable body in their moment of death. As a film of mixed genre (comedy, musical, action film, combat film, and *bourekas*), *Beyond the Walls 2* is less restricted by the codes of realistic style that apply to its predecessor. The plot approximates the carnivalesque and the parodic. As the film was made seven years after the first, it also refers in a comic (and sometimes exploitative) manner to the rapid developments in Israel since 1984, including the Intifada and the move to ultra-Orthodox observance by large numbers of Oriental Jews, expressed mainly by the rise to power of the Shas Party. Thus, for example, Fitussi (Rami Danon), the drug addict of *Beyond the Walls*, becomes in the sequel a caricature of an ultra-Orthodox Shas supporter. The carnivalesque elements also allow the film to dress Issam in an IDF uniform, bringing the inversion of stereotypes begun in *Beyond the Walls* full circle. Furthermore, Issam is wounded by his own people who mistake him, due to his IDF uniform, for an Israeli soldier. The final union of Uri and Issam, in what could have become a powerful, iconic statement on the cruel, shared destiny of these enemy-lovers, becomes an "empty" gesture due to the exploitative nature of the film.

Streets of Yesterday is also rife with homoerotic tones. The romance between Yosef and Nidal is in fact a displacement of the latent erotic friendship between Yosef and Amin, frequently filmed together half-naked in "tight shots." Nidal reinforces this theme by telling Yosef that he is attached to her because she reminds him of Amin.[14] Yosef's love affair with Nidal is part of the web of love and betrayal that underpins the structure of the film. Like the liminal women in the Israeli Jewish/Palestinian forbidden love genre, the "feminized" Yosef continually oscillates between the rival groups, and his love story with Nidal, deeply tainted with the colors of betrayal, comes to symbolize this liminal zone of "forbidden love."

There is a most notable absence of intimacy between women in these movies. Theoretically, intimate relationships in all their gender and national permutations are possible; yet, in the films discussed here only the heterosexual and male homosexual options exist, with the noticeable absence of lesbian love.[15] This economy of "mixing blood" reflects the patriarchal structure of both Israeli and Palestinian society. From the Israeli Jewish point of view, the Palestinian man threatens the continuity and purity of the race because he "steals our women," the exchange objects of patriarchal society. Women, in the words of Mary Ann Doane, are the foundation of the "ethnic-blood group," and "the guarantee of an exogamy without which the family, and society along with it, would suffer an incestuous collapse." [16] Both groups, according to this ideology, as reflected and examined in these films, are controlled by male anxieties regarding the transfer of women from their group to the "enemy" group. *On a Narrow Bridge*, for example, criticizes the ideology of the honor of the Palestinian family (the "Byzantine" family in Dayan's words). Presumably, according to the Israeli patriarchal position, the meaning of a Palestinian man having sex with a Jewish woman is conquest and victory for the Palestinian. It is perceived as revenge against the oppressor. For a Palestinian, however, the meaning of a Palestinian woman having sex with a Jewish man is a violation of national and familial honor and submission to the oppressor.

Within this sexual economy, woman's point of view, or for that matter woman's desire, is completely missing. What does a woman want? What is woman's desire? The women in *Ricochets* and *On a Narrow Bridge* are more symbols than women of flesh and blood. Unlike the Palestinian men in the forbidden love narratives, they are less erotic objects than objects of admiration. In *On a Narrow Bridge*, Taggar tells Azulai that he has never met a woman like Laila, who is for him more an idea than an erotic object. This might explain why Salwa Nakra-Haddad, according to Dayan, decided (despite Palestinian objections) to play the role of Laila because of her feminism. She told Dayan that as "an Arab woman I've got a reason to fight for this." [17] Even the woman's fantasy in *My Michael* is an imagined one, a male fantasy projected into a fictional female consciousness. This patriarchal economy of desire explains the lack of films either on lesbian love or even on relationships of female bonding that represent forms of intimacy involving identification and not necessarily lesbian sexuality based on the fetishistic expression of desire. Woman's love for another woman poses a real threat to the taboo on interracial love. It is the ultimate transgression, more so than male homosexual love, because it threatens the patriarchy of both sides and destroys the status of women as exchange commodities between men. Ultimately women are the weak link in the cohesion of the collective. They are more prone to "betray" the group and move to the enemy side (which is what Miriam in *Crossfire* literally does by crossing the border erected between Jewish Tel Aviv and Arab Jaffa)— hence the importance of controlling the women on both sides. Women in these films, whether Jewish or Arab, are portrayed as liminal, keen on crossing boundaries and trying to live in more than one world. In this respect women are more "cosmopolitan," less border restricted, and freer than the men in these films. They therefore have the potential to become links, albeit tenuous ones, between the Israelis and the Palestinians. Their androgyny, their status as literal and symbolic border crossers, assigns to them a progressive role as agents of change and mobility. Paradoxically their "betrayal" of their "blood" groups creates an opening for communication with the other. Women appear in these films as bearing the tidings of a utopian future of peace and coexistence. Hava, Laila, Nadia, even Hannah in *My Michael*—all are potential bridges for the mixing of blood to create "hybrids." They are thus used as symbols, but their own desires find little or no expression in the films.

Hybrid Hopes?

The fact that all the films in this genre (except *The Lover*) were made by Israeli men dictates to a certain extent the tragic failure (with the exception of *Day after Day*) of the potential coalition between the Jewish women and the Arab men in these films. The inevitable death, madness, and destruction intrinsic to this genre demonstrate the threat posed to Israeli society by the temptation of forbidden love. Through this male anxiety, which haunts the forbidden love films, their creators achieve two goals: first, the continuation and perpetuation of women's "traditional roles"; and second, the positioning of the Arab outside the Jewish national body.

But a consideration of the temporal dimensions sheds a different light on the economy of coupling and desire in these narratives. Could it be that there is a temporal progression, paralleling the political changes beyond the film screen, toward racial tolerance in these narratives, from *My Michael* to the narratives produced during the Intifada and afterward? Do these films express a growing desire to transgress national boundaries or do they, despite the passage of time, reinforce racial taboos? Or perhaps they reflect a deep overall ambivalence toward the other.

From *My Michael* to *Day after Day* we can see a clear transition from fantasy to materialization of fantasy. What was in the realm of the imaginary in the 1960s and 1970s became a reality in the following two decades. Although *Hide and Seek* and its open treatment of doubly forbidden love (homosexual and interracial) constitutes perhaps the ultimate transgression in this genre, *Day after Day* with its matter-of-fact treatment of Mosh/Mussa, the Palestinian-Israeli hybrid, is perhaps the more transgressive.[18] Most of the films discussed here do not have a happy ending. To the contrary, as narratives of forbidden love they are doomed to end tragically. Only *Day after Day* does not end tragically although Mussa/Mosh, like the biblical Moses, is a "wandering Hybrid" who never reaches the promised land.

The final scene of the film leaves the film's "opsimism"[19] open. Ivgi is seen marching in the dark on a road leading to an unknown destiny, and on the soundtrack "Shir LaShalom" (The Song for Peace) is heard: "So just sing a song for peace / don't just whisper a prayer." The history of the reception of this song among the Israeli public assigns ambiguity to the film ending. When the song was first performed by the Israeli military theatrical troupe of the Nachal,[20] with Miri Aloni as the soloist, it was heavily criticized for its "pacifism" and eventually was banned from public performance. With the signing of the Oslo Peace Accords the song regained new life and became the anthem of the peace camp. It was sung by Aloni at the mass peace rally at which Rabin was assassinated. Rabin (well known for his shy and reserved manner) joined Aloni's singing in what, tragically, became his last optimistic public gesture. In the pocket of his jacket a bloodstained sheet of paper with the lyrics of the song for peace was found. Since then the song has become the icon of the peace camp and a locus of public controversies triggered by the objection of the Israeli Right to use of the song in official public events. Ivgi's solitary but determinate march thus becomes a metaphor for the marchers on the slippery road to peace.

In some of the films in the forbidden love genre, particularly in *Hamsin* and *Day after Day*, the love story is mingled with the theme of home.[21] The Israeli-Palestinian conflict in these films is represented through the dominance of the home metaphor. In these films, too, a temporal progression can be discerned. Both *Hamsin* and *Day after Day* deal with disputes over buying and selling houses/homes and with questions related to who is entitled to live in them. These questions are related to the bigger issue of literal and symbolic boundary crossing (whether border crossing or territorial, national, ethnic, class, or gender crossing) with which all the films in the forbidden love genre deal. Yet, the difference between the disputed home in *Hamsin* and that in *Day after Day* reveals the path leading from 1980s Zionism as portrayed in *Hamsin* to late 1990s Zionism as represented in *Day after Day*. Whereas in *Hamsin*, as I have shown, there is still a conflict between old-style Zionism and new-style Zionism, in *Day after Day* the conflict has been resolved with the victory of the latter. The new-style Zionism (or Post-Zionism) is embodied by the character of Nadiv, the nouveau riche contractor who tries to convince Yussef to sell his Arab family home in Haifa where he was born. In the area where this beautiful old house stands, Nadiv plans to build a big mall and a huge parking lot. Nadiv, the greedy contractor (whose name ironically means generous in Hebrew), is the new Zionist, a neocapitalist entrepreneur. Unlike Gedalia, the "Zionist native," Nadiv no longer attempts to buy land from the Arabs in order to live like an ascetic pioneer in the Galilee wilderness, but in order to live like a real capitalist in a huge, nouveau riche villa in Haifa crowded with gaudy European-looking knickknacks. Nadiv is the descendant of *Hamsin's* greedy moshava members who view Arab land as hot property, a real estate investment. The Zionist bulldozer of *Hamsin* turns in *Day after Day* into the real estate bulldozer of brutal and merciless capitalism. Zionism in *Day after Day* has unmasked its idealistic facade. Arab land is no longer bought or expropriated for Jewish settlement inspired by pioneering ideals. Rather, Haifa's remaining Palestinian landscape is brutally "raped" and evacuated of its "natural," pastoral, and nativist meaning, acquiring a new "masquerade" as in the popular Zionist song "Achasech BeSimlat Beton VaMelet" (I Shall Cover You with a Dress of Concrete and Cement).[22] *Day after Day* brings full circle the process begun in *Hamsin*: the complete commodification of the Zionist dream and its transformation (or unmasking) as (post-Zionist?) capitalist enterprise. The forbidden love in these films thus provides the context (or the pretext) for representing the change from a pseudosocialist struggle over land into a capitalist struggle over real estate.[23]

The progression of prevailing attitudes regarding interracial romance can also be discerned from examining how temporality is addressed within these films. Where do the filmmakers choose to temporally anchor the plot? Do they look at the conflict through the prism of the past or the present? Do they posit the past (or some moments of grace affiliated with this past) as a utopia for the present and future, or do they deal with the here and now? The answers to these questions shed light on the way these films reflect and construct the world outside the cinema. Some of the films, such as *Crossfire* and *Hide and Seek*, are displaced to the past, to 1947– 48, those fragile years in which the two populations still lived in mixed neighborhoods in the three major cities— Jerusalem, Tel Aviv–Jaffa, and Haifa—but were already ready to part. These years constitute the point of no return, after which the communities became separated and segregated. They signify the point in time when the two communities became official enemies. *Hide and Seek* and *Crossfire* capture those unique passages of time when and where love stories could still flourish, those fragile moments before the fixing and marking of official borders and boundaries. These films constitute love stories that flourish in the liminal zones of time and space before Tel Aviv–Jaffa became controlled by Jews, before the escape and expulsion of the Arabs from Jaffa, before the official 1948 war, and before the Palestinian Nakba and Jewish independence. Do these impossible liaisons communicate, as Shohat observes in her discussion of *Hide and Seek*, "a sense of lost possibilities on both a human and a political level"?[24] *On a Narrow Bridge*, on the other hand, despite being based on a popular Arab folktale, deals with the here and now, with the reality of the occupation, albeit in a very softened version. The majority of films in this category appeared in the 1980s as part of what Shohat calls the return of the repressed. *Day after Day*, which appeared a decade later and under completely different sociopolitical circumstances, is, strangely enough, the only slightly optimistic film in this category because it implicitly suggests that an Israeli multicultural and binational identity is a tangible and realistic option brought about by the fruit of love that has the potential to become unforbidden and unbinding.

Conclusion

■ It is part of morality not to be at home
in one's home.

Theodor W. Adorno

In his first poetry collection *Kinat HamMhager* (*The Immigrant's Lament*, 1995) Moroccan-born poet Moshe Ben Harosh, who immigrated to Israel with his parents in 1972, describes his sense of alienation from Israel. He writes that, since his immigration to Israel:

> I feel lonely
> in Israeli society
> and even more of a stranger
> with my diaspora family
> or with the diaspora Jews
> and with my family in Israel
> I even developed a chronic estrangement
> from myself.[1]

In this poem the immigrant —the *oleh* who arrives in Israel by ascending (*aliya*), according to the Zionist terminology, and exits the land by descending (*yerida*)—presents himself as a stranger. This poetic articulation of displacement, of being exiled at the very site that signifies the end of exile, of being homeless even at the center of home, is at the core of the "immigrant's lament." It parallels recent developments in Israeli new critical sociology, which no longer discusses Israeli society in Zionist terms (such as "*aliya*" and the Jewish melting pot) but rather analyzes it as a society of immigrants.[2]

The feeling of displacement in Palestine/Israel—in one's own "home"— is not peculiar to Oriental Jews;[3] it has always hovered in the background of the Zionist project. However, it was not openly expressed, discussed, or debated, either in prestate Palestine or in Israeli political public space. Most expressions of displacement, internal exile, and homelessness were articulated in the relatively "safe haven" of the cultural and aesthetic spheres.[4] Although Ben Harosh laments his estrangement from both "home" and the "Diaspora," there is, nonetheless, a nostalgic sentiment toward the Diaspora in his poem. Implicitly the poem suggests that his "homecoming" is to be blamed for creating his feeling of "homelessness." The Israeli home deprived Ben Harosh of the ability to feel at home. Paradoxically the Zionist "homeland" has only sharpened his exilic consciousness and placed him back in the Jew's "natural place," the spiritual Diaspora.

An even earlier immigrant to Palestine than Ben Harosh, the Polish Jewish poet Avot Yeshurun, manages, as Tamar Berger perceptively observes, in a single line, a single metaphor, to connect separate worlds. The identification of the Jewish shtetl with Palestine, Polish Jews with Arabs, is a recurring motif in Yeshurun's writing. "The Bedouins who came from Poland" is the opening line of his poem "A Lullaby to the Nordia Neighborhood."[5] The hybridization of the Polish Jews and the Arab nomads into one entity, recalling both the mythic figure of the wandering Jew and the mythic figure of the Arab nomad, draws attention not only to the "rootlessness" of the two peoples but also to the tragedy inflicted by the diasporic Jew victimized by Europe on the Palestinian Arabs. This tragedy, according to Yeshurun, was twofold because it turned the Palestinians into either homeless refugees or (in the case of those who stayed in Palestine/Israel) exiles in their homeland. Furthermore, the "returning Jews" were not redeemed by the act of "return" either. To the contrary, both missing their diasporic home and consciously (or not) feeling guilty for depriving the Palestinian Arabs of their own home by their act of "redemption," they became "Jewish-Polish Bedouins," forever trapped and locked in the tragic dialectics created by what Rashid Khalidi calls "the contrasting narratives regarding Palestine."[6]

Hannah of *My Michael* is a fictional embodiment of Tel Avivan poet Avot Yeshurun. "Representative of one type of Jerusalemite, the child of European immigrants, Hannah" as Hannah Wirth-Nesher observes, "is identified by her feelings of displacement, of being exiled from the very site that marks the end of exile, of being homeless even at the center of home."[7] This feeling of displacement also is experienced by the film director Hanna Azulay Hasfari as well as by Cheli, her fictional alter ego in *Shchur*, and even by the Palestinian female protagonist she plays in *Nadia*. Feelings of displacement, "one of the most formative experiences of our century,"[8] are pervasive also in the postmemory Holocaust cinema. The metaphor of home, so prominent, in particular in the Israeli films dealing with the Palestinian-Israeli conflict, is yet another expression for the dominance of the politics of displacement in Israeli cinema, which desperately attempts to create imagined homes through narratives about lost, destroyed, or longed-for homes.

In a recent interview that the Palestinian poet and activist Mahmud Darwish[9] gave to the Israeli writer Batya Gur, Darwish articulated the Israeli-Palestinian conflict in terms of a struggle over the construction of the master narrative of place: "Whoever writes the story (of the place) first—owns the place," Darwish claimed.[10] It is in the intimate link between nation and narration, to borrow Homi Bhabha's catchy phrase, that the debate about place, and particularly about place and belonging, place and home, constructs the discussion about identity.[11]

As Israel's sociocultural identity has shifted from one grounded in Zionist nationalism to new identity claims by groups and movements such as the ultra-Orthodox, the religious Mizrahim, and the Russian and Ethiopian immigrants, who were either excluded or appended to its core identity (and who, as yet, have not found "home" in Israeli cinema either), the question of identity will continue to haunt Israeli society in the new millennium as well.[12] As this book has shown, the struggle over Israeli identity is not over; Israeli identity is in the process of becoming rather than in the state of being. Just as Israel is a society in search of an identity, so is Israeli cinema in search of new forms to represent emerging, conflating, and conflictual identities.

Notes

Introduction

1. I am borrowing the term "politics of ideas" from Azmi Bishara's introductory remarks to the conference titled "The Conflictual Construction of Identities in the Middle East," The Jerusalem Van Leer Institute, November 24–26, 1998. Since Bishara defines himself as an old-fashioned modernist (following the tradition of Jurgen Habermas), he renounces this politics as "sectorialism." According to Bishara, this contemporary sectorialism is common to both Jewish and Arab populations in Israel.

2. Edward Said made this claim in a meeting at the Jerusalem Van Leer Institute on November 16, 1998. Despite being hounded by the audience regarding this position, Said steadfastly refused to refer to the topic as worthy of discussion.

3. Stuart Hall, "Introduction: Who Needs 'Identity'?" in *Questions of Cultural Identity*, ed. Stuart Hall and Paul du Gay, 1 (London: Sage Publications, 1996).

4. Paul Gilroy, "Diaspora and the Detours of Identity," in *Questions of Cultural Identity*, 301.

5. Michael Peter Smith, "Transnational Migration and the Globalization of Grassroots Politics," *Social Text* 39 (1994): 23.

6. Stuart Hall, "Cultural Identity and Diaspora," in *Questions of Cultural Identity*, 51.

7. Ella Shohat, *Israeli Cinema: East / West and the Politics of Representation* (Austin: University of Texas Press, 1989).

8. According to Ella Shohat, the Mizrahim (like the Palestinians) are certainly the victims of Zionism. See Ella Shohat, "Sephardim in Israel. Zionism from the Standpoint of Its Jewish Victims," *Social Text*, vols. 19–20 (spring–summer 1988). The title of this article is a conscious ironic reference to Edward Said's article "Zionism from the Standpoint of Its Victims," *Social Text*, no. 1 (1979).

9. In the case of Mizrahim and Holocaust survivors, the anger and the frustration is usually not directly channeled against "Zionism" or the Jewish state but is displaced and disguised in different forms. However, among intellectuals and artists of the second generation of Mizrahim and Holocaust survivors the anger is sometimes openly targeted against Zionism or at least against the "historical mistakes made by the state" with regard to the absorption of immigrants from the Islamic countries and Holocaust survivors from Europe (see chaps. 2 and 3).

10. David Ben-Gurion's famous phrase "without Maki [the former Israeli Communist Party] and Herut [the former Likud Party]" was extensively used in Netanyahu's political rhetoric expressing his unwillingness to forge a political alliance with the Labor Party.

11. Hall, "Cultural Identity and Diaspora," 52.

12. Idith Zertal, *Zehavam shel HaYehudim: HaHagira HaYehudit HaMahtartit L'Eretz Yisrael, 1945–1948 (From Catastrophe to Power: Jewish Illegal Immigration to Palestine, 1945–1948* [Tel Aviv: Am Oved, 1996]), 499. Unless specified otherwise, translated works are in Hebrew.

Chapter One

1. It is interesting to note that the leader of the passengers of *Exodus*, the Zionist Polish Jew Mordechai Rosner, said that members of the Palyam (the navylike branch of the Palmach) who were in charge of the *Exodus* operation looked to the Jewish refugees like demigods. For elaborations on the Zionist body (the new Jew) versus the diasporic body (the old Jew) see among others Daniel Boyarin, *Unheroic Conduct: The Rise of Heterosexuality and the Invention of the Jewish Man* (Berkeley: University of California Press, 1997); Sander Gilman, *The Jew's Body* (London: Routledge, 1991); David Biale, *Eros and the Jews: From Biblical Israel to Contemporary America* (Basic Books, 1992), particularly chapter 8, "Zionism as an Erotic Revolution"; and Judith Doneson, "The Image Lingers: The Feminization of the Jew in *Schindler's List*," in *Spielberg's Holocaust: Critical Perspectives on* Schindler's List, ed. Yosefa Loshitzky, 140–52 (Bloomington: Indiana University Press, 1997). For a comparison between the construction of the Sabra image and the new American Adam, see Ella Shohat, "Columbus, Palestine, and Arab-Jews: Toward a Relational Approach to Community Identity," in *Cultural Readings of Imperialism: Edward Said and the Gravity of History,* ed. Keith Ansell Pearson, Benita Parry, and Judith Squires, 88–105 (London: Lawrence and Wichart, 1997); and Ella Shohat, "Taboo Memories and Diasporic Visions: Columbus, Palestine, and Arab-Jews," in *Performing Hybridity,* ed. Jeniffer Fink and May Joseph (Minneapolis: University of Minnesota Press, 1998). For a discussion of the male body in Israeli cinema, see Yosef Raz, "HaOr HaKarua: Fantaziot Gavriyot, Haradot Gavriyot VeYitzug Guf HaGever HaNashi BaKolnoa HaYisraeli" (Broken Skin: Male Fantasies, Male Anxieties, and the Representation of the 'Feminine' Male Body in Israeli Cinema), *Cinematheque* 94 (March–April 1998): 20–25.

2. For a discussion of the heroic-nationalistic genre in Israeli cinema, see Ella Shohat, *Israeli Cinema: East/West and the Politics of Representation* (Austin: University of Texas Press, 1989), in particular, chap. 2.

3. Yael Munk, "Nireh Otcha Gever" (Let's See If You're a Real Man). *HaIr,* September 27, 1996, 10.

4. A more recent example that demonstrates the power of the popular mythical thinking that nurtures the ideology of the film *Exodus* in the American political sphere is President Clinton's speech over Yitzhak Rabin's grave. Clinton concluded his speech by invoking, like Paul Newman before him in his speech over the shared grave of Taha and Karen, Abraham

the patriarch of both the Jews and the Arabs, thus emphasizing the shared history of the two nations. He also invoked the promised land motif. In light of Rabin's assassination and Clinton's speech, Newman's speech gains a new, prophetic, and tragic meaning despite and perhaps because of its utopian vision of resolution through the symbolic annihilation of difference. For another recent political use of the American/Jewish promised land motif, see Binyamin Netanyahu's statement in an interview to the Spanish daily *El Pais*. In this interview Netanyahu claimed that the United States is the only country that understands Israel, not because of its large Jewish community but because "the Americans identify us with the promised land, like America." See "Eropa Eina Yoda'at Davar al HaMizrah HaTichon: Rak Artzot Habrit Mevina Otanu" (Europe Does not Know Anything about the Middle East: Only the U.S. Understands Us), *Ha'aretz*, March 6, 1998, 3a.

5. On the two possible readings of *Exodus*—liberationist versus chauvinist—see Jonathan Boyarin, "Reading Exodus into History," in *Palestine and Jewish History: Criticism at the Borders of Ethnography* (Minneapolis: University of Minnesota Press, 1996), 40–67. Boyarin submits the hypothesis that "the intimate association of Exodus with the Jewish settlement in Palestine and establishment of Israel is largely a product of the 1940s and after" (59). In his view, the model of the return from Babylon was more prominent than the Exodus from Egypt in early Zionism. For a further discussion of the debate between Said's "Canaanite reading" (in "Michael Walzer's 'Exodus and Revolution': A Canaanite Reading," *Grand Street* 5, no. 2 [winter 1986]: 86–106) and Walzer's liberationist, pro-Zionist reading, see Ella Shohat, "Antinomies of Exile: Said at the Frontiers of National Narrations," in *Edward Said: A Critical Reader,* ed. Michael Sprinker, 121–43 (Oxford: Blackwell, 1992).

6. For more recent accounts of the *Exodus* affair, see Aviva Halamish, *Exodus: Ha'Sipur Humiti (Exodus: The Real Story* [Tel Aviv: Am Oved, 1990]), and the more controversial study (due to its more critical view of the Zionist leadership) Idith Zertal, *Zehavam shel HaYehudim: HaHagira HaYehudit HaMahtartit L'Eretz Yisrael, 1945–1948 (From Catastrophe to Power: Jewish Illegal Immigration to Palestine, 1945–1948* [Tel Aviv: Am Oved, 1996]).

7. See *History and Memory* 7, no. 1 (spring/summer 1995). This special issue is devoted to "Israeli Historiography Revisited," ed. Gulie Ne'eman Arad.

8. See Alison Landsberg, "America, the Holocaust, and the Mass Culture of Memory: Toward a Radical Politics of Empathy," *New German Critique* 71 (1997): 63–86.

9. My account of the *Exodus* affair is based on the description in Tom Segev, *The Seventh Million: The Israelis and the Holocaust,* trans. Haim Watzman, 129–32 (New York: Hill and Wang, 1993). According to the mapping of the post-Zionist debate Segev is, to a certain extent, associated with the new historians.

10. A recent historical drama titled "Egoz," produced and broadcast by Israel's state-controlled Channel One, is another interesting example for the use of boats as symbols of national birth. This television drama is based on the true story of the boat *Egoz,* which on January 11, 1961, embarked from Port Alhuseyma in Morocco to Gibraltar with forty-four Moroccan Jews on board. This illegal operation was organized by the Israeli Mossad in an attempt

to bring the passengers to Israel. Tragically, the boat sank and all the passengers drowned. The scandal surrounding the accident exposed the secret activity of the Mossad among Moroccan Jews and enabled the legalization of mass immigration of Jews from Morocco to Israel. With the rise to power of the formerly suppressed Jewish Moroccan community in Israel, an attempt has been made to commemorate nationally the tragedy of the *Egoz* in order to integrate the Mizrahim into the Zionist narrative of national rebirth. The idea to create a television drama based on this historical event was initiated by Rafi Elul, a Labor Knesset member of Moroccan descent. According to Elul, the transformation of the event into a television drama would help remedy the injustice inflicted upon the Moroccan Jewish community in Israel. This televised act of "redemption" can be seen as a manifestation of "Exodus envy," signifying the growing integration of Mizrahim in Israeli society through their symbolic acceptance and appropriation of Ashkenazi Zionist myths. Implied in this appropriation is a claim to a share of suffering and sacrifice in the Zionist struggle for national rebirth.

11. Ilana Pardes, "The Biography of Ancient Israel: Imagining the Birth of a Nation," *Comparative Literature* 49, no. 1 (winter 1997): 24.

12. I am indebted to Haim Bresheeth for drawing my attention to this fascinating point.

13. Michel Foucault, "Of Other Spaces," *Diacritics,* vol. 16 (1986).

14. The story of Noah's Ark is one example of the death and rebirth of a nation in the Jewish tradition.

15. In *From Catastrophe to Power* (152–53), Idith Zertal reminds her readers that at the time of the *Exodus* affair an analogy was made between that historical event and the "Boston Tea Party." Each was perceived as instrumental to the achievement of national independence. This historical analogy probably was not lost in 1960 on the U.S. audience of *Exodus*, hence further deepening the incorporation of Jewish history into the consciousness and conscience of Americans.

16. Eva Marie Saint was at that time associated in the public mind with Alfred Hitchcock's *North by Northwest* (1959). Her family name in *Exodus*, Fremont, is perhaps inspired by the name of the heroine, Lisa Fremont, played by Grace Kelly, in Hitchcock's *Rear Window* (1954).

17. This quote is taken from Laura Mulvey's now classic essay "Visual Pleasure and Narrative Cinema," *Screen* 16, no. 3 (fall 1975): 417.

18. Benedict Anderson observes:

> The other side of this coin [the rise of nationalism] is the recent emergence in the United States and other older nation-states of an ethnicity that appears as a bastard Smerdyakov to classical nationalism's Dimitri Karamazov. One emblem of the American variant is perhaps the espionage trial of Jonathan Pollard a few years back. In the age of classical nationalism, the very idea that there could be something praiseworthy in an American citizen's spying on America for another country would have seemed grotesque. But to the substantial number of Jewish-Americans who felt sympathetic to Pollard, the resentful spy was understood as representing a transnational ethnicity. (Benedict Anderson, "Exodus," *Critical Inquiry* 20 [winter 1994]: 325)

19. Shohat, *Israeli Cinema*, 66.

20. Ibid.

21. Rachel Weissboard, a lecture on *Exodus* delivered to my class on "The Representation of the Palestinian-Israeli Conflict in Cinema," The Hebrew University of Jerusalem, December 3, 1997.

22. Pardes, "Biography of Ancient Israel," 31.

23. Dov Gruner was a member of the Etzel (the right-wing Jewish military underground during the British mandate) who was executed by the British at the Acre prison.

24. Zahava Solomon, "From Denial to Recognition: Attitudes to Holocaust Survivors," *Journal of Traumatic Stress* 8, no. 2 (April 1995): 215–28.

25. This redemption ceremony assumes additional meaning given the fact that Sal Mineo was a homosexual, and in a number of films he was cast in roles that question his heterosexuality. In *Rebel without a Cause* he plays a character who is a social outcast because he is "queer."

26. In retrospect one cannot but ironically compare these fetishes to the three contemporary objects—yarmulka (*kipa*), pistol, and mobile phone—that have become the new fetishistic paraphernalia of the religious, nationalist Israeli Jew.

27. The idea that a German officer was active in Palestine in 1947 is only one example of the many historical absurdities of the film.

28. Yael Zerubavel, "The Historic, the Legendary, and the Incredible: Invented Tradition and Collective Memory in Israel," in *Commemorations: The Politics of National Identity,* ed. John R. Gillis, 105–23 (Princeton: Princeton University Press, 1994).

29. Similar reservations were raised regarding Richard Attenborough's *Gandhi* (1982). See Akbar Ahmed, "Jinnah and the Quest for Muslim Identity," *History Today* 44, no. 9 (September 1994): 34–40.

30. The fact that part of the film is conveyed through the point of view of Kitty Fremont (Eva Marie Saint) is indebted to the tradition of the woman's melodrama.

31. Hayden White, "On the Value of Narrativity in the Representation of Reality," in *On Narrative,* ed. W. J. T. Mitchell, 300 (Chicago: University of Chicago Press, 1986).

32. Quoted from the Palestinian delegation's address to the Madrid Middle East Peace Conference, delivered by Dr. Haider Abdul Shafi, head of the delegation. For a further analysis of the rhetoric and ideology of this address, see Yosefa Loshitzky, "The Text of the Other, the Other in the Text: The Palestinian Delegation's Address to the Madrid Middle East Peace Conference," *Journal of Communication Inquiry* 18, no. 1 (winter 1994): 27–44.

33. It should be mentioned that the allusion to the Canaanites also invokes the Canaanite movement, a literary and artistic movement active in Israel during the years following the 1948 war, led by the poet and intellectual Yonatan Ratosh. Many of the members of this group were former members of the Etzel and Lehi underground organizations. Canaanite ideology was based on the belief that a new Hebrew nation, culture, and identity, separate and distinct from the historical Jewish people and the Diaspora, had come into being in the land of Israel (Eretz Israel). The Canaanites rejected the cultural heritage of Diaspora Jewry.

34. Saul Friedlander, "Memory of the Shoah in Israel," in *The Art of Memory: Holocaust Memorials in History*, ed. James E. Young, 152 (New York: The Jewish Museum, Prestel, 1994). For a further discussion see Loshitzky, *Spielberg's Holocaust*.

Chapter Two

1. Yechiam Weitz, "Political Dimensions of Holocaust Memory in Israel," in *The Shaping of Israeli Identity: Myth, Memory, and Trauma,* ed. Robert Wistrich and David Ohana, 130 (London: Frank Cass, 1995).

2. Dina Porat, *Hanhaga BeMilkud: HaYishuv Nochach HaShoah 1942–1945 (An Entangled Leadership: The Yishuv and the Holocaust, 1942–1945* [Tel Aviv: Am Oved, 1986]), 12.

3. For a further discussion of the memory of the Holocaust in Israel, see the following: James E. Young, "Israel: Holocaust, Heroism, and National Redemption," in *The Texture of Memory: Holocaust Memorials and Meaning* (New Haven: Yale University Press, 1993), 209–18; Saul Friedlander, "Memory of the Shoah in Israel," in *The Art of Memory: Holocaust Memorials in History,* ed. James E. Young, 149–58 (New York: The Jewish Museum, Prestel, 1994); Tom Segev, *The Seventh Million: The Israelis and the Holocaust* (New York: Hill and Wang, 1993); Anita Shapira, the section on "Zionism and the Holocaust," in "Politics and Collective Memory: The Debate over the 'New Historians' in Israel," *History and Memory* 7 no. 1 (spring/summer 1995): 17–23 (special issue titled "Israeli Historiography Revisited," ed. Gulie Ne'eman Arad); Haim Bresheeth, "The Great Taboo Is Broken: Reflections on the Israeli Reception of *Schindler's List*," in *Spielberg's Holocaust: Critical Perspectives on* Schindler's List, ed. Yosefa Loshitzky, 193–212 (Bloomington: Indiana University Press, 1997); Omer Bartov, "Defining Enemies, Making Victims: Germans, Jews, and the Holocaust," *American Historical Review* 103, no. 3 (June 1998): 771–816 (for an analysis of the Israeli case, see 800–808); Moshe Zuckerman, *Shoah in the Sealed Room: The "Holocaust" in the Israeli Press during the Gulf War* (Tel Aviv: Hotzaat HaMehaber, 1993); Oz Almog, "The Sabra and the Holocaust" (HaTzabar VeHashoah), in *The Sabra: A Profile (HaTzabar: Dyokan* [Tel Aviv: Am Oved, 1998]), 137–47. On the relationship between the Holocaust and post-Zionist debates, see *Post-Zionism and the Holocaust: The Role of the Holocaust in the Public Debate on Post-Zionism in Israel, 1993–1996,* comp. and ed. and with a foreword by Dan Michman, Bar Ilan University, Faculty of Jewish Studies, The Abraham and Eta Spiegel Family Chair in Holocaust Research, The Institute for Research on Diaspora Jewry in Modern Times, Research Aids Series No. 8, January 1997.

4. In recent years the question has repeatedly arisen as to whether the survivors could have told their stories immediately after the Holocaust. The prevailing view today, inspired by growing criticism of the reception and absorption of the immigrants (both from Europe and the Arab countries) by the young Israeli state, maintains that the survivors faced indifference and contempt that kept them silent. The attitudes toward the survivors have recently become a focus of heated debates in Israel. In a symposium about Idith Zertal's book *Zehavam Shel HaYehudim: HaHagira HaYehudit HaMahtartit L'Eretz Israel, 1945–1948 (From Catastrophe to*

Power: Jewish Illegal Immigration to Palestine, 1945–1948 [Tel Aviv: Am Oved, 1996]) that took place at the Van Leer Jerusalem Institute on October 31, 1996, Moshe Zuckerman, a historian at Tel Aviv University, claimed that the moment of meeting between the Yishuv and the survivors was also the moment of contradiction, when the Zionist entity was confronted with its "negation": the survivors who epitomized the diasporic entity. (The title of the symposium was "Did the Yishuv Recognize the Contribution of the Survivors to the Establishment of the State of Israel?") Only in the 1980s, with organized tours to the camps, has this space of contradiction opened up, according to Zuckerman.

In the same symposium Shlomo Ben Ami, a historian at Tel Aviv University and formerly a minister in Ehud Barak's government, argued that the meeting point between the prototype of the Sabra and the survivor was not significantly different from the Sabra's shocking encounter with the Oriental diasporic Jew. Only the magnitude of the tragedy is different. The main structure that characterizes the two encounters is that of the meeting between the new Israeli and the diasporic Jew. And indeed the second "mahapach" (transformation) that was brought about by the rise to power in 1996 of Binyamin Netanyahu's government—the first occurred with the rise of Menachem Begin's Likud government in 1977—signifies the return of the repressed diasporic Jew (the Mizrahi, as well as the ultra-Orthodox and the religious) to the center of Israel's life. Many consider it to be the victory won by Judaism over Israeliness.

In her response Idith Zertal claimed that she did not write a book on the survivors although their presence is interwoven throughout the book. Speaking through their diaries, the survivors' voice is a first-person voice. The survivors exist and they posit themselves as subjects against the Zionist discourse about them. The book, Zertal argued, gives a voice to the survivors and places them at the forefront of the Zionist struggle over the establishment of the Zionist state. According to Zertal, they met two kinds of Israelis: agents of the "Mossad" (HaMossad L'Aliya Bet, the organization responsible for the illegal immigration of European Jewry to Palestine after World War II), who were immigrants themselves, spoke the survivors' languages, and could feel empathy toward them; and the new Israelis, members of the Palmach and Palyam who were raised on the ethos of the negation of exile. Ben-Gurion discovered the "treasure" buried in the Jewish catastrophe and decided to translate it into political power by bringing the survivors to Palestine. In the displaced persons camps, according to Zertal, he could have said "here I have founded the Jewish state." Zertal also claimed that Natan Alterman's poem "Zehavam shel Yehudim" (The Gold of Jewish People), which she used as the title of her book, epitomizes her thesis: "the transformation of the ultimate Jewish catastrophe into Zionist power."

An earlier study of the Yishuv's response to the Holocaust written by Dina Porat, *The Blue and the Yellow Stars of David: The Zionist Leadership in Palestine and the Holocaust, 1939–1945* (Cambridge: Harvard University Press, 1990), tends to justify the reaction of the Yishuv. Israeli writer Hanoch Bartov, a Sabra who fought with the Jewish Brigade, angrily denied the claims (voiced by, among others, the poet Natan Zach in "Mihu Sofer Yehudi, Mahu Sefer Yehudi" [Who Is a Jewish Writer, What Is a Jewish Book?], *Ma'ariv*, November 29, 1991) that the Palmach generation, or "Dor HaMedina," was indifferent to the fate of European Jewry, was focused on "our tiny, Eretz-Israeli, provincial *"pupik"* (navel), and simply were not interested in what was happening there." Hanoch Bartov, "Ein Emet BaDiba Al Adishuteno LaShoah" (There Is No Truth in the Slanderous Accusation of Our Indifference to the Shoah), *Iton 77* 144–45 (January-February 1992): 66.

On the controversy surrounding Ben-Gurion's attitude toward the Holocaust, the refugees, the reception of the survivors in Israel, and the Yiddish language, see Shabtai Tevet (Ben-Gurion's official biographer), *Ben-Gurion and the Holocaust* (Harcourt and Brace, 1998); "'HaHor Hashahor: Ben-Gurion ben Shoah LeTkuma" (The Black Hole: Ben-Gurion between Shoah and Independence), *Alpayim* 10 (1994): 111–95; and other numerous articles published mostly in *Ha'aretz*. For a discussion of the representation of Holocaust survivors in Israeli cinema, see Nurit Gertz, "Ha'Aherim' Basratim Ha'Yisraelim Bishnot Ha'arbaim Ve-Hachamishim: Nitzoley Shoah, Arvim, Nashim" (The "Others" in Israeli Films of the 1940s and 1950s: Holocaust Survivors, Arabs, Women), in *Fictive Looks: On Israeli Cinema,* ed. Nurith Gertz, Orly Lubin, and Judd Ne'eman, 381–402 (Tel Aviv: Open University of Israel, 1998).

5. Zahava Solomon, "From Denial to Recognition: Attitudes to Holocaust Survivors," *Journal of Traumatic Stress* 8, no. 2 (April 1995): 215–28. In the symposium on Zertal's book (see note 4) a Holocaust survivor from the audience said: "Even to this day I find exile here." Another Holocaust survivor from the audience responded to Zertal's justification of her use of the term "mehagrim" (immigrants) instead of the words "olim" or "plitim" (refugees), which are common in mainstream Zionist historiography of the Holocaust, saying: "I did not come here as an immigrant. I came home." Solomon claims that the survivors met a conspiracy of silence and an attitude that implicitly and explicitly blamed them for what happened to them and for surviving. In the first twenty years after the war, the psychiatric community failed to connect the emotional distress and physical problems of the Holocaust survivors to their previous experiences of terror and loss. When they did start to treat Holocaust survivors, therapists found themselves overwhelmed by their patients' suffering, and sometimes resentful of their demand for attention. Tragically, to this very day eight hundred Holocaust survivors who were institutionalized in insane asylums when they immigrated to Israel are still there. Only recently was it discovered that some of them were placed in asylums because they were found socially "unfit." In one publicized case it was clear that there was no psychiatric justification for institutionalization. Due to the intervention of the television crew who interviewed him, the person was released and sent to a regular home for the elderly. Solomon argues that only after the Eichmann trial and the 1967 war was there a marked turnaround in attitudes both generally and in the clinical field. She suggests that the views of mental health professionals have mirrored rather than led those of the general public.

6. Gouri, "Facing the Glass Booth," in *Holocaust Remembrance: The Shapes of Memory,* ed. Geoffrey H. Hartman, 154 (Oxford: Blackwell, 1994).

7. On the appropriation of the Holocaust by the Right, see Laurence J. Silberstein, "Others Within and Others Without: Rethinking Jewish Identity and Culture," in Laurence J. Silberstein and Robert L. Cohn, *The Other in Jewish Thought and History: Constructions of Jew-*

ish Culture and Identity (New York: New York University Press, 1994), 1–34. This appropriation reached its tragic climax with the incitement campaign that preceded Yitzhak Rabin's assassination.

8. For a further discussion of this issue, see *History and Memory* 7, no. 1. See in particular Anita Shapira's section on "Zionism and the Holocaust" in "Politics and Collective Memory," (see note 3).

9. It is important to emphasize that the trendy term "post-Zionism" was coined by the academic/intellectual community. Most Israelis still see themselves and their state as Zionist. In fact, one could claim that Zionism has never thrived so powerfully as in contemporary Israel with its growing ultranationalism and the Zionization of the formerly anti-Zionist and ultra-Orthodox community.

10. For a new publication on this issue, which has generated heated debate in Israel, see Daniel Frenkel, *Al Pi Tehom: HaMediniyut HaTziyonit VeShe'elat Yehudei Germanya, 1933–1938* (*On the Abyss: Zionist Policy and the Question of the German Jews, 1933–1938* [Jerusalem: Magnes, 1994]).

11. Giyora Senesh appealed to the Israeli Supreme Court because of one line spoken in Lerner and Barabash's drama about Kasztner, in which Kasztner claims that Hannah Senesh broke under torture and informed the Nazis about the two other parachutists. Senesh's appeal was dismissed by the judges. However, the creators of the television drama eventually decided to remove the controversial line from the broadcast version. It is interesting to note at this point that Spielberg replaced "Jerusalem of Gold" with Senesh's "To Caesaria" (known in Israel as "Eli, Eli") in the Israeli version of the film. For a discussion of this replacement and its ideological implications, see Bresheeth, "The Great Taboo Is Broken," and Omer Bartov, "Spielberg's Oskar: Hollywood Tries Evil," in Loshitzky, *Spielberg's Holocaust.*

12. It should be noted that the museum's renewed decision to cancel the visit enjoyed the support of Binyamin Netanyahu. On the other hand, the Lohamei HaGetaot Holocaust Museum invited Arafat to visit in reaction to the cancellation of the Washington Museum's invitation.

13. See *Ha'aretz,* April 4, 1995, 1; and "Boots and Leather Fashion from 'Nazi Leather' Sold in Israeli Stores," *Yediot Aharonot,* October 30, 1996, 12. The owner of Grosso Modo, one of the stores implicated, lamely apologized: "If I had not said to my supplier 'Nazi leather' he would not have understood what I was asking for."

14. Moshe Zimmerman and Moshe Zuckerman defined the reaction to the victory of the German team as racism. An internal Ashkenazi ethnic element was introduced into the debate when Irit Linor explained the two researchers' pro-German feelings as deriving from their "Yeke" (German superior) background as opposed to her Polish (inferior) background. Linor does not go to Germany, does not buy German products, and tries not to have contact with Germans. A clause in her contract with her publisher prohibits the translation of her books into German or their distribution in Germany and Austria.

15. *Ha'aretz,* May 5, 1995, 5A.

16. See *Ha'aretz,* June 6, 1997.

17. A discussion of the "Historians' Debate" is beyond the scope of this study. Suffice it to mention that this debate began when Jurgen Habermas published an article on November 7, 1986, in *Die Zeit* in which he attacked an article by the German revisionist historian Ernst Nolte in the *Frankfurter Allegemeine Zeitung*. The core of the debate revolved around the issue of whether the Nazi period and, above all, the Holocaust should be regarded as a unique event that made German history different from that of all other nations, or whether it was just one genocide among others. Nolte favored the latter view and argued in consequence that German history should be "normalized." Historians Michael Sturmer and Andreas Hillgruber expressed views that were seen by some critics as associated with Nolte's. In Habermas's view these revisionist historians wanted to rewrite the Nazi past in order to normalize German national identity in the present. The debate had moved from the academic arena to the forefront of political controversy in Germany.

18. See, for example, the debate between Yehuda Bauer and Yosi Grodzinski in *Ha'aretz*, June 6, 1997, E2.

19. See Moshe Gross's letter to *Ha'aretz*, June 10, 1997, 16B.

20. The opening speeches were delivered by Prime Minister Binyamin Netanyahu and Education Minister Zevulun Hammer.

21. Moli Brug, "Eretz Zion VeAuschwitz" (The Land of Zion and Auschwitz), *Ha'aretz*, October 13, 1996, 3B.

22. Ibid.

23. Other even more striking examples of the "militarization" of the Holocaust occurred in 1998. The General Staff of the IDF gathered for its weekly meeting in "The Valley of the Communities" in Yad Vashem a day before Holocaust Remembrance Day. Chief of Staff Amnon Lipkin-Shahak said: "We came here in order to understand our role as the continuers of the victims, to understand the importance of having a safe home for the Jewish people and the tremendous responsibility which the Holocaust places on our shoulders." See Alex Somech, "HaMatkal Hitkanes LeYeshiva BeYad VaShem" (The IDF Chief of Staff Holds a Meeting at Yad Vashem), *Ha'aretz*, April 21, 1998, 6A. Perhaps the most extreme manifestation of the attempt to "militarize" the Holocaust was expressed by Brigadier General Yossi Ben Hanan, who proposed that IDF elite commando units conduct their swearing-in ceremonies at the extermination camps of Majdanek and Birkenau. See Yossi Melman, "Yossi Ben Hanan Matzia: Tiksey Hashba'a shel Yehidot Elit Yearchu BeMahanot HaHashmada" (Yossi Ben Hanan Proposes: The Swearing-In Ceremonies of Elite Commando Units Will Take Place at the Extermination Camps), *Ha'aretz*, April 24, 1998, 4A.

24. Weitz, "Political Dimensions of Holocaust Memory," 133.

25. Ibid.

26. Gulie Ne'eman Arad, "Rereading an Unsettling Past: The Holocaust in Present-Day Israeli Consciousness," Plenary session 2, "The Holocaust-Memory, History and Politics," Association for Jewish Studies, December 16, 1996, Boston. For a further analysis of commemoration ceremonies conducted in Israeli secular schools, see Avner Ben Amos and Ilana Bet El, "Ceremonies, Education, and History: Holocaust Remembrance Day and the Commemora-

tion Day for The Fallen Soldiers of Israel's Wars," in *Education and History,* ed. Imanuel Atex and Rivka Feldhay, 457–79 (Jerusalem: Merkaz Shazar, 1999). Eyal Sivan, an Israeli filmmaker who lives in France, made *Izkor! Slaves of Memory* (1991), a very critical documentary on commemoration ceremonies conducted in Israeli schools. The film includes interviews with the late professor Yeshayahu Leibowitz, who criticizes the nationalistic, militaristic, and antihumanistic Zionist ideology embedded in the Israeli educational system that nurtures these ceremonies. Sivan also made *The Specialist* (1999), a film composed entirely of excerpts from the 350 hours of raw material filmed by the American director Leo Horowitz in 1961, during the dramatic trial of Adolph Eichmann in Jerusalem. The film was inspired by Hannah Arendt's book *Eichmann in Jerusalem: A Report on the Banality of Evil,* which was heavily criticized by the Israeli Zionist establishment when it first came out. The book appeared in Hebrew translation almost forty years after its publication.

27. Malchei Yisrael is a large square in central Tel Aviv, renamed Yitzhak Rabin Square following Rabin's assassination there.

28. *Ha'aretz,* January 25, 1998, 8A.

29. *Ha'aretz,* April 4, 1997, 7A.

30. "The Reformers Are to Blame for the Holocaust," *Ha'aretz,* December 2, 1996, 7A.

31. *Ha'aretz,* December 29, 1996, 7A. On the extensive use made by the ultra-Orthodox of the Holocaust, see also B. Michael, "La'Asot Din BaReformim VeOzrehem" (To Bring to Judgment upon the Reform Jews and Their Helpers), *Yediot Aharonot,* December 3, 1996, 5.

32. Dina Porat, "L'Oolam lo Darki HaAharona" (It Is Never My Last Road), *Ha'aretz,* January 15, 1997, 5. This is a review of Felix Zandman's *Darki MeVichy le Vichy: MeNeourim BaShoah LeBagrut shel Mada VeTa'asiya* (*My Way from Vichy to Vichy: From Adolescence in the Holocaust to an Adulthood of Science and Industry*), trans. Amos Karmel (Tel Aviv: Keter, 1997).

33. Alain Finkielkraut, *The Imaginary Jew,* trans. David Suchoff (Lincoln: University of Nebraska Press, 1994), 7.

34. Ibid., 10.

35. Ibid., 11.

36. Ibid., 12.

37. Ibid., 14.

38. Marianne Hirsch, "Past Lives: Postmemories in Exile," *Poetics Today* 17, no. 4 (winter 1996), 661.

39. Ibid., 664.

40. Eleonora Lev, *First Morning in Paradise* (Tel Aviv: Keshet, 1996), 55 (translation mine). See also Lev's recent book *Sug Mesuyam shel Yatmut: Edut al Masa* (*A Certain Kind of Orphanhood: Report of a Journey* [Tel Aviv: N. B. Books, 1999]).

41. Yitzhak Laor, "On Relativism," *Ha'aretz* literary supplement, April 21, 1997, 6E (translation mine). In this lecture, delivered as part of a conference on "The Reception of the Holocaust by the Third Generation: Germany, Israel, the USA," Laor claims that the Holocaust was an event alien to the Israeli experience. The survivors, who did not speak Hebrew (many of

them still do not), and who were scattered around the world, posed a threat to the process of nation building. Only during the 1960s, when Israeli hegemony within the Jewish world had been established, could the Holocaust be introduced into the life of the Israelis, first politically and then culturally. Laor's article is an adaptation of a lecture delivered in a conference on "The Reception of the Holocaust by the Third Generation: Germany, Israel, the USA," which was held in January 1997 during the Holocaust Remembrance Day recently established in Germany on the day commemorating the liberation of Auschwitz. The lecture was subsequently published in *Literaturwerkstatt*.

42. Geoffrey H. Hartman, "Introduction: Darkness Visible," in *Holocaust Remembrance: The Shapes of Memory*, 18.

43. See, inter alia: Dina Wardi, *Memorial Candles: Children of the Holocaust*, trans. Naomi Goldblum (London: Routledge, 1992); Helen Epstein, *Children of the Holocaust: Conversations with Sons and Daughters of Survivors* (London: Penguin Books, 1988 [c. 1979]); Rafael Moses, M.D., ed., *Persistent Shadows of the Holocaust,* proceedings of the 1988 conference at Hebrew University's Sigmund Freud Center (International Universities Press, Inc.); Martin S. Bergmann and Milton E. Jucovy, eds., *Generations of the Holocaust* (New York: Basic Books, 1982 and/or New York: Columbia University Press, 1990); Yael Danieli, "Families of the Nazi-Holocaust: Some Short- and Long-Term Effects," in *Stress and Anxiety*, vol. 8, ed. C. D. Spielberger and I. G. Sarson, chap. 46 (New York: Wiley & Sons, 1982); Howard Cooper, "The 'Second Generation' Syndrome," *Journal of Holocaust Education* 4, no. 2 (winter 1995): 131–46; Gaby Glassman, "The Holocaust and Its Aftermath: How Have the Survivors Fared during the Last Fifty Years?" *European Judaism* 29, no. 1 (spring 1996): 52–63. For a very interesting discussion of Israeli female writers and film directors and Holocaust second-generation consciousness, see Ronit Lentin, "Likhbosh MeHadash et Teritoryot HaShtika: Sofrot VeKolnoaniyot Yisraeliyot KeBanot LeNitzolei Shoah" (To Reconquer the Territories of Silence: Israeli Female Writers and Film Directors as Daughters of Holocaust Survivors), in *Memory and Awareness of the Holocaust*, 169–95. In her study (which attempts to break what she calls the three territories of silence related to the Holocaust: sociology, gender, and self-reflexive acknowledgment of the researcher in his/her own personal involvement in the object of his—but mainly her—research) Lentin argues that the construction of male-dominated Zionist identity not only suppressed, discriminated against, and stigmatized Holocaust survivors but also feminized them.

44. Wardi, *Memorial Candles*, 27.

45. Ibid.

46. Ibid., 35.

47. See Loshitzky, *Spielberg's Holocaust*.

48. David Suchoff, "Introduction," in Finkielkraut, *Imaginary Jew*, xvii.

49. Ibid.

50. Ibid., viii–ix.

51. In this study I do not include the more institutionalized expressions of the second generation that have emerged in the last decade in the form of special organizations, conferences,

therapy and support groups, and so forth. One of the more interesting (and in my opinion disturbing) phenomena related to the growing institutionalization of the second generation is the creation of forums between second-generation Jews and Germans (mainly the sons and daughters of high-ranking Nazis). Thus, for example, on Sunday June 2, 1996, at the Royal Geographical Society in London the Second Generation Trust presented a symposium titled "Opposite Sides of a Shared History." The speakers were Samson Munn, the son of Holocaust survivors, and Kirk Kuhl, the son of a high-ranking Nazi. Each year since 1992, as the brochure distributed to the participants revealed, "with others from similar backgrounds, they have been meeting in a group created by the Israeli psychologist, Professor Dan Bar-On. Together, they have reflected on the impact of the Holocaust on their lives, how it has affected them and how their parents' experiences were communicated to them." One of their meetings was documented in a remarkable BBC documentary, *Children of the Third Reich* (1993), produced by Katherine Clay. The London meeting was attended by five hundred people. See also Dan Bar-On, *Fear and Hope: Three Generations of the Holocaust* (Cambridge: Harvard University Press, 1995), and *Legacy of Silence: Encounters with Children of the Third Reich* (Cambridge: Harvard University Press, 1991); and Born Krondorfer, *Remembrance and Reconciliation: Encounters between Young Jews and Germans* (New Haven: Yale University Press, 1995).

52. Finkielkraut, *Imaginary Jew*, 23.

53. Roni Perchak, "HaIntimi Hu HaKolektivi: Al Kolnoa Yisraeli VeNose HaShoah" (The Intimate and the Collective: On Israeli Cinema and the Holocaust), *Dimui* 13A (summer 1997): 38–41. For an analysis of the Holocaust in Israeli cinema (viewed from a right-wing perspective), see Ilan Avisar, "Personal Fears and National Nightmares: The Holocaust Complex in Israeli Cinema," in *Breaking Crystal*, 137–59.

54. Judd Ne'eman, "The Empty Tomb in the Postmodern Pyramid: Israeli Cinema in the 1980s and 1990s," in *Documenting Israel*, ed. Charles Berlin, 130 (Cambridge: Harvard College Library, 1995).

55. The notion of the "negation of exile" is crucial to the conceptualization of Zionism. "Negation of exile," as Amnon Raz-Krakotzkin explains, refers to a mental attitude and ideological position that sees the present Jewish settlement in and sovereignty over Palestine/Eretz Israel as the "return" of the Jews to a land considered to be their homeland and described as empty. According to him:

> "Negation of exile" seems to be the "normalization" of Jewish existence, the fulfillment of and "solution" to Jewish history, whereas "exile" is interpreted as an unsatisfactory political reality that concerns only the Jews. According to this point of view, the cultural framework that Zionists wished to "actualize" was an "authentic" Jewish culture, one that could not develop under exilic circumstances, and which was also considered to be in direct continuity to the ancient "pre-exilic" past. This conception also shaped the image of the "new Jew," defined in contrast of the rejected "exilic Jew." As such, the "negation of exile" demanded cultural uniformity and the abandonment of the different cultural traditions through which Jewish identity had previously been determined. (Amnon Raz-Krakotzkin, "Galut Betoch Ribonut: LeBikoret Shlilat HaGalut BaTarbut

HaYisraelit" [Exile within Sovereignty: Toward a Critique of the 'Negation of Exile' in Israeli Culture], *Teoria VeBikoret* [*Theory and Criticism*] 4 [fall 1993]: 23–56, and 5 [fall 1994]: 113–32)

56. Alongside the official genre there has developed another unofficial "amateur" second-generation film genre. Many children of survivors document on video their visits to their parents' lost world.

57. Feldman, "Whose Story Is It, Anyway?" 238.

58. Perchak, "The Intimate and the Collective."

59. Ibid.

60. Only recently, while staying in cosmopolitan London—which reminded him of cosmopolitan Tangier—and experiencing the joys of voluntary "exile," Tlalim decided to reclaim his original family name, de Bentolila. "Tlalim" is a "Hebraized" version of the Arab-Jewish name "de Bentolila." Like many other immigrants to Israel, both from Europe and the Arab world, Tlalim adopted a new Israeli-sounding name in an attempt to join the Israeli collective by erasing any traces of diasporic roots. It should be noted that during the 1950s many immigrants were actually forced to change their names. Until 1997 people who worked for the Israeli Diplomatic Service were forced to change their names when representing Israel abroad.

Chapter Three

1. Quoted in Ronit Lentin, "Likhbosh MeHadash et Teritoryot HaShtika: Sofrot VeKolnoaniyot Yisraeliyot KeBanot LeNitzolei Shoah" (To Reconquer the Territories of Silence: Israeli Female Writers and Film Directors as Daughters of Holocaust Survivors), in *Memory and Awareness of the Holocaust in Israel,* ed. Yoel Rappel (Tel Aviv: Mod—Publishing House Co., 1998).

2. One example of such audience participation is the common Israeli practice of broadcasting songs of nationalism and heroic events perceived as traumatic on the national and collective level, such as "terrorist" activities.

3. According to Eyal Zandberg, songs from Poliker and Gilead's album *Ashes and Dust* can be divided into three groups: (1) "The Last Stop Is Treblinka" and like songs that are closely linked to the Holocaust and therefore are broadcast only on Holocaust Remembrance Day or in direct relationship to Holocaust observations; (2) songs that do not deal with the Holocaust and are normally broadcast on regular radio programs; (3) "intermediate songs" that deal with the Holocaust indirectly and thus can be connected to the Holocaust but also to other events. These latter songs, according to Zandberg, break the autonomy of Holocaust discourse because they can as easily "enter" and "exit" its boundaries, further accelerating its introduction into everyday "normal" discourse. See Eyal Zandberg, "Lizkor VeDavar Lo Lishkoha? Yahas HaTarbut HaPopolarit BeYisrael BiShnot HaTishim LaShoah" (To Remember and Never Forget? The Attitude of Popular Culture in Israel in the 1990s to the Holocaust), Department of Communication and Journalism, Hebrew University of Jerusalem.

4. See *Spielberg's Holocaust: Critical Perspectives on* Schindler's List, ed. Yosefa Loshitzky (Bloomington: Indiana University Press, 1997).

5. For other discussions of *Don't Touch My Holocaust,* see Regine-Michal Friedman, "Generation of the Aftermath: The Parodic Mode," *Kolnoa: Studies in Cinema and Television,* Assaph Section D, no. 1 (1998): 71–82, and Moshe Zimmerman, "HaShoah 'VehaAherut,' o Erko HaMusaf shel HaSeret *Al Tigou li BaShoah"* (The Holocaust and "Otherness," or the Surplus Value of the Film *Don't Touch My Holocaust),* in *Fictive Looks: On Israeli Cinema,* ed. Nurith Gertz, Orly Lubin, and Judd Ne'eman, 135–59 (Tel Aviv: Open University of Israel, 1998). Another film about *Arbeit Macht Frei,* titled *Balagan* (1994)—"balagan" is slang for disorder—was made by German filmmaker Andres Weiel. Tlalim claimed that the making of this film was based on dishonest and shameful conduct on the part of ZDF, which promised to support his film but instead sent its own director to make a documentary about *Arbeit Macht Frei.* Tlalim felt both cheated and victimized by the German station, and the title of his film (among other things) refers to this experience. It is as if he warns the Germans to keep their hands off the Holocaust and his own film.

6. *Musslman* is a German term meaning "Muslim," widely used by concentration camp prisoners to refer to inmates who were on the verge of death from starvation, exhaustion, and despair. A person who had reached the *Musslman* stage had little, if any, chance for survival and usually died within weeks. The origin of the term is unclear, but it probably derived from an image of Islam as encouraging fatalism.

7. Tzvi Gilat, "Mesibat HaZva'a" (The Horror Party), *7 Yamim* (*Yediot Ha'aronot* weekend supplement, November 4, 1994, 47). Among the testimonies that were collected by the group during their research for documentary materials was one by a woman who hid for two years in the sewage canals of the Warsaw ghetto where her son was born in the dark. When the city was liberated and she saw the light of the sun, the baby cried because he wanted to return to the dark. Darkness was familiar to him, light was threatening.

8. In Tlalim's film Madi Maayan discusses visual similarities between Arab Acre and the ghetto, in particular the Warsaw ghetto.

9. All the citations from Tlalim are taken from a lecture that he gave to my class, titled "Identity Politics in Israeli Cinema," at the Hebrew University on January 8, 1997.

10. Ibid.

11. Tlalim heard through a friend about the performance in Acre and called Dudi Maayan. Madi Maayan answered the phone, and when Tlalim introduced himself she said: "I just cannot believe it. We had a meeting yesterday and decided that we wanted someone to film us and you were suggested as the director."

12. Another example of "marriage" between Mizrahim and children of survivors is Eli Amir's novel *Ahavat Shaul* (Shaul's Love [Tel Aviv: Am Oved, 1998]), in which the protagonist, Shaul Bar Adon, a pure Sephardi (*Samech Tet* in Hebrew), falls in love with Haya, a daughter of Holocaust survivors, who under the pressure of her Polish parents marries Gershon, a Sabra pilot. As a result, the sterility of Shaul, who never marries and has no children,

assumes a deep symbolic meaning. Gilead Ovadia, a clinical psychotherapist of Oriental Jewish descent, claims that the suffering of the Oriental immigrants was dwarfed compared to the survivors' suffering. Consequently, the Mizrahim suffered from unconscious feelings of guilt toward the survivors with whom they competed for resources during the 1950s, the days of mass immigration from Europe and North Africa. Their attraction to the Right and especially to the figure of Menachem Begin, according to Ovadia, can be explained against this background. Begin symbolized a father figure whose diasporic personality, along with the centrality of the Holocaust in his rhetoric, freed them from their unconscious guilt. At the same time, Begin provided for them a non-Sabra, antiheroic role model with whom they could identify. See Gilead Ovadia, "HaKoah ShebaHulsha" (The Strength in Weakness), *Ha'aretz,* November 3, 1997, 2B.

13. Mengele, she tells Muni, ordered her to leave her little son in the hands of an old woman who was behind her and since then she has not seen him. The survivor's daughter who joins her mother tells her "second-generation story." After giving birth to her boy, she suffered from depression. Her boy was born with a defect in his heart. One day she found out that the boy had disappeared. In fact he was taken for an examination. But the daughter repeated her mother's trauma: the loss of her little boy. After experiencing this trauma she was unable for a long time to take care of her little boy, and her survivor mother had to take care of both her daughter and grandson.

14. On the ideologically laden terms "Israeli Arabs," "Israeli Palestinians," etc., see Dani Rabinowitch, "Oriental Fantasy: How the Palestinians Have Become Israeli Arabs," *Theory and Criticism* 4 (fall 1993): 141–51 (in Hebrew). For a very interesting article that explores the highly complex relationships between the Arabs (including the Palestinians) and the Holocaust, see Azmi Bishara, "HaAravim VehaShoah: Nituah Beayatiyuta shel Ot Hibur" (The Arabs and the Holocaust: An Analysis of the Problematics of Conjunction), *Zmanim* 53 (summer 1995): 54–71.

15. Tlalim, lecture (see note 9).

16. Raz-Krakotzkin, "Exile within Sovereignty," 121–22.

17. Gilat, "Horror Party," 44.

18. Khaled, the representative of the oppressed, used to stand twice a week in front of the model of Treblinka at the Lohamei HaGetaot Museum and cry over the Holocaust, which is not *his* people's holocaust. Three days after experiencing the show, and still unable to digest its disturbing impact, the Israeli journalist Tzvi Gilat called Khaled and asked him what he was crying about. "I always have something to cry about," Khaled said. "And the Holocaust belongs to everybody. Even an Arab who lives here lives under its shadow." In one year, he told Gilat, three of his brothers died as a result of illness. His father died and his people are still suffering. That week, he told Gilat, he caught himself crying over the (Jewish) people who died from a terrorist bomb that exploded on bus number 5 in Tel Aviv. Gilat, "Horror Party," 44.

19. Raz-Krakotzkin, "Exile within Sovereignty," 121–22.

20. Michael Handelzaltz, "Tzofim VeMeshatfim Peula" (Observing as Collaborating), *Ha'aretz* literary supplement, April 19, 1991, B2.

21. Nobody from Sakhnin, Khaled's small village in Galilee, saw the show although it ran for three years. Nobody, also, knew that Khaled performed naked. Khaled does not know what would have happened had they known about it, but he made his choice. The Lohamei HaGetaot Museum founded a new project for the teaching of the Holocaust to the Arab and Druze population. The director of the museum said that at first the Palestinian students tend to compare the situation of the Palestinians in the occupied territories to that of the Jews in the Holocaust. The project is modeled on a similar program for African-American youth organized by the Washington Museum. Recently there has been a growth of interest in the Holocaust in Palestinian circles. Some major Palestinian intellectuals, like Edward Said, Mahmud Darwish, and others, have appealed for the recognition of the Jewish Holocaust and for the withdrawal of analogies made by some Arabs and Palestinians between the Holocaust and the Palestinian "Nakba" (catastrophe), the name adopted by the Palestinians to describe the tragedy of 1948. In return they asked that Israelis recognize the Palestinian "Nakba." In a closed meeting at the Jerusalem Van Leer Institute on November 16, 1998, Said (in response to Adi Ophir's question) appealed for the mutual recognition of the irrecoverable loss of both peoples.

22. For further reading on this anxiety, see Moshe Zuckerman, *Shoah in the Sealed Room: The "Holocaust" in the Israeli Press during the Gulf War* (Tel Aviv: Hotzaat HaMehaber, 1993); and Brenda Danet, Yosefa Loshitzky, and Haya Bechar-Israeli, "Masking the Mask: An Israeli Response to the Threat of Chemical Warfare," *Visual Anthropology* 6, no. 3 (1993): 229–70.

23. Maayan refers here to Yitzhak Rabin.

24. Gilat, "Horror Party," 47.

25. Madi Maayan's pronunciations regarding what she regards as the "arousing" pornographic power of the Holocaust are highly disturbing. Her unsettling confessions were given more salience in the German film *Balagan,* a fact that makes this film even more disturbing and ethically problematic than *Don't Touch My Holocaust.* Similar sets of concerns about the use of pornographic imagery in conjunction with the Holocaust were raised with regard to an exhibition by Ram Katzir (a grandson of survivors) titled "Within the Line," which opened at the Israel Museum on January 21, 1997, and became the focus of controversy and survivors' protests, as well as to the even more scandalous exhibition by Roi Rosen (also a son of survivors), "Live and Die Like Eva Braun," which opened at the same museum in December 1997 and provoked a stormy public debate.

26. The survivors in the audience, Tlalim told my class, felt that the film expressed something very truthful about themselves. One of the students commented: "I find it hard to see my parents who are 'Auschwitz graduates' in this performance." Tlalim responded: "I saw 'Auschwitz graduates' in the performance," thus implying that his film is meaningful and acceptable for survivors.

27. The reactions to my paper and the same film clip at the May 15–18, 1997, Society for Cinema Studies Conference in Ottawa, Canada, were, by contrast, very enthusiastic. Many of the audience were American Jews and some of them second generation, and they thanked me after the session. I raise this point to show that response to the film varies depending on different cultural and generational sensibilities.

28. A substantial portion of my discussion of the film is indebted to Levana Nir, "*Choice and Destiny* as a Cultural Document," seminar paper, School of Education, Tel Aviv University, 1996.

29. Quoted in Nir, "*Choice and Destiny*," citing the film's synopsis.

30. Reibenbach, quoted in Maya Bahir, "HaRa'av shel Aba, HaShtika shel Ima" (Father's Hunger, Mother's Silence), *Yediot Aharonot,* April 19, 1995, 8.

31. Bahir, "Father's Hunger, Mother's Silence," 8–9.

32. "Ma'abarot" were the transitory camps where new immigrants were placed by the government during the late 1940s and early 1950s, years of mass immigration to Israel.

33. The red book was "proof" of membership in the Histadrut (the Israeli labor union), which during the 1950s was controlled by Mapai (the current Labor Party). "Protektzia" is a slang word for the use of personal connections. For further discussion see Brenda Danet, *Pulling Strings: Biculturalism in Israeli Bureaucracy* (Albany: State University of New York Press, 1989).

34. Tzipi Reibenbach, "HaHorim Sheli" (My Parents), *Ha'aretz* Friday supplement, October 25, 1996, 26 (special issue on "Ashkenazi Anxiety").

35. See Wallid Khalidi, "The Palestinian Problem: An Overview," *Journal of Palestinian Studies* 21, no. 1 (1991): 5–16. Encouraged by the assimilation of the term "Intifada" into international public discourse, the Palestinians tried, with the approaching fiftieth anniversary of the State of Israel, to internationalize the term "al Nakba" as well.

36. Quoted in Nir, "*Choice and Destiny.*"

37. Ibid.

38. Ibid.

39. Ibid.

40. In Ben Dor's film only Jacko comes close to this type of survivor although he is of Oriental/Greek origin. The Jews of Corfu in Lanzmann's *Shoah* also come close to this type. As Margaret Olin explains, "It was the Jews of Corfu who touched him [Lanzmann] most profoundly. They were his Other." Margaret Olin, "Lanzmann's *Shoah* and the Topography of the Holocaust Film," *Representations*, No. 57 (winter 1997): 6.

41. Quoted in Nir, "*Choice and Destiny.*"

42. Victor Emil Frankl, *Man's Search for Meaning: An Introduction to Logotherapy* (Boston: Beacon Press, 1968).

43. Quoted in Nir, "*Choice and Destiny.*"

44. This was the "81st blow," as the survivor Michael Gilad has termed it. The eighty-first blow refers to the anguish of the survivor Michael Gilad, who as a child in the Holocaust was punished with eighty lashes, but when he told his story to the Israelis they did not believe him. This was his eighty-first blow. His testimony, given during the Eichmann trial, affected the Israeli author Haim Gouri, who with Jacquo Erlich and David Bergman made a film trilogy about the Holocaust. The first film was called *The Eighty-First Blow* (1974).

45. Quoted in Nir, "*Choice and Destiny.*"

46. Ibid.

47. Frankl, *Man's Search for Meaning.*

48. Quoted in Nir, *"Choice and Destiny."*

49. Lanzmann often called his witnesses the "characters" of the film. Moreover, he edited their testimonies very carefully and staged certain scenes in search of a particular "reenacting" of his original interviewees.

50. Reibenbach made another film, *Three Sisters* (1998), on "the people who are not able to tell their story, their trauma." It is a film, Reibenbach told me on October 14, 1997, "on people whom the psychotherapist that I consulted calls 'problematic.'" The film focuses on Fruma, Reibenbach's mother, and her two sisters, Esther and Karola, who are also Holocaust survivors. Originally Reibenbach intended to begin the film the day after *Choice and Destiny* ends. At the end of *Choice and Destiny* the mother tells her daughter "come tomorrow and I'll tell you." Yet, the mother cannot talk the day after her emotional outburst. Instead she begins to write down her memories. Following the daily life of the three sisters, who in their old age devote most of their time to caring for their sick husbands, Reibenbach's new film focuses on the inability of the traumatized survivors to break the silence even on the threshold of death.

51. For a further discussion of the place of the Holocaust in American culture, see James Young, *The Texture of Memory: Holocaust Memorials and Meaning* (New Haven: Yale University Press, 1993). See also Peter Novick, "Holocaust Memory in America," in *The Art of Memory: Holocaust Memorials in History*, ed. James Young, 159–65 (New York: Prestel, 1994); and Jeffrey Shandler, "Schindler's Discourse: America Discusses the Holocaust and Its Mediation, from NBC's Miniseries to Spielberg's Film," in Loshitzky, *Spielberg's Holocaust.*

52. Jack Kugelmass, "Why We Go to Poland: Holocaust Tourism as Secular Ritual," in Young, *Holocaust Memorials*, 175–184.

53. In the political arena this process is most evident in the mobilization of the Holocaust by the Shas (Sephardi-religious) Party, particularly during the trial of its leader Aryeh Derei, which was compared in one of the party's propaganda videos to the Eichmann trial.

54. Finkielkraut, *Imaginary Jew*, 24. Zygmunt Bauman describes Finkielkraut's book as "a bitter book, in which the despair born of the difficulty in spelling out the meaning of Jewish identity after the Holocaust mixes and melts with the frustration left by the dissipation of French intellectual identity after the May 1968 debacle and the abrupt end to the revolutionary-emancipatory-missionary dreams." Zygmunt Bauman, review of *The Imaginary Jew*, by Alain Finkielkraut, *Journal of Holocaust Education* 4, no. 2 (winter 1995): 229.

55. Cooper, "'Second Generation' Syndrome," 133.

56. Ibid., 145.

57. Ibid.

58. Ibid.

59. Ibid.

60. Ibid., 132.

61. Ibid.

62. Rachel Feldhay Brenner, "The Angels of History and the Post-Holocaust Quest for Redemption in Israeli Fiction," presented at the Twelfth World Congress of Jewish Studies, July 29–August 5, 1997, Jerusalem.

63. Laor, "On Relativism," 6E.

64. Mira Hovav, letter to *Ha'aretz*, November 1, 1996, 4.

65. Theodor W. Adorno, "Refuge for the Homeless," *Minima Moralia: Reflections from Damaged Life*, trans. E. F. N. Jephcott (1951; reprint, London: Verso, 1978), cited in *New Formations*, no. 17 (summer 1992): 107–8 (special issue titled "The Question of 'Home'").

66. Aviva Lori, "Ma Omeret HaHotenet KshehaSefer Ne'eleam?" (What Does the Mother-in-Law Say When the Book Disappears?), *Ha'aretz*, November 2, 1994, 3B. For further discussion of this phenomenon, see Kugelmass, "Why We Go to Poland," 175–84; and Segev, *Seventh Million*.

67. This quote is from a text illustrating a photo in which two young Israelis are seen waving the flag of Israel in "Never Say Never," an exhibition of photographs by David Katz at the Beth Shalom Holocaust Memorial Centre, Notts, U.K., April 1996.

68. For a further anthropology-oriented discussion of Israeli youth visits to the camps in Poland, see Jackie Feldman, "In the Footsteps of the Israeli Holocaust Survivor: Israeli Youth Pilgrimages to Poland, Shoah Memory, and National Identity," in *Building History: Art, Memory, and Myth,* ed. Peter Daly (New York: Peter Lang, Inc., forthcoming).

69. Perhaps the most notorious abuse of the Holocaust in the hate and incitement campaign mobilized by the Right against the peace camp was the use of a poster of Yitzhak Rabin wearing an SS uniform. The poster was burnt by a mob in a demonstration in Zion Square in Jerusalem. Binyamin Netanyahu, present at the demonstration, to this day insists that he never saw the poster in this violent context.

70. Doron Rosenblum, "Kama Reflexim Yeshanim" (Some Old Reflexes), *Ha'aretz* weekend supplement, October 28, 1994, 12.

71. Omer Bartov, "Kitsch and Sadism in Ka-Tzetnik's Other Planet: Israeli Youth Imagine the Holocaust," *Jewish Social Studies* 3, no. 2 (winter 1997): 42–76.

72. Ne'eman Arad, "Rereading an Unsettling Past."

73. This example was given by Ne'eman Arad. At the center of the 1998 Holocaust Remembrance Day ceremony that took place at Ankori High School in Tel Aviv were "sick" jokes such as "What is the difference between a Jew and a pizza?" The controversial ceremony also included standup comedy routines. See Yehuda Golan and Eli Bohadna, "HaTekes BeTichon Ankori: Bedihot al HaGhetto VehaNispim BaShoah" (The Ceremony at Ankori High School: Jokes about the Ghetto and the Victims of the Holocaust), *Yediot Aharonot*, April 24, 1998, 3.

74. This example was given by Ne'eman Arad in "Rereading an Unsettling Past."

75. Ibid.

76. For a further discussion of this discovery see Mordechai Alon, "Humor Taei Gazim" (Gas Chamber Humor), *Shiv'a Yamim* (weekend supplement of *Yediot Aharonot*), June 20, 1997, 38–45.

77. Hirsch, "Past Lives," 681–82.

Chapter Four

1. The film leaves it open whether Penina and Ruth are clinically retarded, autistic, or "crazy." "Retarded" in Hebrew is *mefager*. The same word is also used in Hebrew in reference to "undeveloped," or "primitive" ethnic groups. It was common in Israel until the emergence of Mizrahi consciousness to describe Oriental Jews as "mefagrim" (retarded). By questioning, through the characters of Penina and Ruth, the "scientific" definitions of mental retardation and normalcy adopted by the Ashkenazi establishment, Azulay Hasfari demonstrates their oppressive power with regard to ethnic minorities and underprivileged groups. In fact, she implies that what is conceived as primitive by the Ashkenazi establishment, which tends to see itself as the representative of modernity and progress, is indeed a different cultural practice that is no less valid than the Western. In the film Shlomo tells his fiancée Denise: "Do you know what the Moroccan word for psychology is? It is *shchur*"—thus suggesting that traditional Moroccan Jewish practices of healing are no less valuable than those developed by Western modernity. The title of the film itself challenges the ideology embedded in the dichotomy *shchur* versus modernity, or tradition versus progress.

2. A precedent, however, was the short experimental film *Kurdania* (1984) by Dina Tzvi-Riklis. Yet, in the absence of suitable channels of distribution for short films the film, unlike *Shchur*, did not enjoy mass exposure. For further discussion of *Kurdania*, see Orly Lubin, "Min Ha'shulayim el Ha'merkaz" (From Margins to the Center), *Zmanim* 10, no. 39–40 (winter 1991): 140–149.

3. The name *bourekas* derives from a popular Sephardi pastry sold commercially as fast food. For a further discussion of the *bourekas* film genre in Israeli cinema, see Ella Shohat, *Israeli Cinema: East/West and the Politics of Representation* (Austin: University of Texas Press, 1989), in particular chap. 3.

4. For a further discussion see Shohat, *Israeli Cinema*; Ammiel Alcalay, *After Jews and Arabs: Remaking Levantine Culture* (Minneapolis: University of Minnesota Press, 1993); and Yosefa Loshitzky, "The Bride of the Dead: Phallocentrism and War in Kaniuk and Gutman's *Himmo, King of Jerusalem*," *Literature/Film Quarterly* 21, no. 3 (1993): 218–29.

5. Uri Kleine, "Hiyucho HaMistori shel HaTzofe" (The Mysterious Smile of the Spectator), *Ha'aretz* Friday supplement, December 16, 1995, 71.

6. Laura Mulvey, *Visual and Other Pleasures* (Bloomington: Indiana University Press, 1989), 39.

7. *Ha'aretz* Friday supplement (special debate on *Shchur*), December 16, 1995, 60–71.

8. Dov Alfon, "*Shchur*: HaSchita HaGdola" (*Shchur*: The Big Butchery), *Ha'aretz* weekend supplement, 60.

9. Hanna Azulay Hasfari, "Bati Benechem Reeva VeTzmuka" (I Entered Your Midsts Hungry and Shriveled), *Ha'aretz* weekend supplement, March 3, 1995, 32.

10. Ibid.

11. Walter Zenner, "Ethnic Factors in Israeli Life," in *Books on Israel*, vol. 1. ed. Ian Lustick, 48 (Albany: State University of New York Press, 1988).

12. Ammiel Alcalay, "The Keys to the Garden: An Introduction," *Literary Review* 37, no. 2 (winter 1994): 154 (special issue, "The Key to the Garden: Israeli Writing in the Middle East").

13. Yossi Yonah, "Cultural Pluralism and Israeli Society," presented at "Film/Politics/Ideology," a symposium of the Smart Communications Institute, Hebrew University of Jerusalem, April 8, 1992; and Yossi Yonah, "A Visiting Card to the Israeli Collective," presented at a conference titled "Processes of Construction of Collective Identities in Israel and Collective Israeli Identity," Jerusalem Van Leer Institute, November 30, 1994.

14. For an interesting discussion of the notion of the "negation of exile," see Amnon Raz-Krakotzkin, "Galut Betoch Ribonut: LeBikoret Shlilat HaGalut BaTarbut HaYisraelit" (Exile within Sovereignty: Toward a Critique of the "Negation of Exile" in Israeli Culture), *Teoria VeBikoret* (*Theory and Criticism*) 4 (fall 1993): 23–57 and Part 2 in *Theory and Criticism* 5 (fall 1994): 113–32. See also Daniel Boyarin and Jonathan Boyarin, "Ein Moledet LeYisrael: Al HaMakom Shel HaYehudim" (The People of Israel Have No Motherland), *Teoria VeBikoret* (*Theory and Criticism*) 5 (fall 1994): 79–103; and Yoav Peled, "Galut Delux: Al HaRehabilitazia shel HaGalut Etzel Boyarin VeRaz-Krakotzkin" (Luxurious Diaspora: On the Rehabilitation of the Concept of Diaspora in Boyarin and Raz-Krakotzkin), *Teoria VeBikoret* (*Theory and Criticism*) 5 (fall 1994): 133–40.

15. Azulay Hasfari, quoted in Orna Kadosh, "HaZehut HaKfula shel Azulai-Hasfari" (The Double Identity of Azulay Hasfari), *Ma'ariv Sof Shavua,* February 3, 1995, 51.

16. See Issachar Ben-Ami, *Yahadut Morocco: Prakim BeHeker Tarbutam* (*Moroccan Jewry: Some Issues in Their Culture* [Jerusalem: Reuven Mass, 1975]); Eyal Ben-Ari and Yoram Bilu, "Saints' Sanctuaries in Israel Development Towns: On a Mechanism of Urban Transformation," *Urban Anthropology* 16, no. 2 (1987): 243–72; Yoram Bilu and Galit Hasan-Rokem, "Cinderella and the Saint: The Life Story of a Jewish Moroccan Female Healer in Israel," in *The Psychoanalytic Study of Society,* vol. 14., ed. L. Bryce Boyer and Simon A. Grolnick, 227–60 (Hillsdale, N.J.: Analytic Press, 1989); and Yoram Bilu and Eyal Ben-Ari, "The Making of Modern Saints: Manufactured Charisma and the Abu-Hatseiras of Israel," *American Ethnologist* 19, no. 4 (1992): 672–87. In recent years this ethnic revival has been transformed into a significant political power with the emergence of Shas, the highly popular Sephardi-religious party whose slogan is "Lehahzir atara leyoshna" (To revive tradition). The rise of Shas to power further fed the popularity of practical Cabalism, black magic, and other forms of *shchur* among Israeli Orientals. These phenomena have become a locus of public controversy because they have infiltrated into Israel's political life, challenging the legitimacy of the state's legal and democratic institutions, such as the Supreme Court.

17. See Erik Cohen, "Development Towns: The Social Dynamics of 'Planted' Urban Communities in Israel," in *Integration and Development in Israel,* ed. S. N. Eisenstadt et al., 587–617 (Jerusalem: Israel Universities Press, 1970); and Eli Avraham, *HaTikshoret BeYisrael—Merkaz Veperipheria: Sikuran shel Ayarot HaPituah* (The Media in Israel—Center and Periphery: Coverage of the Development Towns [Tel Aviv: Breirot Publishers, 1993]).

18. Ben-Ari and Bilu, "Saints' Sanctuaries," 252.

19. Ibid., 265.

20. Amnon Lourd, "Mizraha Mikan" (East from Here), *Iton Tel Aviv*, February 10, 1995, 74.

21. Agha Shahid Ali, *"The Satanic Verses*: A Secular Muslim's Response," *Yale Journal of Criticism* 4, no. 1 (1990): 295–300.

22. Edward Said, *Culture and Imperialism* (New York: Alfred A. Knopf, 1993), 306.

23. Akeel Bilgrami, "Rushdie, Islam, and Postcolonial Defensiveness," *Yale Journal of Criticism* 4, no. 1 (1990): 301–11.

24. Azulay Hasfari, quoted in Kadosh, "Double Identity," 51.

25. Shohat, *Israeli Cinema*, 126.

26. Alfon, *"Shchur:* The Big Butchery," 60.

27. Umberto Eco, "Postmodernism, Irony, the Enjoyable," *Postscript to* The Name of the Rose (New York: Harcourt Brace Jovanovich, Inc., 1984), 67.

28. As there are no Moroccan actresses in Israel old enough to play the role of the mother, Azulay Hasfari had to choose an Ashkenazi actress.

29. I am indebted to Andre Levy for bringing this point to my attention.

30. The Black Panthers, an Oriental protest movement that emerged in the 1970s, was important in the consolidation of an Israeli Oriental identity.

31. The term "imperfect cinema" (*cine imperfecto*) was coined by Cuban filmmaker Julio Garcia Espinosa in his 1969 essay, "For an Imperfect Cinema." For a further discussion locating the term in a postmodern perspective, see Fredric Jameson, *Signatures of the Visible* (New York: Routledge, 1990).

32. For a further discussion see Yosefa Loshitzky, "More than Style: Godard's Modernism versus Bertolucci's Postmodernism," *Criticism* 34, no. 1 (winter 1992): 119–142; and *The Radical Faces of Godard and Bertolucci* (Detroit: Wayne State University Press, 1995).

33. See Yosefa Loshitzky, "The Tourist/Traveler Gaze: Bertolucci and Bowles' *The Sheltering Sky,*" *East/West Film Journal* 7, no. 2 (July 1994): 110–32.

34. Esther Schely-Newman, private communication.

35. Sammy Smooha, "HaShever HaGadol shel HaMizrahim" (The Big Rift of the Mizrahim), *Ha'aretz* Friday supplement, December 16, 1995, 62.

36. I am indebted to Haim Bresheeth for drawing my attention to this point. Since the release of the film, the word *shchur* has infiltrated Israeli political culture. In most cases it has been used to describe the exploitation of popular Cabalists for political means. It should also be pointed out that Azulay Hasfari herself became a political activist as a result of the consciousness-raising process she underwent through the making of *Shchur.* Along with a group of Oriental intellectuals, she founded *Kedem* (in Hebrew, Ha'Keshet Ha'Democratit Ha'Mizrahit; in English, Mizrahi Rainbow Coalition), devoted to struggle over sociopolitical issues pertaining to the Mizrahim.

37. Azulay Hasfari, "I Entered your Midsts," 32.

38. Yoram Bilu, personal communication.

39. For a further discussion of the representation of Oriental Jews in *Sallah Shabbati,* see Shohat, *Israeli Cinema*, 138–54.

40. Smooha, "Big Rift of the Mizrahim," 62.

41. Dalia Karpel, "Sodo shel HaMenahel" (The Principal's Secret), *Ha'aretz* Friday supplement, December 16, 1995, 70.

42. For an elaboration of the notion of diasporic/exilic, transnational film, see Laura Marks, "A Deluzian Politics of Hybrid Cinema," *Screen* 35, no. 3 (fall 1994): 244–64; and Hamid Naficy, "Phobic Spaces and Liminal Panics: Independent Transnational Film Genre," *East-West Film Journal* 18, no. 2 (July 1994): 1–30.

43. Naficy, "Phobic Spaces and Liminal Panics," 1.

44. Ibid., 3.

45. Yoram Bilu, "The Moroccan Demon in Israel: The Case of 'Evil Spirit Disease,'" *Ethos* 8 (1980): 35.

46. Michael Fischer, "Ethnicity and the Post-Modern Arts of Memory," in *Writing Culture: The Poetics and Politics of Ethnography*, ed. James Clifford and George E. Marcus, 195 (Berkeley: University of California Press, 1986).

47. Trinh T. Minh-ha, "Other than Myself/My Other Self," in *Travellers' Tales: Narratives of Home and Displacement,* ed. George Robertson, Melinda Mash, Lisa Tickner, Jon Bird, Barry Curtis and Tim Putnam, 10 (London and New York: Routledge, 1994).

48. Marks, "Deluzian Politics of Hybrid Cinema," 245.

49. Nancy Miller, "Representing Others: Gender and the Subject of Autobiography," *Differences* 6, no. 1 (1994): 49.

50. Alice Jardine, *Genesis: Configurations of Woman and Modernity* (Ithaca: Cornell University Press, 1985).

51. Kadosh, "Double Identity," 51.

52. For a further discussion see R. Egerman and O. Lofgren, "Romancing the Road: Road Movies and Images of Mobility," *Theory, Culture, and Society* 12, no. 1 (February 1995): 53–79.

53. Minh-ha, "Other than Myself," 10.

Chapter Five

1. Amos Elon, *The Israelis* (New York: Holt, Rinehart and Winston, 1971), 272.

2. Ibid., 271.

3. Judith Williamson, "Woman Is an Island: Femininity and Colonization," in *Studies in Entertainment: Critical Approaches to Mass Culture*, ed. Tania Modleski, 113 (Bloomington: Indiana University Press, 1986).

4. Robert Young, *White Mythologies: Writing History and the West* (London: Routledge, 1990), 128.

5. After twenty years of Israeli occupation resulting from the June 1967 war, the Intifada—the Palestinian popular uprising in the occupied territories—broke out.

6. For a discussion of the genres of the heroic-nationalist films, the *bourekas,* and personal cinema in Israeli cinema, see Ella Shohat, *Israeli Cinema: East/West and the Politics of Representation* (Austin: University of Texas Press, 1989).

7. Although Oz has been many times the target of vicious attacks by the settlers and the Right for publicly criticizing right-wing extremists, he nevertheless has not enjoyed the support of the so-called extremist, anti-Zionist Left either. See, for example, Haim Bresheeth, "Self and Other in Zionism: Palestine and Israel in Recent Hebrew Literature," *Palestine: Profile of an Occupation* (London: Zed Books Ltd., 1989), 120–52; and Yitzhak Laor, "Hayey Hamin shel Kohot Habitahon: Al Gufaniyuto shel HaYisraeli HaYafe VehaBithoni etzel Amos Oz" (The Sex Life of the Security Services: On the Carnal Body of the Beautiful and Security-Conscious Israeli in Amos Oz's Work), *Anu Kotvim Otach Moledet (Narratives with No Natives: Essays on Israeli Literature* [Tel Aviv: HaKibbutz Hamehuad, 1995]), 76–104. For a more recent interview given by Oz to the journalist Ari Shavit, which deals with Oz's reaction to these attacks, see Ari Shavit, "Lo Oto Amos Oz" (Not the Same Amos Oz), *Ha'aretz* weekend supplement, December 11, 1998, 18–26.

8. Within the context of Israeli literature *My Michael* continues the revolution begun in the early 1960s, a revolution that established a tradition of "meta-Zionist narrative" characterized by a sense of disillusionment with the State of Israel and an attempt to challenge Zionist ideology. One of the major consequences of the institutionalization of the "meta-Zionist narrative" in Hebrew literature has been a demythification of the figure of the Hebrew hero. The Israeli writers of the 1960s and 1970s and even after belong to what is often called in Hebrew Dor Hamedinah, the Generation of Statehood. Since the 1960s, the heroes of Hebrew literature have ceased to be mythic Sabras. Furthermore, the Sabra's others—the Sephardi and the Arab—have begun to occupy focal positions on the stage of Hebrew literature. I am borrowing the term "meta-Zionist narrative" (*alilat-al-Tzionit* in Hebrew) from Gershon Shaked, who used it in a lecture titled "Literary and Social Processes in Hebrew Literature" delivered in the colloquium of the Department of Comparative Literature at the Hebrew University on March 19, 1991. For a broad in-depth discussion of Israeli literature from the 1950s to the 1980s, see Nurit Gertz, *Amos Oz: A Monograph* (Tel Aviv: Sifriat Poalim, 1980), 9–43. The book combines ideological, political, sociocultural, and stylistic analyses of Oz's writing.

9. The name Holon is rich in connotations in Hebrew. It comes from the Hebrew word *hol* (sand) as Holon is built on sand dunes. *Hol* in Hebrew also means *hulin* (the opposite of holy), and by implication it means "prosaic," noninspiring, ordinary. Oz has many literary as well as public and publicist pronouncements regarding what he calls *Arey HaShfela* (the cities of the plains). These are new cities in the area of Tel Aviv, built on sand dunes. In an essay on Jerusalem titled "Foreign City," written in 1967 (the year when *My Michael* was written), Oz compares Jerusalem to what he calls "the white and flat commerce cities: Tel Aviv, Holon, Herzelia, Netanya." He says that "Jerusalem was different. It was the negation of the white box-like buildings [typical of the *Shfela* cities]." Amos Oz, "Foreign City," *Under This Blazing Light* (Tel Aviv: Sifriat Poalim, 1979), 209 (translation mine). This essay could be read as Oz's "decoding" of *My Michael.* The binary opposition between Jerusalem and Tel Aviv, discussed by Oz in this short essay, but also in his other works, is transformed into the binary opposition of Michael (Holon) versus Hannah (Jerusalem). The main component of this binarism

is Tel Aviv's flatness versus the depth of Jerusalem. This topographical feature (Tel Aviv is built on a plain whereas Jerusalem is a hilly town) is carried over, especially in Hebrew literature, beyond sheer geography. For an expression of a more recent change in Oz's attitude toward Jerusalem and Tel Aviv, see Shavit, "Not the Same Amos Oz." For a further elaboration on the emergence of Tel Aviv as Jerusalem's opposite, see Nurit Govrin, "Jerusalem and Tel Aviv as Metaphors in Hebrew Literature," *Modern Hebrew Literature*, no. 2 (spring 1989): 23–27. This article is part of a special issue commemorating the eightieth anniversary of Tel Aviv, the first Hebrew city. As Govrin and others point out, contrasting Tel Aviv with Jerusalem is not a new *topos* in Hebrew literature. See also Hana Wirth-Nesher's discussion of Jerusalem in Oz's *My Michael* in *City Codes: Reading the Modern Urban Novel* (Cambridge, Mass.: Cambridge University Press, 1996), 48–64. For another discussion of the binarism regarding Tel Aviv and Jerusalem in Yoram Kaniuk's novel *Himmo, King of Jerusalem* (1966), see Yosefa Loshitzky, "The Bride of the Dead: Phallocentrism and War in Kaniuk and Gutman's *Himmo, King of Jerusalem*," *Literature/Film Quarterly* 21, no. 3 (1993): 219–29.

10. Amos Elon, *Jerusalem: City of Mirrors* (*Yerushalyim: Shigaon LaDavar* [Jerusalem: Domino, 1991]), 76 (translation mine).

11. Fassbinder's melodramas of the 1970s were much in vogue in Israel at the time of the making of *My Michael,* as they were also in the art cinemas of Europe's and America's big cities.

12. Edward Said, *Orientalism* (New York: Random House, 1978), 167, 190. See also Ali Behdad, "The Discursive Formation of Orientalism: The Threshold of (Pseudo) Scientificity," *Peuples mediterraneens* 50 (January–March 1990): 163–69.

13. For a very interesting discussion of this issue and related topics, see James Roy MacBean, "Between Kitsch and Fascism: Notes on Fassbinder, Pasolini, (Homo)sexual Politics, the Exotic, the Erotic, and Other Consuming Passions," *Cineaste* 13, no. 4 (1984): 12–19.

14. MacBean, "Between Kitsch and Fascism," 15.

15. For a further analysis of *The Sheltering Sky,* see Yosefa Loshitzky, "The Tourist/Traveler Gaze: Bertolucci and Bowles' *The Sheltering Sky*," *East-West Film Journal* 7, no. 2 (July 1993): 111–37.

16. Millicent Dillon, "The Marriage Melody," in *The Sheltering Sky: A Film by Bernardo Bertolucci Based on the Novel by Paul Bowles,* devised, edited, and produced by Livio Negri, coeditor Fabien S. Gerard, 47 (London: Scribners, 1990).

17. Paul Bowles, *The Sheltering Sky* (1949; reprint, New York: The Ecco Press, 1978), 272–73.

18. Oz's short story "Nomad and Viper" in his collection of stories titled *Where the Jackals Howl* (1963) is an even more explicit example of Orientalist rape narrative. It is a story of a young kibbutz woman, Geula, who has a sexually ambiguous encounter with a Bedouin, is bitten by a snake, and dies.

19. Amos Oz, *My Michael,* (London: Chatto and Windus, 1972), 18.

20. See, for example, the description on 47.

21. Rana Kabbani, *Europe's Myths of the Orient* (London: Pandora Press, 1986), 63.

22. Abdul R. JanMohamed, "The Economy of Manichean Allegory: The Function of Racial Difference in Colonialist Literature," *Critical Inquiry* 12, no. 1 (fall 1985): 68.

23. Said, *Orientalism*, 167, 188, 190.

24. Ibid., 190.

25. Yigal Zalmona, "The Tower of David Days: The Birth of Controversy in Israeli Art in the Twenties," *The Tower of David Days: First Cultural Strife in Israel Art* (Jerusalem: Tower of David Museum of the History of Jerusalem, 1991), 69. See also Ehud Ben-Ezer, ed., *Bmoledet HaGaguim HaMenugadim: HaAravi BaSifrut HaIvrit* (*In the Homeland of Competing Longings: The Arab in Hebrew Literature* [Tel Aviv: Zmora, Bitan, 1992]).

26. Zalmona, "Tower of David Days," 69.

27. Ibid.

28. Tragically and ironically Yosef Haim Brenner was murdered by Arabs in 1921. According to Ammiel Alcalay, Brenner is an early instance of the tendency in Hebrew literature to represent Arabs and non-European Jews as others. This tendency, Alcalay observes, "can be seen, as well, in the work of a contemporary writer such as Amos Oz." Ammiel Alcalay, *After Jews and Arabs: Remaking Levantine Culture* (Minneapolis: University of Minnesota Press, 1993), 229.

29. Zalmona, "Tower of David Days," 69.

30. Ibid.

31. Ibid., 68.

32. Elon, *The Israelis*, 273.

33. Robert Alter, "Fiction in a State of Siege," *Defenses of the Imagination: Jewish Writers and Modern Historical Crisis* (Philadelphia: The Jewish Publication Society of America, 1977), 221.

34. Shohat observes that "the psychoanalytical postulation of id and superego parallels, to some extent, the primitive/civilized dichotomy permeating colonial discourse." Ella Shohat, "Imagining Terra Incognita: The Disciplinary Gaze of Empire," *Public Culture* 3, no. 2 (spring 1991): 66.

35. Alter, "State of Siege," 224.

36. JanMohamed, "Economy of Manichean Allegory," 72.

37. See Frantz Fanon, *Black Skin, White Masks*, trans. Charles Lam Markmann (London: Pluto Press, 1986).

38. See Albert Memi, *L'Homme Dominc* (Paris. Gallimard, 1968).

39. Edward Said, "Orientalism Reconsidered," in *Literature, Politics, and Theory: Papers from the Essex Conference, 1976–84*, ed. Francis Barker, Peter Hulme, Margaret Iversun, and Diana Loxley, 224 (London: Methuen, 1986).

40. Homi Bhabha, "The Other Question: Difference, Discrimination and the Discourse of Colonialism," in *Literature, Politics, and Theory*, 166–67.

41. Ibid., 166.

42. Ibid., 165.

43. From the mid-1980s up to the present one can detect the emergence of films (inter alia, *Heat and Dust, The Gods Must Be Crazy, A Passage to India, Out of Africa*) that portray imperialism with nostalgia. See Renato Rosaldo, "Imperialist Nostalgia," *Culture and Truth: The Remaking of Social Analysis* (Boston: Beacon Press, 1989), 68–87. Edward Said points out: "In 1984, well before *The Satanic Verses* appeared, Salman Rushdie diagnosed the spate of films and articles about the British Raj, including the television series *The Jewel in the Crown* and David Lean's film of *A Passage to India*. Rushdie noted that the nostalgia pressed into service by these affectionate recollections of British rule in India coincided with the Falklands War, and that 'the rise of Raj revisionism, exemplified by the huge success of these fictions, is the artistic counterpart to the rise of conservative ideologies in modern Britain.'" Edward Said, "Two Visions in *Heart of Darkness*," *Culture and Imperialism,* 21. The 1990s witnessed a new wave of French films (*L'Amant, Indochine,* and *La Guerre Sans Nom*) on the French colonial experience in Indochina and Algeria. Much like *The Sheltering Sky*, these films' plots involve doomed love affairs used to allegorize, nostalgically, the French colonial experience.

44. Emily C. Bartels, "Imperialist Beginnings: Richard Hakluyt and the Construction of Africa," *Criticism* 34, no. 4 (fall 1992): 519. Edward Said claims that the form of Conrad's narrative in *Heart of Darkness* has "made it possible to derive two possible arguments, two visions, in the post-colonial world." According to the first argument, "the colonial world was in some ways ontologically speaking lost to begin with, irredeemable, irrecusably inferior." The second argument is less imperialistically assertive and represents the colonial world as "local to a time and a place, neither unconditionally true nor unqualifiedly certain." Said, "Two Visions," 25.

45. Bartels, "Imperialist Beginnings," 519.

46. JanMohamed, "Economy of Manichean Allegory," 63.

47. Vijay Mishra and Bob Hodge, "What is Post(-)colonialism?" *Textual Practice* 5, no. 3 (winter 1991): 404.

48. Andreas Huyssen, "Mass Culture as Woman: Modernism's Other," in *Studies in Entertainment: Critical Approaches to Mass Culture*, ed. Tania Modleski, 189 (Bloomington: Indiana University Press, 1986). Virginia Woolf writes: "Have you any notion of how many books are written about women in the course of one year? Have you any notion of how many are written by men? Are you aware that you are, perhaps, the most discussed animal in the universe? . . . Women do not write books about men. . . . Why are women . . . so much more interesting to men than men are to women?" Virginia Woolf, *A Room of One's Own* (1929; reprint, London: Grafton, 1977), 31–32. And she adds: "A very queer, composite being thus emerges. Imaginatively she is of the highest importance; practically she is completely insignificant. She pervades poetry from cover to cover, she is all but absent from history." Ibid., 49.

49. Jean-Paul Sartre, "Flaubert and Madame Bovary: Outline of a New Method," in *Madame Bovary, Gustav Flaubert: Backgrounds and Sources Essays in Criticism*, Norton Critical Edition, ed. Paul De Man, 302 (New York: W. W. Norton & Company, 1965).

50. Huyssen, "Mass Culture as Woman," 189.

51. Oz, *My Michael*, 26.

52. Ibid., 222.

53. On the autobiographical level one cannot resist the temptation to analyze Oz's projection of his own mother, who committed suicide in 1952, "deserting" him when he was only twelve years old. Oz keeps silent about this traumatic event, but one may argue that Hannah Gonen is an amalgam of his mother and himself. In this respect, her imaginary femininity, loaded as it is with self-hate, is "justified." She is both man and woman, mother and deserted son, and, as such, she brings full circle the built-in ambivalence of the real son toward his real/imaginary m/other. Two years after his mother's suicide, Oz joined Kibbutz Hulda, where he attended classes in socialism that were in sharp contrast to the nationalist right-wing (revisionist) education that he absorbed at home during his childhood in Jerusalem. For further biographical information that supports my earlier interpretation, see Shavit, "Not the Same Amos Oz."

54. JanMohamed, "Economy of Manichean Allegory," 75.

55. Said, *Orientalism*, 170.

56. Robert Briatte, "The Territories of the Sky," in *The Sheltering Sky: A Film . . .* , 35.

57. Quoted from publicity release by Palace Pictures for Bertolucci's *Sheltering Sky*, 32.

58. It should be pointed out, however, that in the sphere of public life Oz expresses very progressive ideas in regard to women. Both Oz and Yehoshua have declared, publicly, that the prime minister of Israel should be a woman. As a mother, they claimed, she would be more in tune to the situation of the son/soldier. Her ability to demonstrate affection would cause her to prefer a policy of peace to one of brute force. This "idealist" essentialist view of women is obviously polemical in itself and certainly demands a thorough examination.

59. "Following the Dreams: A Conversation with the Poet Dalia Rabikovitch on Amos Oz's novel *My Michael*," *Mahashavot* 2 (August 1974): 69 (special issue on art and cinema; translation mine). In this interview Rabikovitch celebrated the novel stressing that "this is the first time that somebody recognizes the right of a woman to be completely cut off from reality" (70, translation mine). Rabikovitch said, though I could not find supporting evidence for her statement, that Amos Oz even used the term "glass jar" to express the idea of Hannah's clinical detachment from reality. This term recalls the title of the American poet Sylvia Plath's novel *The Bell Jar*. (Plath, like Oz's mother, committed suicide.) Some critics in Israel like to compare Rabikovitch to Plath. Also, it should be pointed out that Oz's mother, Fania, wrote poetry. It is also interesting to note that together with Oz, Rabikovitch was awarded the 1998 Israel Prize for Literature.

60. Wolman said this in a television program on "Women in Israeli Film and Literature," produced by the Open University, Tel Aviv. The panelists were Wolman and Yosefa Loshitzky, interviewed by host Miri Talmon.

61. In still another scene, the pregnant Hannah is seen sitting on an armchair observing her husband scrubbing the floor. This is a very unusual scene in the "real" life of many Israelis. Mopping the floors—or as it is called in Israeli slang, "sponja"—is typically considered by Israeli men to be a very dirty job suitable to women and Arabs only. One can safely assume that it was viewed as an even less respectable form of housework for men during the fifties.

62. Hannah's short haircut in this scene is definitely not typical of the average Israeli woman in the fifties. However, it recalls Jean Seberg's hairstyle in Godard's *Breathless*, which introduced a new type of feminine beauty to the cinema. Israeli personal cinema was Francophile, heavily influenced by the French New Wave. Some of the prominent directors even lived in Paris during the fifties. As short hair has psychoanalytic connotations of self-castration, it strengthens the argument for viewing Hannah as the personification of Jerusalem. This idea is propagated by Gila Ramras-Rauch in *The Arab in Israeli Literature* (Bloomington: Indiana University Press, 1989), 157–58. Ramras-Rauch describes Jerusalem in the novel as a "wounded woman." To my mind the wounded woman is a "castrated woman." Burton Pike, in his book *The Image of the City in Modern Literature* (Princeton: Princeton University Press, 1981), 127–28, points out that the cities in *Invisible Cities* by the contemporary Italian writer Italo Calvino all bear female names, and that they all seem to be the same city, perhaps Marco Polo's native Venice. Marco Polo, we should bear in mind, revealed China to the West and furnished it with a stock of dreams, fantasies, and utopias of otherness. The typing of cities as female, Pike observes, "recalls on one hand Mumford's depiction of early settlements as containers, symbolizing the female principle, and on the other hand Balzac's Paris and Angouleme, cities also under the sign and domination of woman. (Women in Balzac's cities are the divinities of place, the sacred goddesses whom his upward-striving hunter-heroes must both propitiate and conquer in order to possess *le monde.*)"

63. Ramras-Rauch, *The Arab in Israeli Literature*, 148. Gilead Morahg claims that in the fiction of the 1960s and early 1970s "Israel's transition from a state of war to a state of siege" is marked by "the transformation of fictional Arab characters from realistic signifiers of national moral choices to symbolic embodiments of universal existential concerns." Morahg claims that in the literature of the Palmach generation and the fiction of the sixties and early seventies the fundamental mode of Arab characterization is virtually the same. Most Arab characters in Israeli fiction until the early seventies "are stereotypical abstractions whose characterization is limited to superficial externals. They are, for the most part, depersonalized figures that serve as schematic catalysts for the internal dilemmas of their fictional Jewish counterparts whose inner worlds are much more deeply penetrated and extensively portrayed." Gilead Morahg, "The Arab as 'Other' in Israeli Fiction," *Middle East Review* 22, no. 1 (fall 1989): 36.

64. Indeed, as JanMohamed observes: "the colonialist text is in fact antagonistic to some of the prevailing tendencies of realism." "The Economy of Manichean Allegory," 68. Frederic Jameson observes: "Nothing is more alien to the windless closure of high naturalism than the works of Joseph Conrad." "Romance and Reification: Plot Construction and Ideological Closure in Joseph Conrad," *The Political Unconscious* (London and New York: Routledge, 1981), 206.

65. For a discussion of the representation of homosexuality in Israeli cinema and in particular in the work of Amos Guttman (the only Israeli director who was open about his own homosexuality, which he also expressed in his films), see Loshitzky, "Bride of the Dead."

66. Wimal Dissanayake, editor's note, *East-West Film Journal* 5, no. 1 (January 1991): 1 (special issue on melodrama and cinema). Another valuable source on melodrama in the non-Western world is *Screen* 30, no. 3 (summer 1989; special issue on "Indian and European Melodrama").

67. Edward Said refers to this indirectly saying: "For a while, then, Zionist doves like Amos Oz spoke—in Avineri's formula—of the conflicts in Palestine as the struggle of two competing national movements, of right versus right." "An Ideology of Difference," *Critical Inquiry* 12, no. 1 (fall 1985): 50.

68. Ibid., 43.

Chapter Six

1. Ilan Pappe, "Mada v'Alila bSherut Haleumiyout: Historiographia v'Kolnoa BSichsuch HaAravi-Yisraeli" (Science and Plot in the Service of Nationalism: Historiography and Film in the Arab-Israeli Conflict), in *Mabatim Fictiviyim: Al Kolnoa Yisraeli* (*Fictive Looks: On Israeli Cinema*), ed. Nurith Gertz, Orly Lubin, and Judd Ne'eman, 108 (Tel Aviv: Open University Press, 1998).

2. Ibid., 110.

3. Bill Ashcroft, Gareth Griffiths, and Helen Tiffin, *Key Concepts in Post-Colonial Studies* (London: Routledge 1998), 142.

4. Quoted in Joan Borsten, "An Israeli Self-Portrait: It's Not Pretty," *Los Angeles Times*, December 12, 1982. It is interesting to note that the reaction of the Arab audience was completely different. In a screening in Nazareth (the largest Arab city in Israel) attended by the director and the actors, the audience responded with enthusiasm. Each time the Palestinians were treated badly by the Jews, or when the Israeli bulldozer razed confiscated land, the audience reacted with anger. When a Palestinian character made love with a Jewish woman, the audience responded enthusiastically. The mayor of Nazareth, who was interviewed for the daily newspaper *Ma'ariv*, said: "[T]his is a breakthrough in Israeli cinema. The film is important because it faithfully reflects the land problem and the relationships between Jews and Arabs particularly around the issues of Arab labor and land confiscation. It is also the first time that we see a Jewish-Arab cast." Quoted in Shayah Segal, "Tzofim Aravim BeNazaret Hegivu BHitragshut Al HaSeret *Hamsin*" (Arab Spectators in Nazareth Respond with Excitement to *Hamsin*), *Ma'ariv*, April 14, 1989.

5. The name Uri is rich in associations in the context of Israeli culture. It is the name of the mythological, epic Sabra protagonist of Moshe Shamir's now-classic play from the Palmach period, *He Walked through the Fields*, as well as the name given by the poet Rachel to the son she longed for but never had in her famous poem "Akara" (Barren Woman). The name Uri has thus come to symbolize the "new Jew," the "Sabra."

6. *Hamsin* refers to the dry, oppressive heat wave that originates in the desert and frequents the region, particularly during the transitional periods. The oppressive heat, which be-

comes the controlling metaphor of the film, recalls the use of heat as a dramatic device and sexual/political metaphor in a number of American films, notable among them Elia Kazan's *Streetcar Named Desire* (1951), the movie adaptation of Tennessee Williams's steamy play, and Spike Lee's *Do the Right Thing*. The latter, like *Hamsin,* deals with ethnic tensions. Kazan's film, on the other hand, deals mainly with class tensions. To the ethnic and class tensions *Hamsin* adds the national tension, which is the cause for the other two in the Israeli case.

The word *hamsin* recalls also the Hebrew word *hamas,* meaning violence, injustice, oppression, wrong, cruelty, injury. All these wrongs are inflicted by the Jews on the Palestinians in *Hamsin.*

7. Galilee is the only region in Israel with an Arab majority. Over the last three decades successive Israeli governments have tried to change the demographic balance of the region by using a racist strategy, "Yihud HaGalil" (the Judaization of Galilee). This racist policy has gained a greater level of support since the outburst of the Al-Aqsa Intifada in late September 2000.

8. The tension between Galilee and Jerusalem occupies a major role in the history of ancient Israel, as well as in the development of early Christianity. Wachsmann, who lives in Galilee, made a fascinating film about this continuing historical tension called *The Song of Galilee* (1996).

9. David Biale, *Eros and the Jews: From Biblical Israel to Contemporary America* (New York: Basic Books, 1992), 176.

10. Ibid., 203.

11. This land-oriented ideology is grounded in the belief that, as Jonathan Boyarin observes, it would "revitalize both Jewish bodies and Jewish culture." Jonathan Boyarin, "In Search of 'Israeli Identity': Anecdotes and Afterthoughts," *Palestine and Jewish History: Criticism at the Borders of Ethnography* (Minneapolis: University of Minnesota Press, 1996), p 195.

12. The ethos of home, strengthened among Palestinian Israelis during the 1950s, was reproduced after the 1967 war by the Palestinians in the Gaza Strip and the West Bank. There, the Tsumud attained almost mystical/erotic proportions as reflected in the Palestinian "resistance literature." The cases of murder of Palestinians who sell property to Jews are another manifestation of the Tsumud ideology.

13. It is not surprising that the most racist member of the Moshava is Yossi, an Oriental Jew. In the 1980s the stereotype of the Oriental Jew as Arab-hater was very common among Ashkenazi leftists. For further discussion see my analysis of *On a Narrow Bridge* in chapter 6.

14. Horses play a major role in Jewish Orientalist discourse. In the beginning of the Yishuv, when the Arab was the prototype of the new Jew, the horse and Arab paraphernalia were adopted by the first Jewish military organization, HaShomer. However, with the gradual increase of anti-Arab feelings and Jewish racism, the horse came to symbolize a menacing Arab presence. Hannah Gonen's fantasies about her Arab twins in *My Michael* involve horses. In the film *My Michael* the entrance of the twins into the narrative phantasmagoric space is introduced through the sound of riding horses. In *Hide and Seek* the Arab lover enters the spectator's scopic regime riding a horse.

15. The Bilu colonies were the first Jewish settlements in Palestine. They were sponsored and supported by the Rothschild family.

16. The most erotic encounter between Hannah and the Arab twins in the film *My Michael* also occurs in the shower. Hannah has short hair there like Hava.

17. See Baruch Kimmerling and Joel S. Migdal, *Palestinians: The Making of a People* (Cambridge: Harvard University Press, 1993). For a more recent study of Palestinian identity, see Rashid Khalidi, *Palestinian Identity: The Construction of Modern National Consciousness* (New York: Columbia University Press, 1997).

18. Edward Said, "Camus and the French Imperial Experience," *Culture and Imperialism* (New York: Alfred A. Knopf, 1993), 185.

19. Quoted in Irit Shamgar, "Eretz lelo Motza" (Dead-End Land), *Ma'ariv*, October 14, 1982. For a less favorable criticism of the film's presumed radicalism, see Ella Shohat, *Israeli Cinema: East/West and the Politics of Representation* (Austin: University of Texas Press, 1989), 160–61.

20. For a further discussion of the contradictions inherent in the production of this film, see Shohat, *Israeli Cinema*, 242–46.

21. Quoted in Meir Schnitzer, "Gesher Tzar Midai" (A Too Narrow Bridge), *Hadashot*, November 29, 1985, 51. This is what Palestinian director Michel Khleifi did in *Wedding in Galilee*, where Arab extras were dressed in IDF uniforms, to their great amusement. It should also be noted that Khleifi made a documentary on forbidden love titled *Forbidden Marriages in the Holy Land* (1995).

22. Quoted in Schnitzer, "A Too Narrow Bridge," 51.

23. In *Wedding in Galilee* there is a similar scene in which the beautiful daughter of the Mukhtar is erotically teasing one of the Israeli soldiers and tells him that she will dance with him only if he takes off his uniform. When Noa, the Israeli female soldier, faints during the wedding of the Mukhtar's son, the women of the village undress her and later give her more feminine, civilian clothes. This scene is also invested with sexual undertones. Benny Taggar's red phallic car is also related to the sexual fetishization of the uniform. "Get jealous of my new red car!" he "orders" Amnon Abadi, the military governor. The red car with which Taggar is seen throughout the whole film is his phallus, Dayan said. "And like any average Israeli man, when he takes off his uniform and goes home he feels humiliated when his wife asks him to take out the garbage. In Ramallah, in the occupied territories, Taggar is the occupier. He moves freely and does not fear the stone-throwers. But on his own territory, without the uniform, he is lost and his private world collapses." Quoted in Rachel Ne'eman, "Ein Ahavot Politiyot" (There Are No Political Loves), *Koteret Rashit*, November 20, 1985, 33.

24. For a further discussion of *Light Out of Nowhere* in the context of the representation of Oriental Jews, see Shohat, *Israeli Cinema*, 173–178.

25. Schnitzer, "A Too Narrow Bridge," 51.

26. Quoted in Nahman Ingber, "Romeo MeRamat HaSharon VeYulia MeRamallah" (Romeo from Ramat Hasharon and Julia from Ramallah), *Sheva Leilot*, 12.

27. See Marsha Pomerantz, "Preoccupation," *The Jerusalem Post Magazine,* November 22, 1985, A.

28. Although Dayan has acknowledged the fact that he filtered the political situation through allegorical and symbolic lenses, he has refused to acknowledge symbolic dimensions such as those associated with Tony's first entry into the spectator's scopic regime. In this highly dramatic scene Tony is seen emerging from a huge old rock in the Palestinian village Ein Arik, as if he is being born from the Palestinian land from which he was expelled by the Israelis. Dayan claims that if the Palestinian villages convey a sense of rootedness and connection to the land in contrast to the transitoriness conveyed by the Jewish settlements, it is because this is how they are "objectively" seen by the observer. See Irit Shamgar, "Aggadah BaGadah" (A Legend in the West Bank), *Ma'ariv,* November 29, 1985.

29. Quoted in Schnitzer, "A Too Narrow Bridge," 51.

30. Ne'eman, "There Are No Political Loves," 33. It would be interesting to apply the same analysis to the phenomenon of mixed couples in Israel. Many Oriental intellectuals are married to Ashkenazi or American Jewish women.

31. Most Mizrahi intellectuals will not agree with this assumption, which represents a very naive self-perception constructed by Israeli Zionist ideology.

32. Quoted in Ingber, "Romeo from Ramat Hasharon," 12.

33. Lea Tzemel is a famous anti-Zionist Israeli lawyer whose expertise is defending Arab and Palestinian "terrorists."

34. From the Mate Binyamin (a regional district of settlements in the West Bank) settlers' publication: Hava Pinhas-Cohen, "Gesher Tzar M'Ahorei HaKlaim: LaGa'at BaEsh" (A Narrow Bridge beyond the Screen: To Touch Fire), January 2, 1986, 12.

35. Shamgar, "Legend in the West Bank."

36. Ibid.

37. Quoted in Schnitzer, "A Too Narrow Bridge," 51.

38. Ne'eman, "There Are No Political Loves," 33.

39. Quoted in Schnitzer, "A Too Narrow Bridge," 51.

40. Ibid. Rachel Ne'eman wrote: "Now that he is being blamed for filming at the house of Khalil Janho, the son of the head of Agudot HaKfarim [the peasants' association] who was murdered for collaborating with the military government, and not in an authentic Palestinian home, he asks what is authentic? A collaborator is not authentic? Ironically, Janho's house is used as the location for the house of Anwar Mansour, Ramallah's feudal lord, who also collaborates with the military governor" ("There Are No Political Loves," 33)

41. Zyad Fahoum, "Pituya shel Araviyah" (Seduction of an Arab Woman), *Koteret Rashit,* December 11, 1985, 4. The research findings are quoted by Fahoum from the *New York Times* (December 27, 1983).

42. Fahoum, "Seduction of an Arab Woman," 4.

43. *The Lost Lover,* another adaptation of A. B. Yehoshua's novel by the Italian director Roberto Panza, was released in the autumn of 1999.

44. Dan Fainaru, "Ray of Hope," *Jerusalem Post Magazine,* May 16, 1986. Despite its "Disney spirit" the film, initially used by the Jerusalem Van Leer Institute as part of an educational kit aimed at fighting racism among Israeli Jewish high school students, was withdrawn from the kit in response to hostile reactions voiced by Jewish parents worried about what they saw as the film's legitimation of mixed couples.

45. Quoted in *Lahiton.*

46. After Rabin's assassination, Ne'eman published an essay discussing the political assassination portrayed in his film, which was made seven years before Rabin was shot and killed by a religious ultranationalist. In this essay, "Ha'Zeev Shetaraf Et Rabin" (The Wolf that Ate Rabin), *Plastica*, vol. 3 (summer 1999), Ne'eman examines the political and social undercurrents linking the film with Rabin's assassination and illuminating it as a mytho-historical event.

47. The name Nidal recalls the name of Abu Nidal, the head of the Democratic Front for the Liberation of Palestine.

48. Related to the theme of betrayal is Amin's ambiguous identity. It is not even clear if Amin—whose name in Hebrew means reliable, trustworthy, one who does not betray—is a Palestinian living in Israel, a Palestinian from annexed East Jerusalem, or a Palestinian from the occupied territories.

49. The theme of betrayal echoes Bernardo Bertolucci's free adaptation of Jorge Borges's short story "Theme of the Traitor and the Hero" in *The Spider's Stratagem* (1970). For a further discussion of this film and its complex relationship with themes of political and national betrayal, the presence of the past in contemporary political debates, the role of commemoration in the struggle of contested pasts, and suppression of the mutable potential of the past (yesterday's heroes as today's or tomorrow's traitors and vice versa), see Yosefa Loshitzky, "The Politicization of Memory: From *Partner* to *The Conformist,*" *The Radical Faces of Godard and Bertolucci* (Detroit: Wayne State University Press, 1995), 56–68. The tango scene with Yosef and Nidal is a conscious reference to the famous tango scenes in Bertolucci's *Spider's Stratagem, The Conformist* (1970) and *Last Tango in Paris* (1972). In Bertolucci's cinema the tango scenes, interwoven with the theme of betrayal, are always invested with sexual and political meaning.

50. The scene invokes the murder of Professor Luca Quadri by the Fascist death squad in *The Conformist*, a film centered around the question of political betrayal and collective memory. Ne'eman, a professor of film studies at Tel Aviv University, has discussed *The Conformist* on many occasions. See Rachel Giora and Judd Ne'eman, "Categorical Organization in the Narrative Discourse: Semantic Analysis of *Il Conformista,*" *Journal of Pragmatics* 26, no. 6 (December 1996): 715–35. The structure of *Streets of Yesterday*, which makes extensive use of flashbacks, also recalls the structure of *The Spider's Stratagem* and *The Conformist*. In Bertolucci's films the flow of flashbacks generated by the protagonist's free associations emulates the associative process of psychoanalytic therapy, which enables the patient to respond to present circumstances in light of past experiences. These flashbacks also problematize the relationship between memory and history. For further reading see Yosefa Loshitzky, "'Memory of My

Own Memory': Processes of Private and Collective Remembering in Bertolucci's *The Spider's Stratagem* and *The Conformist*," *History and Memory* 3, no. 2 (fall 1991): 87–114.

51. While in the film version the woman is persecuted by both the Haganah and the Lehi, the historical truth is that she was executed by the Lehi only. She was not tried but shot while kneeling down like an animal. Historically, she has never been cleared of the unproven charges, and the Lehi members, some of whom were still alive during the shooting of the film, never expressed remorse or regret at the execution.

52. During the Intifada, Palestinian youth (Shabab) frequently provoked Israeli soldiers by shouting, "I'll fuck your sister," thus making a conscious political use of the sexual dimension inherent in Israeli Jewish racism.

53. Benny Barabash, the scriptwriter of Gideon Ganani's *Crossfire* (1989), quoted in Oshra Schwartz and Yael Shov's interview in *Dvar HaShavua,* April 7, 1989, 24.

54. Ibid.

55. For a much more favorable view of the film's critical stance, see Pappe, "Science and Plot," 108–14. Pappe draws similarities between what he sees as the courageous and groundbreaking stance of the film in regard to the conflict and the attitudes of the new Israeli historians with whom he is affiliated. Pappe views the film as challenging the tenets of established Zionist historiography and showing empathy toward the Arab and Palestinian position regarding the 1948 war.

56. *Ricochets* by Eli Cohen was produced by the Film Unit of the IDF and shot on location in Lebanon during the last month of the Israeli invasion. It depicts the moral dilemmas that Israeli soldiers faced during the war. The film contains the seeds and shades of a forbidden love story between one of the soldiers, Efi Mizrahi (Boaz Ophri), who, as his name clearly indicates, is an Oriental Jew, and a young Shiite woman villager. The beautiful woman casts what seems to Efi like a very seductive gaze each time the Israeli soldiers pass near her house while she is hanging laundry. Efi leaves her sweets each time his unit passes by, and on one occasion she leaves him cherries. Efi interprets the exchange of gazes and sweets as a sign of desire and seduction. However, eventually he finds out that the woman had been spying on the Israeli forces and actually collaborated with "terrorists," using her seductive gaze as a decoy.

57. For a further discussion of this film, see Orly Lubin, "Dmut HaIsha BaKolnoa HaYisraeli" (The Image of Woman in Israeli Cinema), in Gertz, Lubin, and Ne'eman, *Fictive Looks,* 231–33.

58. A previous film, *The Wet Nurse (HaMeneket,* 1993) also dealt with this topic, but indirectly. The film, directed by the Palestinian Israeli Ali Naser, who a few years later made *The Milky Way* (1999), revolves around an Israeli couple who go to Romania in order to adopt a baby. The couple find out that the baby is in fact the illegal son of a Palestinian man and Israeli Jewish woman.

59. Hannah Meron, the first lady of the Israeli theater, played the girl in Fritz Lang's *M.*

60. Juliano Merr, an actor with a reputation for being violent, was himself born to a Jewish mother and an Arab father. His father, Saleeva Hamis, was one of the leaders of Maki, the

Israeli Communist Party (later Hadash). His mother, Arna Merr, was also a member of the Israeli Communist Party and a prominent activist in dialogues between Israeli Jews and Palestinians. She was also very active in promoting such dialogues during the Intifada. The obvious question, posed by Israeli film critic Uri Kleine, is "Why didn't Gitai choose Merr for the main role?" Gitai answered, "I didn't choose Juliano to play the main role because the result would have been one-to-one and that's less interesting." Instead, as Kleine suggests, "there's a feeling in the film that Merr is examining Ivgi—who plays a role identical to him, yet different—and that the audience is examining both actors. The whole film breaks up into a series of mutual reflections that contradict and complement each other and constitute the routine, daily reality described in the film." Uri Kleine, "Round and Round They Go," *Ha'aretz* Magazine, July 31, 1998, 19. The phenomenon of mixed couples was more pervasive in Israel during the 1950s, in particular among Palestinian intellectual men who married Ashkenazi Israeli Jewish women. It was especially common in the Communist Party, which advocated collaboration between Jews and Arabs. Tufik Tubi, the legendary leader of the party, was himself married to a Jewish woman. *Day after Day* hints that Hannah and Yussuf belong to this milieu. When Yussuf tells Mosh/Mussa the story of his and Hannah's meeting on a bus in Haifa he says that she took the initiative because she saw him reading Dostoyevsky. "An Arab who reads Dostoyevsky, why not?" Yussuf adds ironically. Another less-known phenomenon is that during the 1950s the Israeli Secret Services (the Shabak) sent Jewish agents disguised as Arabs to live in Arab villages in Israel. Some of these agents married Arab women and established families. When this secret unit was disclosed, many families were destroyed.

61. Kleine, "Round and Round They Go," 19.

62. For further reading see Paul Willemen, ed., *The Films of Amos Gitai: A Montage* (London: BFI, 1993).

63. In his role as a "nebech" Ivgi continues the new stereotype of the nebech that was established in 1990s Israeli cinema in such films as "Holeh Ahava BeShikun Gimel" (Lovesick in the Projects), *Shuru,* and *Nikmato shel Itzik Finkelstein* (The Revenge of Itzik Finkelstein). Ivgi was cast as the leading actor in all these films. I am indebted to my students Meytal Alon and Roni Livni for bringing this point to my attention in their seminar paper "The Palestinian Lover in Israeli Cinema," Department of Communication and Journalism, Hebrew University of Jerusalem, 1998.

64. Kleine, "Round and Round They Go," 19. The Israeli urban trilogy is composed of *Zichron Devarim/Past Continuous* (Israel, 1995), *Yom Yom/Day after Day* (Israel, 1998), and *Kadosh* (Israel, 1999). Each of the films in this trilogy takes place in a different Israeli city. *Past Continuous* takes place in Tel Aviv, *Day after Day* in Haifa, and *Kadosh* in Jerusalem. For a critical discussion of this trilogy, see Yosefa Loshitzky, "A Tale of Three Cities: Amos Gitai's Urban Trilogy," (*Framework*, forthcoming).

65. Kleine, "Round and Round They Go," 19. It should be noted that despite what Gitai describes as Haifa's ethnic peaceful coexistence, this city's history is immersed with national, ethnic, and class struggles. In 1948, a large portion of Haifa's Palestinian population was ex-

pelled and its urban intelligentsia destroyed, and on July 8, 1957, Mizrahi social unrest exploded in the Wadi Salib riots. As a mixed city, Haifa also witnessed some Jewish-Palestinian conflicts during October 2000 when the Al-Aqsa Intifada broke out. For further discussion see Loshitzky, "Tale of Three Cities."

Chapter Seven

1. When Miriam and George swim to the Andromeda Rock near the Jaffa beach, Miriam asks George: "How did Andromeda feel while she waited for the monster?" George replies: "And I wonder how the prince felt when he came to save her." Miriam is the sacrifice for the fathers' sins, the Jews who took the land from the Palestinian people. Miriam (Andromeda) is punished for her mother's foolishness. Yet, George, the prince, does not save Miriam. To the contrary he brings about her demise. Israeli society sacrifices Miriam to calm the wrath of the monster of racism and ultranationalism.

2. *Fictitious Marriage* (1989) by Haim Buzaglo is yet another example of a film that deals critically with a Tel Aviv–style, Yuppie fantasy of forbidden love, attempting to expose the seductive power of this fantasy. It is also the first film dealing with the theme of forbidden love that was made after the Intifada. Israeli cinema hardly dealt with this popular uprising despite (and perhaps because of) the prominence of Intifada images on Israeli television news. *Fictitious Marriage* is about Eldi (Shlomo Bar Aba), a high school teacher from Jerusalem, who upon embarking on a plane to New York decides not to go to America but to become a "tourist" in his own country. There is a vague allusion in the film to Eldi's military reserve service during the Intifada as leading to his "identity crisis." Eldi checks into a Tel Aviv hotel where he is mistakenly taken for a *yored* (an Israeli émigré). Later, he begins to work with Palestinians from Gaza who mistakenly identify him as one of them. A woman painter, Avigail (Idit Teperson), who lives near the construction site in a Yuppie neighborhood of Tel Aviv, and who often exposes herself to the workers, takes Eldi to her flat to have sex with her, or as she puts it, "to fix a crack in my wall." Avigail's sexual excitement derives precisely from her mistaken belief that Eldi is a Palestinian worker, and she even composes a song for him titled "My Own Private Sabotage." The parody here derives from the process of deconstructing the mystique surrounding the power of the taboo on interracial romance. The notion of mistaken identity exposes this taboo precisely as a catalyst for fantasies on and of otherness. Avigail is a sort of female Pygmalion. She shapes the character of Eldi the Jew as a Palestinian lover. She dresses, feeds, and sleeps with him, turning him into her source of artistic inspiration. Yet, her "original" Palestinian native lover is eventually found to be an impostor, a Jewish imitation of a "real" Palestinian.

3. Alon and Livni, "The Palestinian Lover."

4. See Ella Shohat, *Israeli Cinema: East/West and the Politics of Representation* (Austin: University of Texas Press, 1989), 160–61.

5. Quoted in Baruch Naeh, "Naim," *Ma'ariv*, February 10, 1986.

6. The confiscation of Palestinian land by the Israeli government, as well as processes of urbanization and modernization, and the abolition of the martial law rule over the Arab population living in Israel in December 1967 forced many Palestinians to seek work in Israel's big cities, particularly in Tel Aviv. The situation changed after the 1967 war when Palestinians from the occupied territories replaced the Palestinians living in Israel (and the Mizrahim) as a cheap source of labor. Currently foreign workers from East Asia, Eastern Europe, Latin America, and Africa are displacing some of these Palestinian workers.

7. The final scene in Amos Guttman's *Nagua* (*Drifting*, 1983) depicts homosexual anal intercourse between the protagonist, a young Jewish Israeli filmmaker (an alter ego of Guttman himself), and a Palestinian worker from Gaza played by the Palestinian filmmaker Rashid Mashrawi. Despite the explicitness of this relationship, it does not constitute the core of the narrative but rather one of its dramatic shifts. In *Hide and Seek*, on the other hand, the forbidden relationship is the cause for all the dramatic turns in the narrative.

8. Here the epic Uri (see chap. 6, n. 5) is transformed into the new Israeli, the Oriental Jew.

9. Shohat, *Israeli Cinema*, 268. For a further critique of the Ashkenazi perspective of the film, see in particular 268–71.

10. The film was universally condemned by all the Israeli critics as exploitative and professionally poor. It was also a disaster at the box office. Even the producer Doron Eran acknowledged that the film was very bad and decided to withdraw it from the competition for the Israeli Oscar in 1992.

11. *Beyond the Walls* won the First Critics' Prize at the 1984 Venice Film Festival and was nominated for an Academy Award in the category of foreign films. Thus far it has been the most commercially successful Israeli film abroad.

12. A similar metaphor is used in Gur Heller's *Night Film* (*Seret Laila*, 1986).

13. This was also an ironic reference to the confusion caused at the 1984 Venice Film Festival when the blue-eyed blond Bakri was taken to be the Jew and the dark-skinned Tzadok was mistaken for the Palestinian.

14. Ne'eman has written on the representation of the Israeli-Palestinian conflict in Israeli cinema as recalling the genre of the medieval romance. See Judd Ne'eman, "HaKad, HaLahav, VeHaGavia HaKadosh: Sirtei HaSichsuch HaYehudi Aravi VeHaromansa" (The Jar, the Knife, and the Holy Grail: Films on the Jewish-Arab Conflict and the Romance," in *Fictive Looks: On Israeli Cinema*, ed. Nurith Gertz, Orly Lubin, and Judd Ne'eman, 403–425 (Tel Aviv: Open University of Israel, 1998).

15. There are, however, lesbian undertones in *Wedding in Galilee*.

16. Mary Ann Doane, "The Economy of Desire: The Commodity Form in/of the Cinema," *Quarterly Review of Film and Video* 11, no. 1 (1989): 23. In this article Doane relies heavily on Claude Levi-Strauss.

17. Quoted in Schnitzer, "A Too Narrow Bridge," 51.

18. It is interesting to note in this context that in the *bourekas* films mixed marriages between Ashkenazim and Sephardim provided the safety valve for the melting pot Zionist ide-

ology. Mixed marriage in these films guaranteed for the Sephardim social mobility and smooth integration in the Ashkenazi-dominated establishment. See Shohat, "The 'Bourekas' and Sephardi Representation," *Israeli Cinema*, 115–18.

19. *The Opsimist* (a pessimistic optimist, or optimistic pessimist) is the title of Emil Habibi's famous novel that recounts the tragedy of the Palestinians who remained in 1948 in Palestine/Israel. Habibi, a Palestinian who lived in Haifa, was one of the notable Palestinian intellectuals affiliated with the Communist Party.

20. This unit is part of the "Nachal," a special division of IDF affiliated with the kibbutz movements.

21. The theme of home/house is quite prominent in Gitai's films where it is used as a metaphor for the complexity of the Palestinian-Israeli conflict. This is most evident in his film *House* (*Bayit,* 1980).

22. There has been a lot of talk, lately, in the Israeli public space about the transformation of "HaHazon LeMamon" (that is, the transformation of the Zionist dream into money and real estate investment). Many real estate ads in the newspapers use the phrase "Hafoch et Ha-Hazon LeMamon" (Transform the dream into money), consciously playing with the growing popularity of the neocapitalist trend in Israel, which advocates privatization, competition, and a free-market economy. The privatization of what is called in Israel "national land" (mostly the land of the kibbutzim and moshavim, which in most cases is confiscated Palestinian land) is only one of the prime examples of the privatization, commodification, and "destruction" of so-called socialist Zionism. The opposition to this policy (supported by Israel's neoliberal discourse) is led by the Mizrahi Rainbow Coalition.

23. On yet another, more concrete allegorical level, the negotiations over the purchase of Yussuf's house in *Day after Day*—perhaps it is not accidental either that Yussuf is also the name of the Palestinian in *Hamsin* who owns the land that Gedalia wants to buy—can be seen as an allegory to the land-for-peace negotiations taking place between the Israelis and the Palestinians during the making of the film.

24. Shohat, *Israeli Cinema*, 218.

Conclusion

1. Moshe Ben Harosh, *Kinat HaMeHager: Dyokan Atzmi shel HaMeshorer B'Re'i HaMishpaha* (*Immigrant's Lament: The Poet's Self-Portrait in the Family's Mirror* [Tel Aviv: Yaron Golan, 1994]; translation mine).

2. For recent developments in Israeli critical sociology, see Uri Ram, *The Changing Agenda of Israeli Sociology* (New York: SUNY Press, 1995). The rise of Israeli critical sociology followed (or, some would argue, capitalized on) the rise of the Israeli new historians. For an excellent review for the English-speaking audience of new developments in Israeli historiography, see *History and Memory* 7, no. 1 (spring/summer 1995), a special issue on "Israeli Historiography Revisited," ed. Gulie Ne'eman Arad.

3. In a column in the Israeli popular newspaper *Yediot Aharonot*, Ben Harosh complained that the Ashkenazi-dominated literary establishment discriminates against Oriental and especially Moroccan Jewish writers. See Moshe Ben Harosh, "Teguva: Yesh, Yesh Aflaya" (Response: Yes, Yes There Is Discrimination), *Yediot Aharonot* weekend supplement, December 11, 1998, 27.

4. Even artistic and essayist expressions of exilic consciousness have never been tolerated by the Israeli-Zionist mainstream. The history of the negative reception of diasporic writers (Arnold Zweig, Max Brod, Hannah Arendt, and Philip Roth) who criticized the Zionist entity during the prestate period and after is a case in point.

5. See Tamar Berger, *Dionysus BaCenter* (*Dionysus at Dizengoff Center* [Tel Aviv: Hakibbutz HaMeuhad, 1998]), 144. Berger's book also provides a fascinating historical, political, and literary/cultural account of the Nordia neighborhood, which was destroyed in order to build the Dizengoff Center (Israel's largest mall).

6. Rashid Khalidi, *Palestinian Identity: The Construction of Modern National Consciousness* (New York: Columbia University Press, 1997), 14. Amnon Raz-Krakotzkin's fascinating polemic against German-Jewish Orientalism further illuminates this tragic dialectic of exile and the Orient:

[Edward] Said was born in Jerusalem, not far from where Yitzhak Ba'ar [one of the prominent Zionist scholars who established and shaped the discipline of Jewish Studies at the Hebrew University of Jerusalem] lived. Most of the scholars who shaped the character of Israeli-Zionist research lived in Talbiya, the neighborhood where Ba'ar lived, and in Rehavia, the nearby neighborhood. Many of them advocated positions which, relatively speaking, supported equality between Jews and Arabs, and most of the members of the "Brith Shalom" movement, who sincerely aspired to build the new Jewish entity in Palestine on the basis of the acknowledgment of the rights of the Palestinian inhabitants of the land, lived in those neighborhoods. Yet, even they did not succeed in shaping a consciousness that takes into account the existence of Said, who, obviously, does not represent only himself in this matter. The exit/expulsion of Arabs from the Arab-Jewish neighborhoods of Talbiya and Rehavia (and from the surrounding neighborhoods and villages) was suppressed and silenced. Said's house, like other houses in those neighborhoods, was later inhabited by Jews, some of them refugees of the German-Nazi hell. In this context, the rejection of Said's arguments regarding Orientalism, on the basis of the absence of a discussion of German Orientalism in his writing, is rather bizarre. To the contrary, the addition of the context of German Orientalism may contribute another dimension to the framework of the discussion on Orientalism proposed by Said. This contribution is related to the duality based on the memory of the minority, which was a victim of this historical approach [Orientalism], and the commitment which this memory pleads for. . . . Developing a committed consciousness towards this memory and its relationships with German-Jewish-Zionist Orientalism may help us in establishing a different definition of the Jewish-Israeli collectivity—one which recognizes the existence of the land, and negates the prevailing dichotomy of West-East. (Amnon Raz-Krakotzkin, "Orientalism, Madaey HaYahadut, VeHaHevra HaYisraelit: Mispar Hearot" [Orientalism, Jewish Studies and Israeli Society: Some Comments], *Jamaah* 3 [November 1998]: 57; translation mine)

It is interesting to note in this context that in August 1999 Said's own biography, and particularly his Rehavia home, became a locus of political debate. Justus Weiner, an American Jewish researcher (affiliated with an obscure research institute in Jerusalem), reported in the arch-conservative American magazine *Commentary* that Said had not lived in, nor was obliged to leave, Jerusalem; that he and his family were not refugees from Palestine; and in short that Said is "a liar." Ironically, the Israeli media coverage of Weiner's "discovery," published "coincidentally" at a time when the Palestinian right of return has started to infiltrate Israeli public debate, has not called into question Weiner's right to be called an Israeli citizen. The researcher's own place of birth (which is obviously not Israel/Palestine) has never been raised as an issue in the Israeli public space, which rarely questions the ethics and ideology of the "Law of Return" as the "moral" foundation of the Jewish state.

7. Hana Wirth-Nesher, "Amos Oz's Jerusalem, *My Michael*," *City Codes: Reading the Modern Urban Novel* (Cambridge, Mass.: Cambridge University Press, 1996), 56.

8. Angelika Bammer, "Introduction," in *Displacements: Cultural Identities in Question*, ed. Angelika Bammer, xi (Bloomington: Indiana University Press, 1994).

9. Until this very day Israel does not allow Darwish, who currently resides in Ramallah, to enter the country, even to visit his ailing mother. A recent film by the Moroccan-born Israeli Simone Bitton, who divides her time between Jerusalem and Paris, *Mahmoud Darwich et le Terre comme la Langue* (*Mahmoud Darwish, Land like Language*, 1998) examines the processes of displacement, immigration, and exile as they relate to the construction of Darwish's individual identity as well as to Palestinian collective identity.

10. See Batya Gur, "Kol Ehad Rotzeh Lichtov et HaMakom" (Everybody Wants to Write the Place), *Ha'aretz*, January 10, 1997, D2.

11. To strengthen this point see Susan Slyomovics, "The Memory of Place: Rebuilding the Pre-1948 Palestinian Village," *Diaspora* 3, no. 2 (fall 1994): 157–68; and Yosefa Loshitzky, "The Text of the Other—the Other in the Text: The Palestinian Delegation's Address to the Madrid Middle East Peace Conference," *Journal of Communication Inquiry* 18, no. 1 (winter 1994): 27–44.

12. A few films, however, have already been made on religious issues, among them Dani Wachsmann's *Hameyuad* (*The Messenger*, 1990), Hagai Levi's *Sheleg BeAugust* (*Snow in August*, 1993), Yossi Zomer's *Ahavah Asura* (*Forbidden Love*, 1997), and Amos Gitai's *Kadosh* (1999). There also have been a few films made on immigrants from the former Soviet Union, such as Ari Fulman and Ori Sivan's *Saint Clara* (1995), Yossef Fichhadze's *In Front of Western Eyes* (1997), and Erik Kaplun's *Yana's Friends* (1999). Both *In Front of Western Eyes* and *Yana's Friends* were made by immigrants from the former Soviet Union. Dan Wolman's most recent film, *Foreign Sister* (2000), tells the story of a woman foreign worker from a community of several thousand Ethiopian Christians, which is perhaps the smallest group of foreign workers living in Israel. Currently there are approximately 300,000 foreign workers in Israel.

Index

Italic page numbers indicate illustrations

Ben-Ari, Eyal, 80
Ben Dor, Orna, xvi, 17, 28, 32, 33–36, 53, 63, 64, 80
Ben-Gurion, David, 4, 16, 20
Ben Harosh, Moshe, 169, 170
Ben-Hur, 8
Benjamin, Walter, 160
Berger, Tamar, 170
Bertolucci, Bernardo, 82, 97, 99, 100–102, 106, 207–208nn49,50
Beyond the Walls (Barabash), 17, 131, 146, 160–161, 162, 163
Beyond the Walls 2, 162–163
Bezalel Academy, 96
Bhabha, Homi, 101, 102–103, 171
Bhaji on the Beach (Chadha), 85, 86
Biale, David, 119
Bilu, Yoram, 80, 83–84
Birenbaum, Hellina, 34–35
"Boat film" genre, 5–6
Boats, as national symbols, 4–6, 175–176n10
Das Boot, 5
Borges, Jorge, 207n49
Botticelli, Sandro, 1
Bourekas films, 74, 76, 81–83, 84, 91, 211–212n18
Bowles, Paul, 94–95, 99, 101, 105, 106
Brenner, Rachel Feldhay, 65–66
Brenner, Yosef Haim, 97
Briatte, Robert, 106
Brug, Moli, 19, 20, 22
Burton, Richard, 95
Buzaglo, Haim, 154, 157, 210n2

Camus, Albert, 126
Canaanites, 3, 14, 177n33
Casablan, 76
Casablanca, 13, 31
Cast a Giant Shadow, 14
Chadha, Gurinder, 85, 86
Chateaubriand, François-Auguste-René de, 106
Choice and Destiny (Reibenbach): body language in, 53–55; and daily life, 47, 48–

49, 50, 51, 61, 62; and food, 56–59, 60, 61; and Holocaust representation, xvi, 28, 32, 47–62; scenes from, *48*, *57*; and second generation of Holocaust survivors, 63–64; and silence, 48, 51, 54, 55–56, 58, 64; time in, 50–51; and Yiddish language, 47, 51–53, 67
Class: and *Crossfire*, 146; and diasporic/exilic transnational films, 86; and *Hamsin*, 123; and Holocaust survivors, 34–35; and identity, xiii; and *My Michael*, 99, 109
Clinton, William Jefferson, 71, 174–175n4
Cohen, Eli, 28, 148, 164, 208n56
Colonialism: and ambiguity, 102–103; and *Exodus*, xvi, 3, 8, 13, 14; and feminism, 90; and *Hamsin*, 118; and miscegenation, 113; and *My Michael*, 90, 94, 98, 99; and *On a Narrow Bridge*, 136; and Orient, xvii, 94–95, 103; and other, 105–106; and Said, 101, 200nn43,44; and *The Sheltering Sky*, 99, 100, 101, 102, 105; and Zionism, 119
The Conformist (Bertolucci), 207nn49,50
Conrad, Joseph, 94, 100, 105, 142
Cooper, Howard, 65
Costa-Gavras, Constantin, 135
Crossfire (Ganani): and forbidden love, 144–147, 149; and Greek mythology, 154, 210n1; scene from, *148*; time in, 167; and victimhood, 155, 156; women in, 146, 147, 164
Cultural identity, 52
Cultural pluralism, 79
Culture war, xi, 3
Cyprus, 4

Daddy Come to the Amusement Park (Gonen), 28, 29–30, 64
Darwish, Mahmud, 119, 171, 189n21, 214n9
Day after Day (Gitai): and forbidden love, xvii, 149–153, 168; and hybrid, 165–166; scenes from, *152*; and Zionism, 166–167
Dayan, Nissim, 112, 127–137, 159, 164. *See also On a Narrow Bridge* (Dayan)
Development towns, 79, 82–83, 85

and horses metaphor, 204n14; scene from, *116*; time in, 167–168; and voyeurism, 125

Hirsch, Marianne, xvi, 24–25, 33, 67, 71

Hitchcock, Alfred, 147

Hitler, Adolph, 18

Hodge, Bob, 103

Holocaust: and culture war, 3; and *Exodus,* 14; and immigration, 10, 178–179n4; and Israel, 15–16, 19–20, 22, 32, 35–36, 40, 183–184n41; and Israeli cinema, xv, 23; and Israeli identity, xiii, xvi, 63; and Israeli Left/Right schism, 12, 15, 68–69; militarization of, 20, 182n23; nationalization of, 29; normalization of, 35–36, 71, 186n3; and State of Israel, 15, 19–20; and *Streets of Yesterday,* 142–143; and victimhood, 10; and Zionism, 16–17, 19, 20, 30–31

Holocaust memory: and Arabs, 41, 44; and *Because of That War,* 34; and *Choice and Destiny,* 47–48; and *Don't Touch My Holocaust,* 38–42, 43, 46, 63; and Israeli cinema, 27; and Israeli identity, xvi, 65–68; and Israeli society, 15, 19, 32, 40–41; and Palestinians, 40–41, 43–44, 50; privatization of, 20–21, 22, 27, 29, 30, 32, 63, 64–65, 68; and second generation of Holocaust survivors, 25–27, 28, 33, 63, 65–68, 69; and third generation of Holocaust survivors, 69, 71; and Zionism, 42, 50, 64

Holocaust Remembrance Day ceremonies, 19, 20, 21, 22, 35, 45, 70, 71

Holocaust representation: and *Because of That War,* xvi, 28, 32, 33–36; and *Choice and Destiny,* xvi, 28, 32, 47–62; and *Don't Touch My Holocaust,* xvi, 28, 30–31, 32, 36–46; and Israeli cinema, xiii, xvi, 23, 27–31, 32; and Israeli identity, 46; and Morocco, 28, 30, 39; politics of, 35

Holocaust survivors: attitudes toward, 16, 51, 52, 53, 56, 62, 70, 178–179n4, 180n5,

190n44; and *Because of That War,* 17, 34–35, 63; and *Choice and Destiny,* 50, 51, 52, 53, 54, 58–59, 61, 62, 63; and *Don't Touch My Holocaust,* 46, 63, 189n26; and *Exodus,* 7, 8, 9–13, 14; and Holocaust memory, 22, 34–35; identity of, xiii, xiv, 26–27, 34; and Israel, 19; and Israeli cinema, xv, 28, 34; and Orientalism, 188n12; and victimization, xiv, 9, 173n9; Zionization of, 9–13

Homophobia, 12, 115, 116

Homosexuality: in *Hamsin,* 124, 162; in *Hide and Seek,* xv, 110, 114–116, 162, 165; in *My Michael,* 110, 114; in *Streets of Yesterday,* 162, 163

Hovav, Mira, 66–67

Hugo (Lev), 28, 29

Huyssen, Andreas, 103–104, 107

Hybrid survivor, 43

I Am Ahmed (Levi), 159–160

Identity: and *Day after Day,* 153; and diasporic/exilic transnational films, 85; and *Don't Touch My Holocaust,* 38, 63; Hall on, xii, xiv, xv; and *Hamsin,* 125–126; of Holocaust survivors, xiii, xiv, 26–27, 34; and home, 171; and *I Am Ahmed,* 160; and inclusion/exclusion, xiv; and *On a Narrow Bridge,* 130–131, 137, 162; and Palestinians, xiii, xiv, 9, 125–126; and second generation of Holocaust survivors, 26, 27, 52, 79; and subjectivity, xii; and victimhood, xiii–xiv. *See also* Ethnic identity; Israeli identity; Israeli identity politics

The Immigrant's Lament (Ben Harosh), 169

Immigration: attitudes toward immigrants, 49; and culture war, 3; and *Exodus* (film), 14; and *Exodus* (ship), 3–4; and Holocaust, 10, 178–179n4; immigrant as stranger, 169; immigrants' stories, 80; and name changes, 186n60; of new Jews, xiv–xv; and *New Land,* 80; and silence, 56; and Yiddish language, 67